DARK
SUMMIT

DARK SUMMIT

THE EXTRAORDINARY TRUE STORY OF

EVEREST'S MOST CONTROVERSIAL SEASON

NICK HEIL

Published by Virgin Books, 2008
Published simultaneously in the United States by Henry Holt and Company, LLC

2 4 6 8 10 9 7 5 3 1

Copyright © Nick Heil, 2008
Maps © Jeffrey L. Ward, 2008

Designed by Meryl Sussman Levavi

Nick Heil has asserted his right under the Copyright, Designs
and Patents Act 1988 to be identified as the author of this work

First published in Great Britain in 2008 by
Virgin Books
Thames Wharf Studios,
Rainville Road
London, W6 9HA

www.rbooks.co.uk

Addresses for companies within The Random House Group Limited can be found at:
www.randomhouse.co.uk/offices.htm

The Random House Group Limited Reg. No. 954009

A CIP catalogue record for this book
is available from the British Library

HB ISBN 978-1-905264-25-4

PB ISBN 978-0-7535-1359-0

The Random House Group Limited supports The Forest Stewardship Council [FSC], the leading
international forest certification organisation. All our titles that are printed on Greenpeace approved
FSC certified paper carry the FSC logo.
Our paper procurement policy can be found at www.rbooks.co.uk/environment

Mixed Sources
Product group from well-managed
forests and other controlled sources
www.fsc.org Cert no. TT-COC-2139
© 1996 Forest Stewardship Council

Printed and bound in the UK by CPI Mackays, Chatham ME5 8TD

For Mom, Dad, Kayte, Jon, Taylor,
Tannis, Ginny, and Minnie. My family.

"A certain Samaritan, who was on a journey, came upon him; and when he saw him, he felt compassion, and came to him, and bandaged up his wounds, pouring oil and wine on them; and he put him on his own beast, and brought him to an inn, and took care of him."

—*Luke 10:33–34*

CONTENTS

Partial List of Teams and Climbers on Everest's North Side, 2006

7 Summits
Alex Abramov
Kevin Augello
Michael Dillon
Lincoln Hall
Christopher Harris
Richard Harris
Harry Kikstra
Sergei Kofanov
Ludmila Korobeshko
Vladimir Lande
David Lien
Ronnie Muhl
Igor Plyushkin
Andrey Selivanov
Slate Stern
Thomas Weber
Kirk Wheatley
Mingma Sherpa
Pasang Sherpa
Pemba Sherpa
Lakcha Sherpa
Dawa Tenzing Sherpa
Dorje Sherpa

Project Himalaya
Laurie Bagley
Duncan Chessell
Chris Klinke
Jamie McGuinness
Anne Parmenter
Hans Fredrick Strang
Scott Woolums
Chhiri Sherpa

SummitClimb
Andrew Brash
Phil Crampton

Dan Mazur
Juan Pablo Milana
Myles Osborne
Jangbu Sherpa

Asian Trekking Permit
George Dijmarescu
Lakpha Sherpani
Dave Watson
David Sharp (climbing
   independently)

Himex
Wayne "Cowboy" Alexander
Marcel Bach
Gerard Bourrat
Russell Brice
Max Chaya
Bill Crouse
Kurt Hefti
Shaun Hutson
Mark Inglis
Mogens Jensen
Bob Killip
Tim Medvetz
Brett Merrell
Terry O'Connor
Ken Sauls
Mark Whetu
Mark "Woody" Woodward
Tuk Bahadur Sherpa
Lhakpa Sherpa
Dorje Sherpa
Phurba Tashi Sherpa
Tashi Phinjo Sherpa
Sonam Sherpa

DARK
SUMMIT

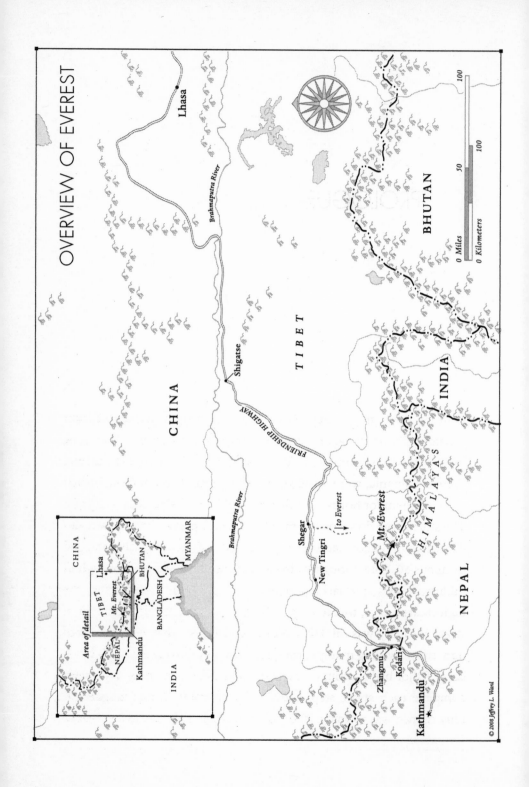

OVERVIEW OF EVEREST

Lhasa

Brahmaputra River

CHINA

TIBET

Shigatse

FRIENDSHIP HIGHWAY

Brahmaputra River

Shegar

New Tingri

to Everest

Mt. Everest

H I M A L A Y A S

Zhangmu

Kodari

Kathmandu

NEPAL

INDIA

BHUTAN

100

100

50

0 Miles

0 Kilometers

CHINA

TIBET   Lhasa

Area of detail   Mt. Everest   BHUTAN

NEPAL   BANGLADESH   MYANMAR

Kathmandu

INDIA

© 2008 Jeffrey L. Ward

PROLOGUE

Late on the night of May 10, 1996, a twenty-eight-year-old Ladakhi named Tsewang Paljor struggled slowly down Everest's Northeast Ridge. The two teammates he'd been climbing with, Dorje Morup and Tsewang Smanla, were somewhere behind him, perhaps dead; he had not seen them for hours. Not that he could have helped them anyway. The storm bore down on the mountain with a primordial intensity unlike anything Paljor had ever experienced. The temperature plunged to minus 50, cold enough to freeze exposed flesh straight through in minutes. Gusts approaching eighty miles per hour ripped across the high escarpments, threatening to fling Paljor off the ridge like a bit of straw. Visibility was nil. His world extended just a few feet in front of him, snow swirling madly through the fading yellow beam of his headlamp. Paljor had run out of oxygen hours earlier, and now, fighting to complete each ataxic step, battered by dehydration and fatigue, his only chance was to make it to high camp, still a thousand feet below, where others would be waiting with extra gas and hot tea. If he remained here, above 28,000 feet, in such desperate conditions, he was doomed.

Paljor belonged to a proud expedition, some forty men strong, led by Mohinder Singh, a commander for the Indo-Tibetan Border Police and one of India's most accomplished mountaineers. Singh was vying to put the first Indian on the summit of Everest via the legendary Northeast Ridge—the route where Mallory and Irvine had vanished in 1924, a line of ascent that would thwart attempts for another thirty-six years. The Chinese had been the first to complete the ridge, in 1960, and many teams and individuals had ascended the route since, but it would hardly diminish the accomplishment pending for Singh and his climbers. Theirs had been an auspicious enterprise, almost entirely without setbacks during the two months they had been on Everest. Finally, at around six P.M. on May 10, Singh's radio had crackled to life: Smanla, Paljor, and Morup reported that they were standing on the summit.

The tempest was approaching its crescendo, but Singh and the others gathered at Advanced Base Camp erupted into cheers. *This is a magnificent achievement, for our expedition and for our country!*, Singh shouted into the handset, the wind roaring, bowing the tent walls. Now, he urged, the climbers must hurry down without delay.

The next morning, Singh received word from high camp, at 27,300 feet, that the trio had not returned. This was devastating news, with an added complication since he had already phoned the Indian prime minister, Narasimha Rao, to inform him of their success; telling Rao that the three men were now lost was not a task Singh relished. But he didn't give up hope. Although there had been no contact since the evening before, it was possible his men had been able to ride out the night.

That day, increasingly desperate to act, Singh approached a cluster of neighboring tents in Advanced Base Camp occupied by a Japanese expedition. The weather had still not relented, but word was circulating that two Japanese climbers, Hiroshi Hanada and Eisuke Shigekawa, and three Sherpas were in position at high camp and planning to depart for a summit attempt that night. Singh's own climbers were of no use. Those back in their tents were exhausted from their aborted efforts on the ridge, and it would take at least two days for anyone from Advanced Base Camp to reach the stranded men. Singh had no option but to implore the Japanese expedition leader, Koji Yada, to assist him; if his men were still alive they most certainly wouldn't be after a second night, and the Japanese summit team—relatively fresh, strong, and well supplied—might be their last chance. The conversation took place in three languages, English, Japanese, and Hindi, but Singh came away believing that the Japanese would do their best to provide whatever assistance they could.

The ensuing twenty-four hours were fraught with confusion. Communication on Everest was problematic even in the best conditions, and the storm had reduced radio contact to the most basic and sporadic dialogue. What few reports filtered down the mountain convinced Singh that a rescue was under way, yet he also learned that the Japanese had pushed on to the summit. How could this be? By 5:30 P.M. on May 12, as the last of the Japanese summit group pulled back into high camp, it became clear that none of the Indians were with them. There had been no rescue.

When the Japanese descended to Advanced Base Camp the following afternoon, the news was grim. They had, in fact, encountered Singh's men, and while their lead Sherpa had helped free one of them, probably Smanla, snared in a tangle of fixed lines on the Second Step, little else could be done, they insisted. "They were Indian climbers—we didn't know them," Hanada told Richard Cowper, a journalist for the *Financial Times* in London who was accompanying a British expedition on Everest that year. "No, we didn't give them any water. We didn't talk to them. They had severe high-altitude sickness. They looked as though they were dangerous."

"We climb by ourselves, by our own efforts, on the big mountains," Shigekawa added. "We were too tired to help. Above 8,000 meters is not a place where people can afford morality."

Singh was apoplectic. How could a strong team of five have passed his men and done nothing? When had the summit become more important than another man's life? There was still more bad news. Hanada and Shigekawa said that there had been no evidence of the Indians on the summit—no footprints, no prayer flags, no empty oxygen canisters. They speculated that in the poor weather and dwindling light of May 10 the Indians had mistakenly pulled up short, some one hundred vertical feet below Everest's apex.

On May 13, Singh, still fuming, convened a meeting of expedition leaders at Advanced Base Camp, urging them to endorse a statement condemning the Japanese for neglecting his men. This was an outrage and a disgrace—tantamount to murder, Singh said. But the other team leaders, while sympathetic, weren't so quick to take sides. It was a seasoned group, including veteran British climber Simon Lowe and Slovenian Viktor Groselg, and they understood the extenuating circumstances at altitude—the stark Darwinian reality climbers confronted above 8,000 meters. Several people at the meeting cited previous examples of individuals who had been left for dead on the mountain. They pointed out that Singh's six-man summit party had left high camp at eight A.M. on May 10, dangerously late by any standard. What's more, Smanla, Paljor, and Morup had continued to push upward in abysmal conditions despite protests from their three climbing partners, who had turned back midway up the ridge.

Even though he had garnered little support from the other team leaders, Singh released his accusatory statement to the press. If the

Japanese believed there was no morality above 8,000 meters, then the world was going to know about it.

Singh's plight might have drawn more attention had other dire events not been taking place simultaneously on the opposite side of the mountain. By the time the May 10 storm had cleared out, five more people had died, including commercial clients Yasuko Namba and Doug Hansen, veteran guide Andy Harris, and two expedition leaders, Scott Fischer and Rob Hall. It was a disaster of such magnitude that it would eclipse everything else happening on Everest for months, even years.

Before long a small library of firsthand accounts emerged, most notably Jon Krakauer's *Into Thin Air,* Anatoli Boukreev's *The Climb,* Beck Weathers's *Left for Dead,* Kenneth Kamler's *Doctor on Everest,* and Matt Dickinson's *The Other Side of Everest.* The mountain hadn't seen such publicity since it had first been scaled by Edmund Hillary and Tenzing Norgay in 1953, but the new light shining down on the world's highest peak illuminated a very different place. Gone were the tweedy gentlemen climbers of yesteryear pioneering their way across a virgin landscape; this modern, commercialized Everest was overcrowded and largely unregulated, a high-altitude playground where conga lines of novice clients clogged the route, where deep-pocketed dilettantes of dubious ability were short-roped to well-compensated Sherpas and guides.

Mountaineering had long championed a keen sense of ethics and style, and this contemporary tableau represented the worst of all scenarios. Veteran climbers sniffed that Everest had become a "slag heap," as Krakauer wrote in *Into Thin Air,* athletically and aesthetically unworthy, "debased and profaned" by the sheer number of amateurs flocking there, relying on regressive siege tactics, defiling the campsites and trailsides with their waste. And filth wasn't the only problem. As more people showed up at Everest each season, the most serious hazards were less objective—rockfall, avalanche, weather, the vagaries of altitude—than *subjective:* misguided decision making, personal agendas, professional rivalries. The communal nature of climbing—the so-called fellowship of the rope—was frayed nearly to the snapping point. By the end of the 1996 season, the public perception of Everest had been altered for good. What had once stood as a symbol of what was best in mankind—determination, tenacity, teamwork—now represented something much darker: ego, hubris, greed.

After 1996, it was clear that the business of Everest had become deadly folly; given the enormously high stakes, it was amazing that anyone continued to show up at all. But show up they did. At first with some trepidation—the number of climbers on Everest dropped slightly in 1997 compared with the year before—but over the next few years business began to resurge dramatically. Despite the fact that Nepal, the port of entry for most climbers regardless of their intended route, was convulsing with civil war, effectively cutting tourism by as much as half, the number of Everest permits issued by the Nepal Mountaineering Association soon reached an all-time high. Between 2000 and 2005, more people climbed to the top of the world than had summited during the previous fifty years.

When I traveled to the Everest region in the spring of 2005, en route to a neighboring 21,000-foot peak called Cholatse, more than four hundred people had already descended on Everest Base Camp in Nepal. Another four hundred were stationed on the north side, in Tibet. My expedition was composed of big-mountain veterans, many of them sponsored athletes, including Pete Athans, who had made a total of fifteen trips to Everest and summited seven times. Another team member, filmmaker Michael Brown, had summited three times. Five others had each summited once: Conrad Anker, who had discovered George Mallory's body in 1999; Geoff Tabin, an American ophthalmologist; Brown's business partner David D'Angelo; and two Sherpas—Dawa and Ang Temba. The climbers claimed a grand total of fifteen Everest summits among them. Naturally, we were all interested in the activity taking place on Everest that year, and we entertained ourselves by monitoring radio traffic on the mountain from our own Base Camp, just twelve miles away.

Despite the cumulative experience of the climbers on my trip, no one could venture a concise explanation for Everest's ever-expanding allure. If anything, this particular group seemed more puzzled and cynical about the mountain's rapidly burgeoning popularity, perhaps because of the seriousness with which they approached climbing but also because they shared an acute awareness of the sustained misery, hard labor, and unnerving risk of high-altitude mountaineering—its propensity to freeze digits and delete brain cells by the millions, the way it could snuff out the lives of friends, acquaintances, and team-mates with cold, capricious indifference.

That spring, during a brief side trip from the Cholatse expedition, I caught my first glimpse of Everest from a lofty knob called Gokyo Ri, a favorite trekking destination at the head of the Gokyo Valley. As is true for many scenic wonders, pictures hardly do Everest justice. I'd hiked up in the early-morning dark with half a dozen people I didn't know, switchbacking up a trail through thick fog. We emerged from the cloud layer a little before dawn as if breaching a sea, just a few hundred feet from the top, our viewpoint the smallest island floating among an archipelago of 7,000- and 8,000-meter peaks—Makalu, Cho Oyu, Lhotse, Nuptse. Above them all: Everest, a soaring black dorsal fin etched against the gloaming.

It was astonishing to me that anyone could climb that high; even where I stood at 18,000 feet, a relatively modest elevation by Hi-malayan standards, I was loopy with altitude, my temples thudding from the steep trail. I'd already spent a grueling night at a similar elevation wedged into a two-man tent halfway up Cholatse, catatonic in my sleeping bag, cymbals crashing inside my skull, waves of nausea welling up in my throat as the night stretched on interminably. The few times I dozed, the sleep was fitful, wracked by vivid and bizarre dreams, like one in which my dog, a perfectly sweet and healthy rottweiler mix in real life, had somehow acquired a peg leg and stainless-steel fangs and turned on me, drooling, ready to pounce. I descended the next day and quickly recovered, but that experience was as unpleasant as any I'd ever had in the mountains. The notion of ascending another 11,000 vertical feet into darker nightmares and more prolonged suffering was inconceivable in a way that no amount of goose down, fixed ropes, or bottled oxygen could alter.

By 2005, at age thirty-eight, I had acquired a moderate amount of climbing experience, mostly on glaciated North American peaks like Mount Rainier and assorted rock crags around the West, where I'd lived since my twenties. I had done just enough mountaineering to develop a dabbler's appreciation for it, in the same way, I suppose, that receiving your driver's license gives you an inkling of Formula One racing—the fundamental activity was similar but the intensity differed by considerable degrees. Cholatse provided my first exposure to Himalayan climbing, and I began to understand just how formidable it could be. On our trip, five of my team members managed to summit, but it required a strenuous twenty-hour push from the highest camp. One of those who made it, Abby Watkins, a professional climber from Golden, British Columbia, and as capable and fit a mountain athlete as I've ever met, told me later how someone at high camp had handed her a cup of hot tea as she'd collapsed in her tent on the way back down. She woke up the next morning wearing her boots and parka, a full cup of tea in her hand—frozen solid.

Few experiences rival a serious climb for bringing us into close contact with our own limitations. Part engineering project, part chess game, part ultramarathon, mountaineering demands of us in a way that other endeavors do not. After my trip to Cholatse, I came to think of high-altitude climbing not so much as a sport but as a kind of art or even, in its purest form, rugged spirituality—a modern version of secular asceticism that purifies the soul by stripping away worldly comfort and convenience while forcing you to stare across the threshold of mortality. It is our effort to toil through these hazardous and inhospitable landscapes that culminates with such potent effect, what humanistic psychologists have described as the attainment of self-actualization, a pinnacle of personal expression that dissolves the constraints of our ordinary lives and allows us, even if fleetingly, to "become what we are capable of becoming." This transformative power is, in a way, why summits have taken on so much symbolic importance for those who pursue them. As the reigning mythology suggests, the higher the peak—Rainier, Cholatse, Everest—the more it fires the imagination.

In 2006, as the spring Everest season was winding down, I was asked to write a brief story about some breaking news just emerging from the mountain. Several deaths had occurred near the summit during the preceding weeks, but one in particular had sparked renewed outrage and righteous indignation. According to various reports, forty climbers had walked past a dying man on their way to the top. In the crosshairs of controversy was the "mayor of the north side," New Zealander Russell Brice, Everest's most successful commercial operator. Brice's team was among those who had written off the dying man alongside the route. What might have been done to help him, and why more hadn't been, became the focus of wild speculation, but it also served to confirm the hushed predictions that had been percolating for years: Everest's problems were still on the rise, and another disaster was overdue. By the end of the season, eleven people had died (and another should have but had miraculously lived)—the second-deadliest year in

Everest's history, and arguably the most controversial: This time there had been no killer storm; this time the weather had been nearly perfect.

We produced our story, which quickly mushroomed to more than four thousand words, in just over a week, in the white heat common to magazine deadlines, but even that barely began to scratch the surface. Soon enough, I found myself immersed in the larger tale, embarking on a journey that would take me around the globe in search of the full account, leading eventually to Everest's soaring north side and up its flanks, toward a small rock alcove where the destinies of a dozen climbers had braided together and sparked the debate that had resonated around the world. It was here that a young British climber named David Sharp had died, alone, next to the frozen body of another mountaineer who, years before, had also been abandoned to his own fate.

To most who ascended Everest's Northeast Ridge, the figure next to Sharp in the alcove was known only as Green Boots, a nickname that illustrated mountaineering's fondness for gallows humor but also reminded climbers of the peril they faced when ascending to such heights. By 2006 only a few individuals could recall Green Boots' real name: Tsewang Paljor, the Indian who had remained where the Japanese team had last seen him alive ten years earlier, his ordeal long since swept away in the spindrift of the seasons.

PART ONE

DAVID SHARP

"The great flood-gates of the wonder-world swung open, and in the wild conceits that swayed me to my purpose, two and two there floated into my inmost soul, endless processions of the whale, and, mid most of them all, one grand hooded phantom, like a snow hill in the air."

—*Moby Dick*

CHAPTER 1

KATHMANDU

First, the climbers bought bottles of beer in the lobby; then they hiked the five flights of stairs to the hotel's rooftop terrace, where they faced west to watch the eclipse begin above Kathmandu. It was March 29, 2006, and at five P.M. that day the moon began to drift in front of the sun, casting the buildings in shadow. The blocky contour of the city's skyline was swept into silhouette, the distant foothills fading to a suggestion. This was the first instance when an eclipse like this had been visible from Nepal at the beginning of an Everest expedition. How could you not take it as a sign?

"At the time I was asked if this was a good or bad omen," Russell Brice, the fifty-three-year-old expedition leader, wrote in a press release that summer, after the season had ended, after David Sharp was dead, after the finger-pointing and accusations and incredulity, after he had hand-carried Sharp's passport to England and returned it to his parents and told them what had happened. "My reply was that it was good, but at the time my heart suggested that it was not to be. My inner instincts were to be true."

Astrologers had long held that a solar eclipse portended the overthrow of a ruler or king or, at the very least, that it signified changes to come. Not that Brice was particularly superstitious or inclined to buy the nutty prognostications of pseudoscientists who studied the alignment of stars. But big mountains were unpredictable, human beings even more so. Combine the two and the potential for catastrophe was always right around the corner. During his lifetime of climbing and skiing and ballooning and paragliding and high-altitude skydiving, Brice had known more than a dozen people whose lives had come to a premature end. These friends and acquaintances of his had exploded in their jumpsuits, or fallen into oblivion, or been swept away in a roaring wall of snow and ice, or simply sat down and never got up again. Brice had been lucky. He had not only walked through the valley of death, he'd scrambled up its slopes and ridges and stood on its summit and had never so much as lost a fingertip to frostbite. More important, on his watch as an expedition guide and leader, he had never lost a client—or another guide or a Sherpa, for that matter—though there had certainly been some close calls.

Brice was the founder and owner of Himalayan Experience, better known simply as Himex, one of the largest and most successful outfitters on Everest. He had been running guided expeditions on the mountain since 1994, exclusively on the north side, in Tibet. Over the years, Brice had poured millions into his business, building a small fiefdom that was the envy of many other operators, a source of inspiration and—sometimes—exasperation. The accommodations during a Himex expedition, both on and off the mountain, were some of the best available. He ran a top-notch kitchen, marshaled sophisticated weather data, employed the strongest Sherpas, and hosted raucous parties. During his twelve-year tenure on the hill, Brice had put more than 270 people on the summits of 8,000-meter peaks, more than any other single outfitter.

Brice had twice summited himself, in 1997 and 1998, but now he orchestrated his show perched on the North Col, at 23,000 feet, from which he had an unobstructed view of the Northeast Ridge, the most dangerous part of the route. He tracked his climbers' progress like a ship captain on the bridge, following them through a telescope peeking out of his tent vestibule, remaining in constant communication via two-way radio or, when that failed, satellite phone. His expeditions were emphatically not a democracy; if he believed a client wasn't going to make it, he would promptly turn him around. Ignore him and Brice insisted he would "pull the Sherpas off you and deal with it later in court."

Brice wasn't particularly imposing—about five-nine, 165 pounds—but he could be intimidating. He was barrel-chested and fit, strong enough to outpace Sherpas half his age while hauling a fifty-pound pack. No Westerner was more at home on Everest than he, and he comported himself with the air of a seasoned army general, even while he clung to the youthful persona of a mountain guide. On Everest, his typical uniform consisted of a rugby shirt beneath a down-filled parka, knit ski cap pulled low, wraparound sunglasses tilted high. Though he still had his roguish good looks and wry sense of humor, there was no mistaking his seniority and clout. Brice's temper could be swift and intense, but so could his sociability. Few climbers escaped a visit to the Himex camp without sharing a beer or a belt of whiskey— or both. The other guides on Everest almost universally respected him, even those who didn't particularly like him. The Sherpas simply gazed upon him with awe. *Ban Dai*, they called him: "Big Boss."

His years in the Himalayas had been rewarding, to be sure, but that hadn't made them any less rough. The dry air and harsh weather had etched his skin and silvered his hair. His teeth had been stained by countless cups of coffee and tea. He had ferried so many spine-crushing loads between camps that he had ground away the cartilage in his knees. By 2006 he had begun to contemplate selling the business, moving on to the next thing. But what was next? He didn't know. Brice had gotten married a couple of years earlier, though he didn't have kids. He was too young to retire but too old to truly enjoy the punishing work of high-altitude climbing anymore—or the heated controversies that often accompanied it.

Brice wasn't sure what to make of the coming season. He had agreed to participate in a television documentary being produced by the Discovery Channel—a six-part series in which he would feature prominently. The crew planned to follow the Himex team all the way to the top, replete with high-altitude cinematographers and Sherpas kitted out with helmet-mounted cameras. It was one of the most ambitious documentary projects the mountain had seen, and things were already shaping up to make it a highly promising year—for television audiences, anyway. Brice's client roster included, among others, a double amputee; an asthmatic who intended to summit without using oxygen; and a 220-pound biker from California whose back, knee, and ankle were bolted together with metal screws.

It was going to be either the best year in Himex history or the worst.

The day after the solar eclipse, the team members—most of them, anyway—gathered on the bougainvillea-draped patio of the Hotel Tibet, a day before their departure for Everest. It was the first time they had assembled as a group, and although they were intimately familiar with their itinerary by now, Brice introduced each person and reviewed the agenda for the coming week. On April 1, they would fly from Kathmandu to Lhasa, where they would be met by a liaison officer and a driver from the Chinese Tibetan Mountaineering Association (CTMA), both of whom would accompany them for the next five days during their ascent to Base Camp. Brice himself would travel overland, accompanying a convoy of trucks full of expedition supplies along the Friendship Highway. Traveling by road was cheaper, but sending his clients through Lhasa ensured them of a more gradual acclimatization and, typically, high-quality accommodations and meals, with a little sightseeing thrown in for good measure. In general, the trip in from Lhasa was a more expensive but preferable warm-up for the next two months, during which they would endure steadily increasing discomfort and deprivation.

Himex had signed up ten clients, from all around the globe. Two of them were returning after a swing-and-miss the year before, including the asthmatic climber Mogens Jensen, a tall, tawny thirty-three-year-old Danish endurance athlete. Jensen was phasing out of his career as a professional triathlete and committing himself to high-altitude mountaineering. He had a generous sponsorship from the pharmaceutical company GlaxoSmithKline, which relished the idea that someone using its asthma drug Seretide was going to climb Everest emblazoned with the GSK logo while singing the benefits of the product. Jensen was relatively new to climbing, but he'd made a hard-charging debut on Everest in 2005: He'd run and cycled more than six thousand miles from his home in Denmark to Base Camp in Tibet before attacking the mountain. It was a noble effort, especially considering that he had forgone bottled oxygen. In the end, though, Jensen had pulled up shy of the top, at 27,700 feet, when frozen toes forced him to turn around.

The other repeat client was Brett Merrell, a forty-six-year-old captain in the Los Angeles Fire Department. Merrell was a strapping SoCal native with a powerful sense of fraternal devotion. He had grown up in a large family, and the emotional bonds he had experienced at home had laid the groundwork for his loyalty to his colleagues in the fire department. Merrell had been deeply affected by the terrorist attacks in New York City and Washington, D.C., in 2001, and he had been vocal about dedicating his climb "to the men and women who sacrificed their lives on September 11, 2001." Merrell was articulate, patriotic, sensitive, and a natural on camera. The documentary crew was already counting on him to be one of their stars.

No one on the expedition, however, had generated more preclimb media attention than New Zealand native Mark Inglis. Inglis was an experienced climber and former search-and-rescue professional who, in November 1982, had been stranded in a storm near the summit of 12,316-foot Mount Cook, the highest peak in his home country. Inglis and his climbing partner, Phil Doole, burrowed into an ice cave barely larger than a refrigerator, dubbing their shelter the Middle Peak Hotel because of its proximity to the mountain's central spire. Their ordeal lasted thirteen days while the storm dragged on, keeping help at bay. They managed to stretch their meager supply of food—half a package of cookies, a can of peaches, a single chocolate bar, and two packets of drink mix—over six days, using their body heat to melt water. A brief lull in the weather on the seventh day allowed rescue workers, in touch with the men by radio, to air-drop additional supplies. But by the time the search party finally reached them, the climbers were hypothermic, emaciated, and suffering from frostbite so severe that Inglis and Doole ended up having both legs amputated just below the knees.

Inglis was in frequent pain for years afterward, but it hardly slowed him down. He went on to earn a degree in biochemistry while conducting cancer research at the Christchurch School of Medicine. In 1992, he made a dramatic career change, soon emerging as one of New Zealand's top vintners. It was almost as though his disability had become the source of his motivation: Inglis intended to set the world on fire—while standing on twin prosthetics. In 2000, he won a silver medal in track cycling at the Paralympic Games in Sydney. Two years later, fitted with special limbs that allowed him to attach crampons, he again climbed to the top of Mount Cook. When he reached the summit, on January 7, he burst into tears.

For his attempt on Everest, Inglis was accompanied by Wayne Alexander, a forty-four-year-old engineer from Christchurch, New Zealand, whom everyone called Cowboy. It was Cowboy who'd built the legs Inglis had used on Cook in 2002, and now he had fashioned an even sleeker pair, sculpted from carbon fiber, especially for Everest. Cowboy had limited climbing experience himself—he'd been to the top of only two peaks in New Zealand, Cook and 8,120-foot Mount Aspiring—but Inglis and other Kiwi climbers had vouched for his competency. Cowboy knew that this was going to be the most significant challenge of Inglis's life. If Inglis made it, he would become the first double amputee ever to stand on top of Everest. Cowboy was going to make sure his friend didn't fail because of the equipment.

Brice continued the roll call of clients: Max Chaya, forty-four, a sports retailer from Lebanon, was attempting to complete the Seven Summits and, on this trip, to become the first Lebanese to summit Mount Everest. Bob Killip was a fifty-two-year-old businessman from New South Wales making his second attempt on the mountain. Three of the team members remained in absentia: Kurt Hefti, a forester, and Marcel Bach, a real estate broker, who both lived in Switzerland, and Gerard Bourrat, a sixty-two-year-old retired computer salesman from Cannes, France. When Bourrat had gone in for his preclimb physical shortly before the expedition, his doctor had discovered a malignant tumor on his kidney. Instead of preparing for Everest, Bourrat prepared for surgery. The surgeon removed the cancerous kidney from the front, through Bourrat's abdomen, so that carrying a backpack would not aggravate the surgical wound. The procedure went so well that the doctor soon gave Bourrat the green light for the climb. It would take him a couple of weeks to recover from the operation, but then he would be hopping the first plane to Nepal and joining the expedition as soon as possible.

Brice came to the last client in the room, Tim Medvetz, a former bouncer who helped customize Harley-Davidsons in Los Angeles for celebrities like Mel Gibson and the professional wrestler Hulk Hogan. When Brice introduced him, some of the Himex climbers were confused; they couldn't recall having seen Medvetz's name on any of the pre-expedition e-mails.

Medvetz had been a late addition—extremely late. In fact, he had paid Brice the fee for the trip—in full and in cash—just that day. Everything about him seemed unusual. Most strikingly, he was six feet, five inches tall and 220 pounds, much bigger than the typical mountaineer. He sported a goatee and straight, jet-black hair that fell to his shoulders. His skin was deeply tanned, almost brown, and his eyes were so green they looked like emeralds pressed into his skull. He was dressed in camouflage pants, pink Converse high-tops, and a black T-shirt over a white long-sleeved thermal top. A bandanna was cinched around his head, do-rag style, holding his long hair away from his face. "We kind of looked around at each other," Brett Merrell recalled, "and we were like, Who the hell's *that* guy?"

Medvetz didn't care what the others thought; he deserved to be there as much as anyone. With the exception of Inglis, no one at the meeting had endured what he had to reach this point, an odyssey that had begun five years earlier, on September 10, 2001. Medvetz had been roaring down a county highway near Los Angeles, on his way to meet a friend for dinner. It was a glorious Southern California evening, and he was letting his hog run, as he was wont to do—seventy, eighty, pushing ninety miles per hour. He certainly wasn't expecting the pickup truck in front of him, piloted by a gray-haired lady, to make a sudden U-turn.

Medvetz torpedoed into the side of the vehicle, the impact so forceful it broke the truck's rear wheel clean off its axle. He crumpled to the pavement, his bike finally spinning to a stop fifty feet away. Medvetz looked over at his busted rig lying on its side. Something wasn't right. *I need to get my bike out of the road before someone hits it,* he thought. But when he tried to get up he discovered he had no feeling below his waist. He fished his cell phone out of his vest pocket and called a friend. "Hey, man," he said. "You better come down here."

The next morning, when he woke up from surgery, Medvetz was intubated, connected to a respirator. He was extraordinarily groggy but aware enough to look down toward his feet. His left foot had been almost entirely torn off in the accident, and—he could remember this much—the doctor had told him they weren't sure if they could save it. Medvetz had pleaded with him before they rolled him into the OR: Whatever you do, save the foot. And there it was, wrapped in a cast, his toes, swollen and purple, peeking out from the end of the plaster. A group of doctors and nurses were with him in the room, but they were focused on the TV bolted to the wall. Medvetz followed their gaze to the screen. Through his medicinal fog, he dimly recognized the twin towers, smoke pouring from gashes in the side of each building. As he watched, to his astonishment, one tower collapsed in a billowing column of ash. He wanted to speak but couldn't. Was he dreaming? No, no. He was conscious, he knew that much. Something horrible was happening—he would learn later of friends and acquaintances who were killed that day—but at the time all he could think was *Christ, people, turn that shit off. Can't you see I've got my own problems here?*

For the next year, Medvetz grimaced his way through the long recovery. He would go through half a dozen operations; by the time the doctors were done with him, he had a metal plate installed in his head, a titanium cage wrapped around his lower spine, half a dozen screws in his knee, and bolts holding his ankle together, fusing his foot into a nearly immobile ninety-degree angle. "Airport security was going to be an issue for the rest of my life," he said later.

But, then, so would the pain. That first year, Medvetz endured bouts of despair, craving normalcy, dosing himself with Vicodin, sometimes twenty pills a day, chasing it down with Jack Daniel's. Then one afternoon, sitting glumly in his apartment, pondering what his future held, he spied the copy of *Into Thin Air* on his bookshelf, given to him by an ex-girlfriend. He rarely read books—they just didn't interest him—but he had devoured this one, dreaming about one day climbing in the Himalayas himself. The fantasy had faded years ago, but now it came surging back, the tumblers clicking into place. That was it—the ultimate rehab. He was going to go climb Mount Everest.

By March 2006, Medvetz was on the verge of turning his big idea into an even bigger reality. He had reserved his place on an Everest expedition with an Ashford, Washington, outfitter called International Mountain Guides, which was leading a trip that spring up the South Col route, in Nepal. He'd already paid a $6,000 deposit but now the balance for the $30,000 trip was past due. Medvetz had wrangled several sponsors, sold his bike, and scraped together his own cash, but he was still more than $15,000 short. Eric Simonson, IMG's owner and a veteran Everest guide, had stretched the deadline as far as he could. Medvetz had someone lined up to buy his truck; he'd have the balance in two weeks, tops, he assured Simonson—but Simonson needed to purchase the permits the next day. The clock had run out; Medvetz was off the expedition. "Maybe the mountain gods are trying to tell you something," Simonson said, politely, over the phone.

Fuck that, Medvetz thought. He wasn't upset with Simonson; the guy had done what he had to do. But Medvetz already had his plane ticket (a buddy pass he'd wrangled through a friend) and his equipment, and soon he'd have enough money to cover the expedition costs. Hell, he would just show up at Base Camp if that's what it was going to take. Money was powerful persuasion. If IMG wouldn't have him, surely someone else would.

In late March, he flew to Paris, where he holed up and waited two days on standby for his next flight. It was here that he remembered

Russell Brice. They had met a couple of years earlier, in a bar in Kathmandu, and Brice had provided all kinds of salient advice, including suggesting that Medvetz consider a south-side operator because that pitch of the mountain would favor his injured left leg. Medvetz not only had been impressed by the generous free counsel, he'd admired the number of drafts Brice had consumed while dishing it.

"Shouldn't you be preparing for the climb?" Medvetz had asked near the end of their conversation.

"This is preparing," Brice had said.

In Paris, Medvetz tracked down Brice's e-mail address and sent him a note explaining his situation. Brice was already in Kathmandu, but he replied almost immediately. He wasn't sure he could help, but he told Medvetz to call him as soon as he arrived in Nepal.

Even that would prove difficult. When Medvetz reached Mumbai, he was promptly deported—his itinerary required him to enter the country but he didn't have a visa for India. Authorities put him on the first flight back to Paris. By the time he touched down at Charles de Gaulle, he'd almost given up. Maybe the mountain gods *were* trying to tell him something, but then again, maybe the gods needed to see just how badly he wanted it. Medvetz was back on a plane three days later, rerouted directly to Kathmandu.

He called Brice as soon as he got to town. The team was meeting the next day, Brice informed him, and would be departing for Tibet the day after. Medvetz would have to wire the funds directly to the Himex account, a task that would prove to be yet another roadblock. Medvetz couldn't process the transfer while abroad, so on March 30 he walked into the Standard Chartered Bank in Kathmandu and asked to see a manager. He told her he needed to withdraw $40,000 in cash. She nodded slowly. Yes, they could help him. Within the hour, a bank clerk wheeled the money out on a cart, 2.8 million Nepali rupees bound in fat bricks, which they soon loaded into his backpack. They stuffed and stuffed, the sides of the pack bulging. Medvetz could barely fasten the top by the time they were done. The pack had been empty when he came in; now it rose over his head. He shouldered the bag and strode out of the bank, walking proudly toward the Hotel Tibet.

Brice was in the lobby when Medvetz arrived. "I've got something for you," Medvetz told him, and he dropped the pack on the floor by Brice's feet. Brice unhooked the straps and looked inside.

"It's all there," Medvetz reassured him.

Brice laughed, then extended his hand.

"Welcome to the team," he said.

Everest suffered no shortage of eclectics, eccentrics, and wannabes, but even Brice had to admit, once his team was all assembled, that he had attracted a particularly colorful group this year. But if anyone had constructed a foolproof system, it was Brice. He had been running expeditions on Everest for twelve years, and he had debugged the process as much as the process could be debugged. Each client would be paired with a personal Sherpa, and each summit team was typically bracketed by Western guides. Everyone would carry a radio, and the guides and lead Sherpas would bring satellite phones as backup. On summit day, Brice would diligently follow his team from his post on the North Col, charting his clients' pace and oxygen supply as they made their way up and down the ridge. And he wouldn't be bashful about pulling the plug if someone appeared to be climbing his way into trouble.

In 2006, Brice charged $40,000 for a full-service Everest trip—the only kind of Everest trip he ran. Because Himex operated exclusively on the north side, Brice was able to take advantage of the lower permit costs and pass the savings along to his customers. Navigating the

Chinese bureaucracy had never been simple, but over the years he had developed a civil, if not friendly, rapport with the CTMA. Preserving that relationship was one of the reasons he'd grown so annoyed with the low-budget operators and half-baked private expeditions that were descending on the north side in ever-increasing numbers. Never mind that they had a troubling propensity to leave corpses behind; they also tended to cut corners or dodge CTMA officials, who controlled access to the mountain and monitored Base Camp during the climbing season.

Competing operators occasionally crabbed that Brice was a megalomaniac trying to establish a monopoly on the north side, controlling the fixed ropes, crowding out the little guys who threatened to take business away from him. Brice, not surprisingly, countered that he was simply trying to establish safe protocols and promote reasonable cooperation among all those sharing the route. He was appalled by the shoddiness of some of the expeditions, and it peeved him that others would criticize his operation while simultaneously exploiting his largesse—the equipment and manpower he paid for to establish the route each year, the medical services he provided to those climbing without a doctor or adequate first-aid supplies, hell, even the bottles of beer he handed out liberally at Base Camp.

Brice had done much, perhaps more than any other single individual, to commercialize the north side, and with that understanding came the realization that he was not entirely unaccountable for the problems that persisted there. But he had built his empire with a seriousness of purpose focused on safety and climbing success, not just fiscal gain. He had parlayed the business into a decent living, yes, but he ground his teeth over those who approached it with less commitment than he did. They were all playing an extraordinarily dangerous game, and if it was going to continue they couldn't go around losing climbers.

Those who signed up for a Himex expedition generally understood that Brice's experience and resources were unrivaled on the north side, and they either wanted or needed a little extra help if they were going to get to the top. Historically speaking, Himex offered its clients a 42 percent chance of success and a 100 percent chance of survival—attractive odds on Everest. Brice didn't apologize for the amenities he worked hard to provide along the way. After all, Everest expeditions had a long history of lavish support. On Brice's balance sheet, the material luxuries were not intended to pamper a spoiled clientele. The climb entailed an arduous two months, during which you endured a steady process of physical attrition while scraping your way slowly up the mountain. The whole point was to be able to position yourself near the top with enough energy left to dash through the death zone and back before your oxygen, energy, and ability to walk under your own power petered out.

"The real problems aren't the obvious ones—the oxygen, that sort of thing," Brice said. "It's the not-so-obvious stuff that is making these people so weak. They haven't been eating well because they haven't been on an expedition with a budget to afford proper food. They're always cold. They don't have any support—no Sherpas, no guides. These are the things that are killing people. It's out of control."

No one had shown Brice how to climb Everest; he had figured it out during a long process of trial and error. Brice had been born in Christchurch, on New Zealand's South Island. In 1954, when he was eighteen months old, his mother died of pneumonia and he was sent to live with his grandparents on their farm outside of town. He would not see his father or his sister again until he was seven, and by then that part of his family had become strangers.

Brice's early upbringing may have been unorthodox, but it was also idyllic and enriching. Young Russ rode along on a horse-drawn hay rake, sitting in his grandfather's lap. He shouldered the various chores required around the farm. He rode a horse to grade school. The ebb and flow of this rural life instilled self-discipline, focus, and the intrinsic value of a hard day's work.

As a teenager, he was bored by book learning, but he took quickly to experiential education. He had spent a few years in the Boy Scouts, where he'd gotten his first exposure to outdoor adventure: rafting, camping, and tramping around the South Island. By high school he had joined the Venturer Scouts, a nonprofit organization that sought to teach kids vocational and life skills through mountain activities. The group introduced Brice to climbing, but—the scarce population near his home being what it was—it lacked an adult leader and could rally only a small core of club members. The instruction was haphazard and improvisational. Seasoned guides and formal courses were hard to come by, so the scouts made it up as they went along—an alfresco school of hard knocks, with Brice at the helm.

When he wasn't running around the mountains with his friends trying to kill himself, Brice wrangled jobs working construction. He learned how to pour concrete and tie steel, how to service a diesel engine, how to operate heavy machinery like cranes, backhoes, and bucket loaders. One summer, he and a few of his mates were hired to build a bridge in the middle of the bush. Every week or so, after dinner at their small encampment, they would ramble down the dirt road with rifles and shoot a deer so they'd have meat for the coming days.

By his late teens, Brice had racked up enough experience and mileage in the mountains that he started teaching climbing courses for the local chapter of the New Zealand Alpine Club. Formalized mountaineering programs were still in their infancy; the NZAC would import the occasional European guide to teach classes, but quality instruction was hard to find.

One of the regular instructors was Paddy Freaney, a gregarious forty-two-year-old former British Special Air Service (SAS) officer and expat Irishman who managed a restaurant in Christchurch. Brice had signed up for one of Freaney's "mountaincraft" courses at Arthur's Pass, where Freaney had established the Outdoor Education Centre. Brice was a bright, motivated student, and he and Freaney became close friends. Brice even looked like a younger version of Freaney, with his shaggy hair, square chin, and bold nose. Save for the accent, the two might have passed for brothers.

When Freaney left to spend several months training SAS troops in Antarctica, Brice took over running the center and teaching its courses. Working out of tented camps, Brice and another instructor or two would bring half a dozen students into the mountains. They'd go bouldering one day, bivouac under a rock the next. On long, multi-pitch snow and ice climbs, Brice would set the students up in two-person teams, then scramble among them, unroped, checking belays and providing pointers about their techniques. By today's standards, the courses would give a liability lawyer an ulcer, but they fostered in Brice the kind of self-reliance that would be invaluable in the years to come.

Brice had begun to earn money as an instructor at an early age, but it was clear that he would need a more reliable and consistent vocation if he wanted to make it on his own. After high school, he obtained his electrician's license, taking night classes and working as an apprentice with contractors he had met on job sites. The electrician's work filled the seasonal gaps between summer and winter, when he could scrounge up guiding and instructing jobs. He found work managing a ski area in the winter, and began teaching himself to ski. In the off-season, he got a job as a technician at a community theater in Christchurch, helping build stage lighting. It was unique and creative work—fun, at least for a little while. But scrambling over ceilings and rooftops, running wire and splicing cable, hardly measured up to the freedom and joy he felt in the mountains.

Ultimately, Brice knew, his prospects were always going to be limited in New Zealand. He hadn't taken his home turf for granted; it was a stunningly beautiful place, and it had taught him much. But living on an island had its own issues, not the least of which was relentless wanderlust among young men. Brice needed to see what else was out there, so in 1974, at age twenty-two, he and two friends bought 365-day open-route airline tickets and lit out to see the world.

Patagonia, Yosemite, Alaska, the Alps: so many mountain playgrounds, so little time. Off to South America and the 6,000-meter peaks of the Andes—Yerupaja, Siula Grande—then up through North America and the granite walls of California. Over to Europe now, where one of the trio met a girl and fell in love and stayed behind while Brice and his other friend pushed on to Asia. In Nepal, they met the most famous Kiwi of them all, Sir Edmund Hillary, who was climbing less now but helping more through his nonprofit agency, the Himalayan Trust.

Brice had written to Hillary before the trip, informing him that they would be coming through and asking if they could assist him in any way. He'd outlined his journeyman skills, which he'd hoped could be of use, and they were. In Phaplu, they helped Sir Ed build a hospital, one of the most important community projects to come to the region but one that would be tainted by tragedy in 1975 when Hillary's wife and youngest daughter, Louise Mary Rose and Belinda, were killed in a plane crash en route to the village from Kathmandu. Later, Brice hiked upland, deeper into the Khumbu, Nepal's famous trekking region and the gateway to Everest, where he helped build a water system for the Hillary School in Khumjung, not far from the giant white fang of Ama Dablam. Though Hillary's altruism has never quite outshone his historic climb in 1953, his regard for the Sherpa people is hardly a secret; without them, he's often pointed out, there would be no Everest expeditions. Hillary's attitude made a deep and lasting impression on Brice.

Home again: through Thailand and Australia and finally back to New Zealand. Brice and his buddy arrived at the Christchurch airport exactly 365 days after they'd departed, exhausted, blissed out, flat broke. Between the two of them they couldn't even scrape together enough loose change to cover the bus fare to town, so, fittingly perhaps, they hoisted their rucksacks and walked the last five miles of their journey to Brice's father's house.

Plenty of experiences would resonate long after the trip, but none so much as Brice's time in Nepal. Never mind that the Himalayas were the roof of the world; there were more practical reasons to contemplate a return. While most climbing seasons around the globe peak during summer and winter, high season in the Himalayas occurs in the spring and fall, between the summer monsoons and winter snow. For a young climber facing his future as a commercial guide and expedition operator, here was a place to connect the seasons and build a year-round business.

Brice made his first trip to Mount Everest in 1981, at age twenty-nine, not as a guide or Big Boss but as the younger half of a two-man Kiwi team with an ambitious goal: to reach the summit via the daunting West Ridge—without oxygen. His partner was Paddy Freaney.

By the late 1970s the pair had distinguished themselves as two of New Zealand's strongest climbers. Between December and February—summer in the Southern Hemisphere—of 1977–78, they'd scaled all thirty-one of New Zealand's 3,000-meter peaks in a single season, a first in the history of Kiwi climbing. Their peak-bagging project required them to string together multiple ascents and traverses on dangerous technical routes, and they often found themselves riding out storms in moldy mountain huts, trying to stretch a few days of provisions over two weeks or more. "Sometimes, we just didn't eat," Freaney told the *Press*, Christchurch's daily paper, after they were done.

Their New Zealand exploits brought local fame, but success on the West Ridge would install their names among mountaineering's elite in perpetuity, so daunting was their objective. The West Ridge had first been climbed in 1963 by two Americans, Tom Hornbein and Willi Unsoeld, a feat that is still considered one of the greatest achievements in the annals of climbing. Everest is, essentially, a three-sided pyramid, the summit formed by the intersection of three distinct ridges. By the time Hornbein and Unsoeld arrived, the two most accessible ridges had already been completed—the Southeast Ridge, famously, by Hillary and Tenzing Norgay in 1953, and the Northeast Ridge, in 1960, with slightly less fanfare (the *New York Times* gave the story all of eighty words), by a three-man Chinese team. The southeast and northeast routes weren't exactly easy, but they were considerably easier than the saw-toothed blade that confronted Unsoeld and Hornbein when they reached Everest's west shoulder and looked up.

"The cloud cauldron of the great South Face boiled, accentuating the black, twisting harshness of the West Ridge," Hornbein wrote later. "We stared. . . . Our eyes climbed a mile of sloping sedimentary shingles, black rock, yellow rock, grey rock, to the summit."

Negotiating the route was even worse than the Americans had anticipated. Their high camps were fully exposed to Everest's brutal weather, and during the ascent a tent containing four Sherpas blew off the ridge and went tumbling down the north side. (Miraculously, the Sherpas survived.) On the climbers' final stretch, their progress slowed to an agonizing 100 vertical feet per hour while they chopped ice steps up a broad chute. Farther on, they clambered over turrets of rock so loose and rotten that holds slipped away underfoot, like bricks in a wall with no mortar. The ridge was too treacherous to permit a retreat, so their plan was to cross over the summit and descend the south side, where they hoped to encounter other members of their team on the Southeast Ridge.

Hornbein and Unsoeld topped out at 6:15 P.M. on May 22, and headed down the Southeast Ridge as planned. But soon it grew dark, and when they found their two teammates, Lute Jerstad and Barry

Bishop, the men were bunkered into the snow about 1,000 feet below the top, desperately ill, out of oxygen, and lacking headlamps of any sort. The four men passed a calm but bitterly cold night on the ridge. When Hornbein's feet went numb, he removed his boots and socks so Unsoeld could hold them inside his jacket, against the skin of his belly. Hornbein offered to return the favor, but Unsoeld declined. "I'm okay," he told his friend. All four men survived, but Unsoeld lost nine toes.

The 1963 ascent was one for the record books, but with the seemingly infinite capacity of mountaineers to quibble with and continuously revise the milestones of their sport, some people began to sniff that the original West Ridge climb needed to be "straightened out," that it had not been truly complete—or, in the sport's parlance, "direct." The Americans, critics pointed out, had accessed the route from the Western Cwm, skipping the lower ridge altogether. Farther up, they had bypassed some of the most technical sections by scooting out onto the North Face and slashing their way up a broad couloir that now bears Hornbein's name. By the time Brice and Freaney arrived, nearly twenty years later, five teams had tried the West Ridge Direct, and only one had succeeded—a group of Yugoslavians, in 1979. All of them had used supplemental oxygen.

The 1970s and early '80s had seen a kind of modern renaissance for mountaineering. Advances in hardware design and materials made equipment lighter and more reliable, helping open the door for face climbing—long, audacious lines on nearly vertical walls of rock, ice, and snow. As the technical frontiers evolved, so did the attitude. Alpine style, a self-reliant strategy that involves carrying all of your own gear, became de rigueur—and led to a seismic philosophical shift in the way climbs were done. On traditional expeditions, fixed camps, fixed ropes, and platoons of high-altitude porters provided maximum support for the summit team. Alpine style embodied an entirely different approach: light, fast, and self-contained—a test of an individual's endurance and experience. Mountain climbing was no longer about the mountain; it was about the mountaineer.

Arguably, no single individual represented the alpine-style ethos better than Reinhold Messner. Messner was a mop-haired quasi mystic who'd grown up in northern Italy, under the thumb of a strict and stern Austrian father. He had learned to climb in the Dolomites, making his first summit at age five. As an adult, he had become one of the world's foremost alpinists, adopting a climbing creed that was equal parts asceticism and competitive bravado. In essence, Messner asserted, any given climb should rely on as little aid as possible. Taken to the extreme, some joked, this implied climbing naked, alone, and with your bare hands. But Messner, ever serious, explained that it meant simply "by fair means."

"In us all the longing remains for the primitive condition," he wrote in *The Crystal Horizon,* "in which we can match ourselves against Nature, have our chance to have it out with her and thereby discover ourselves."

By the mid-1970s, Messner had provided numerous examples of what alpine style could achieve. He had flown up the Matterhorn and the Eiger, in the Alps, in less than half the time it typically took other climbers. Inevitably, the media began pressing him about Mount Everest. Messner said he would try it, but only without oxygen.

At the time, it wasn't yet clear if it was physiologically possible to reach the summit of Everest without supplemental oxygen; many scientists were convinced it wasn't. At 29,000 feet, the atmosphere contains only about 30 percent of the oxygen available at sea level. That might provide just enough oxygen to survive at rest, the experts surmised, but not nearly enough to support the strenuous demands of mountaineering. If the direct effects of oxygen deprivation, like cerebral and pulmonary edema, didn't kill you, then the indirect effects—hypothermia, exhaustion, a fall—probably would. If you somehow managed to survive, you might get off easy and only sustain permanent brain damage.

When Messner and his climbing partner Peter Habeler topped out on Everest on May 8, 1978, without using oxygen, they not only stunned the mountaineering community, they changed the rules of the game. Granted, they had been part of a larger expedition, and they had climbed Everest's most established route—the Southeast Ridge via the South Col—but the duo had completed the round-trip from the last camp in a mere nine hours, less time than it took many climbers using oxygen just to reach the top.

The expedition hadn't concluded without its controversies. A faction of Sherpas tried to dispute the Austrians' claims of success—even though Messner had returned with summit photos. Some felt that the issue was motivated largely by an incident earlier in the trip when Messner and two Sherpas had been caught in a storm on the col. It was all they could do to survive the next two days, blasted by 125-mile-per-hour winds, nearly freezing to death in their tents. The Sherpas all but gave up, lying catatonic in their sleeping bags, waiting for the end. Messner flew into a rage, screaming at them to help him keep the tent from collapsing, to keep fighting. Later, in formal depositions with Nepal's minister of tourism, his accusers would describe Messner as a madman who had "subjected Nepalese nationals to inhuman treatment," including, according to one, urinating in their cook pot. However, nothing ever came of these charges.

When Russell Brice and Paddy Freaney traveled to the Himalayas in the fall of 1981, they were fresh off a successful climb of the north ridge of Ama Dablam the year before, and brimming with confidence. The technical ascent had taken thirty-two days. It was the second ascent of the ridge (a French team had put up the first ascent a year prior), but it was the first successful climb of a Himalayan peak by a team of Kiwis in more than twenty years.

Despite their growing notoriety, Brice and Freaney's expedition to the West Ridge set out with little fanfare. They knew what they were up against, and thought it was prudent to keep the pre-expedition hype to a minimum. They were approaching the route from the south, in Nepal, and at Base Camp they were neighbors with the American Medical Research Expedition, an eighteen-person team conducting studies on altitude and acclimatization, led by the prominent high-altitude physician John B. West. This was a boon for the New Zealanders. They were surrounded by doctors, but, more important, the large expedition had already installed ropes through the notorious Khumbu Icefall. Since they were well provisioned, in the Kiwi tradition, they sent the Americans a case of Khukri Rum in exchange for use of the ropes. "Of course they were mostly medical students, so they didn't really drink," Brice recalled. "Freaney and I drank most of it."

Their climb took them through the icefall, across the Western Cwm, and up the southern face of the Lho La, the same route Unsoeld and Hornbein had taken back in 1963. They established their high camps and made two separate pushes up the West Ridge, both times turned back by high winds and dangerous cold.

On the second attempt, they returned to the high camp only to be stranded there in a gathering storm, Brice, Freaney, and two Sherpas stuffed inside a single tent on a tiny ledge. They braced their backs against the tent walls to keep it from collapsing; they plugged ice screws through the nylon floor and tied themselves in. After four days, they ran out of food and water, their shelter now in tatters. They would perish if they didn't get off the mountain soon, so they roped up and began downclimbing the steep slope, now a boilerplate of ice, the conditions so severe that Brice couldn't see the next man on the rope above him. Making matters worse, Freaney had become ill. "He couldn't even take his own crampons off," Brice recalled. "So we crawled into a

crevasse and I put him in a sleeping bag and gave him a couple of ciga-
rettes to warm up his core."

Many veteran mountaineers have at least one story of extraordinary,
even inexplicable good luck—the avalanche that swept within feet of
their tent, the sketchy anchor that held them during a fall—and here
was one of Brice's. As he led the way down, facing the slope, the blizzard lashing them, he bumped into a bamboo wand marking the edge
of a bergschrund, an ice cliff that fell away into the murk. It was as
though some invisible hand had reached out to prevent him from simply stepping backward into space, yanking his rope team with him.
"We could have all died there," Brice recalled. "But we kept on and
camped a little further down, and took care of ourselves."

To have come so close on the West Ridge was technically a failure,
but practically it was a fine success. Brice had learned plenty about the
intensity of extreme altitude and the unpredictability of weather. Surviving such an ordeal, summit or no, was more empowering than dis-
couraging. He still felt "bulletproof," as he called it, bent on wilder
outings and more audacious climbs. His business with Everest was just
beginning.

It would take Brice seven years to return to the mountain, and when
he arrived for his second time, in the summer of 1988, it was under considerably different circumstances. Brice was part of a large British expedition, run by a retired SAS sergeant and an old friend of Paddy Freaney's
named John "Brummie" Stokes. It was Freaney who had recruited Brice,
and it was Freaney who bailed out at the last minute when he tripped
over his dog and injured his back. Within a few weeks, Brice would be in
unfamiliar territory, Everest's north side—the only Kiwi on a predominantly English expedition. What's more, the team was attempting a first
ascent of the entire Northeast Ridge, a daunting objective that involved
traversing three infamous spires known as the Pinnacles.

The Pinnacles jut out of the ridge at 27,000 feet, silhouetted against the southern sky like a cluster of shark's teeth. No mountaineer had ever crossed them, and, in 1984, two of the world's most famous climbers, Peter Boardman and Joe Tasker, had died trying.

If Messner was the lone wolf of alpine style, Boardman and Tasker were its legendary partnership, and they'd pioneered climbs that had no rival. In 1976, their ascent of the west face of Changabang, in the Indian Himalayas, was trumpeted as the most daring ascent of its time. The pair had employed new gear and bold techniques, bivouacking in hammocks dangling from Changabang's massive granite face. On climbs, they were fantastically strong and imaginative, even though they tended to taunt each other, fueling their interpersonal rivalry. They were competitors, but they were also friends; each man held his partner's life, literally, in his hands. They often climbed with little spoken communication, but their ability to read each other as they moved swiftly through dangerous places bordered on a kind of telepathy.

They were also deft, prolific writers, and by the end of their truncated careers they had produced a small body of work that would be anthologized in the *Boardman Tasker Omnibus,* works that penetrated beyond the romanticism and idealism that characterized so much of the climbing canon. Peter Boardman was particularly predisposed to introspection, and it colored the accounts of his climbs with blunt honesty and self-deprecation.

"Courage. Endurance. Those words drifted across the office and mocked my bitter mood of discontent—meaningless," he wrote in *The Shining Mountain,* his account of the Changabang climb.

> Courage is doing only what you are scared of doing. The blatant drama of mountaineering only blinds the judgment of these people who are so loud in praise. Life has many cruel subtleties that require far more courage to deal with than the obvious dangers of climbing.

Endurance. But it takes more endurance to crush the hopes and ambitions that were in your childhood dreams and to submit to a daily routine of work that fits into a tiny cog in the wheel of western civilization. "Really great mountaineers." But what are mountaineers? Professional heroes of the west? Escapist parasites who play at adventures? Obsessive dropouts who do something different? Malcontents and egomaniacs who have not the discipline to conform?

That the Pinnacles had snuffed out Boardman and Tasker at the height of their ability and ambition made the ridge fearsomely intimidating. Brummie Stokes had already tried a run at it, two years before, but his team had been soundly beaten back by bad weather and dangerous conditions. Now he'd returned with an even stronger squad. The eighteen-member team included, among other luminaries, Harry Taylor, twenty-nine, a veteran of Stokes's '86 expedition, who had high-pointed at 26,200 feet; Joe Brown, fifty-seven, who had made the first ascent of Kangchenjunga, the third-highest mountain in the world, in 1955; and Mo Anthoine, forty-seven, a teammate of Taylor's in 1986.

The squad was stacked, but the expedition was snakebit from the start. They were turned back at the Friendship Bridge, at the Nepal-Tibet border, because a convoy of trucks loaded with arms and headed for Nepal was idling there.—something the Chinese were not eager to show to a busful of "tourists"—The expedition was rerouted through Lhasa but suffered dismal food, promptly followed by bouts of gastroenteritis and dysentery, as they hopscotched through grotty villages on their way up to Base Camp.

The group arrived at Everest Base Camp in Tibet on June 18, planning to climb through the summer monsoons. Climbing during the summer typically meant more precipitation, but it had its advantages as well—most significantly, longer days and warmer nights. In the beginning, Brice fell into a support role, helping with the hard work required to establish their Advanced Base Camp (ABC) at 21,500 feet. The monsoons were ramping up to full force, dropping copious amounts of precipitation around the Himalayas and requiring the climbers to forge troughs up the route through snow that had piled waist-deep in places.

Brice and a teammate pushed high enough to establish a first camp at 23,000 feet, on a buttress heading up toward the lower section of the Northeast Ridge. Brice, who'd managed to dodge the intestinal bugs that had plagued his colleagues, was now stricken with diarrhea, forcing him all the way back down to Base Camp. While he recuperated, his friendship with Harry Taylor galvanized. The Brit was six years Brice's junior, but they shared a lively sense of humor and had hit it off in Kathmandu, barhopping and chasing girls. In Base Camp they found themselves bonding over a bottle of whiskey, celebrating Brice's thirty-sixth birthday.

By July 12, Brice and Taylor had moved back up to ABC, where the work installing high camps had been frequently interrupted by violent storms and heavy snow. Fresh and rested, the two new friends, along with a handful of Sherpas, took over the lead, wading through new-fallen powder with heavy packs. At times, the work was nearly Sisyphean. The snow piled up to their chests, forcing them to claw and shovel their way forward mere inches at a time. Though the climbers couldn't know it then, they were persevering through one of the worst monsoons on record. That same summer, the flooding in Bangladesh, which sits in the path of the monsoonal flow off the Bay of Bengal, was so severe that it killed more than two thousand people and left thirty million homeless.

It took two weeks before Brice and Taylor were positioned for their historic shot at the Pinnacles, during which the horrendous weather forced them to retreat, yet again, all the way to Base Camp.

They arrived at BC the same day more bad luck hit the expedition: Brummie Stokes had to be evacuated home with cerebral edema, a dangerous swelling of the brain. Stokes was replaced by the expedition's deputy director, Paul Moores. By the time they returned to ABC on July 27, it was obvious who had best weathered the team's six weeks on the mountain. Brice and Taylor had emerged as the most fit and capable of the lot, and they were eager to get their shot at the ridge.

"I would often chuckle to myself as people who were having trouble with the altitude at ABC, and who had been no higher than Camp One to take a load, discussed how they were going to be in the summit team," Brice wrote later. "As it turned out, Mo Anthoine, Joe Brown, Davey Jones, Ian Nicholson, and Sam Roberts were all at Camp One. We watched their attempts to reach Camp Two with interest from ABC, before deciding that it was time some more push was injected into the lead team."

Brice and Taylor caught up to the others at Camp One two days later, their teammates now beginning to wilt back to ABC. On August 3, the pair found themselves tucked into Camp Three, at just above 26,240 feet, alone now on the upper ridge.

By the end of the next day the climbers had strung a fixed line up the First Pinnacle and caught their initial glimpse of what lay ahead. Brice radioed ABC and brashly described the pending terrain as a "piece of weasel piss," but he later revised his assessment: "The route along to the Second Pinnacle looked daunting, even if I was quoted as saying 'a piece of piss' over the radio that evening." Still, "daunting" was doable—not that they had much of a choice at this point—and they climbed into their bags, intending to complete the route the next day.

The pair set out from their high camp on August 5 at six A.M.

They were traveling as light as they thought prudent: one stove and a 150-foot coil of rope between them, plus a headlamp, bivy sack, food, and a single ice ax apiece. Each man also carried one small bottle of oxygen—a provisional backup that would last about three hours; they were planning to climb without using it. The backup canisters were almost a joke; they estimated that their summit push could last as long as thirty-six hours, since it involved crossing the Pinnacles, then traversing the low-angle remainder of the Northeast Ridge to the summit and back.

By the time Brice and Taylor had pulled up the fixed lines from the day before and crossed over the First Pinnacle, they began to realize just how ambitious a plan they'd contrived. The ridge between the First and Second Pinnacles pinched to a few feet, even less in places. The exposure was nauseating; even the rickety ladders in the Khumbu Icefall seemed like a sidewalk by comparison. To their right, steep gullies fell away toward the East Rongbuk. To their left, the fluted wall of the Kangshung Face plummeted 5,000 vertical feet to the glacier below. More troubling yet, the recent storms had foamed the ridge with eighteen inches of fresh snow, which the high winds had sculpted into fragile cornices curling out into space on both sides. For the next four hours, the two men traded leads in a delicate balancing act between the rock towers. Each step was heel to toe, one arm outstretched for balance, the other sweeping the loose snow away with an ax.

At last the climbers skirted the base of the Second Pinnacle, ascending a steep ramp of snow and ice before dropping down into a gully, where they found a small ledge. They had been climbing for fourteen hours. It was nighttime now, and the wind had come up again, and with it more snow. They had hoped to reach the Third Pinnacle that afternoon, but it was suicide to try to keep moving through the dark in such conditions. Brice attempted to dig a snow cave, only to hear the pick of his ax clank against rock just two feet below the surface. It was going to be a long night.

Taylor fired up the stove, but the heat it generated was so feeble that he was able to melt only one cup of water. The men slipped into their bivy bags and hunkered down in their meager hole next to each other. When they pulled out their oxygen, they realized that one of the regulators had busted, so they were forced to pass a single mask between them. The pair was able to take in just enough air to stave off frostbite, though not enough to keep the cold at bay. They tried to protect themselves against the elements, but the wind hammered at them and the snow sifted inside their clothing. Though they did not know it at the time, not far from their frigid bivouac, Joe Tasker's corpse sat serenely in the snow.

Brice and Taylor had hoped to take a relatively brief rest and get moving again by midnight, but the weather continued to deteriorate. Finally, at five A.M., there was just enough light to reveal that the conditions had become a complete whiteout; a fresh eighteen inches of snow had fallen overnight. It took them nearly four hours to reach the Third Pinnacle that morning, slogging up an avalanche-prone gully. Several slides released around them, threatening to sweep them down the mountain, but they clung to the rocks along the edge of the gully until they regained the ridge.

It was an anxious morning for the other team members, too, riding out the storm down at ABC. The weather had completely obscured their view of the ridge, and Brice and Taylor had been out of radio contact since the night before. Boardman and Tasker's fate a few years earlier weighed on everyone's mind. It was eleven A.M. when Taylor's voice crackled over the radio at ABC.

"Harry!" It was Joe Brown, loud and clear. "We were gettin' worried. Over."

"Yeah, bit dodgy up here," Taylor said. "We're just below the First Step. Found some shelter, so we're going to brew up. Over."

"Good idea. Weather's clearing here, so you might want to sit tight for a bit, see if you get a break."

"Roger. Pretty bad up here still. Gonna be a piece of work getting down."

When the weather finally eased, the summit emerged, so tantalizingly close it looked as though they could reach out and touch it. But there was no chance of pushing farther up the mountain, not unless they wanted to stay there for good, and so they began their retreat.

The pair clomped slowly down the North Ridge, an easier line of descent than the lower section of the Northeast Ridge, which led directly to the North Col. From there they saw no clear way down. This stretch was the last real hurdle between them and the sanctuary of ABC, and Brice and Taylor radioed down to see if their teammates could provide any direction. This time, Mo Anthoine directed the climbers to a line down from the col that started steeply but eased to what he described as a "bum slide," where he said they could glissade with minimal risk.

When they reached Anthoine's so-called bum slide they found that it was, in reality, a 1,500-vertical-foot ice wall laced with crevasses and cornices, slickened with an inch-deep coating of snow. They would be lucky to get down it alive, let alone try to glissade. By now, Brice and Taylor were beyond exhausted. Their progress was excruciatingly slow, especially since they had left their precious coil of rope behind, anchored to the col's steepest pitch. They climbed down without protection, tacked to the headwall by only the front points of their crampons and a single ax. A slip now would be fatal—an undeserving end to such a grand outing.

When they finally reached the bottom—wasted, parched, giddy— John English, Davey Jones, and a few Sherpas met them with hot tea, biscuits, and bottles of beer. It was too soon to appreciate the full magnitude of their accomplishment, but for now they could savor the simple fact that they'd survived it.

Within days, Brice and Taylor were making headlines. "Everest's Toughest Route Is Conquered," rang out one. "Britons Beat Last Everest Frontier," declared another. The climb had not been without a twinge of the bittersweet—it was Brice's second near miss at the summit, Taylor's third—but no matter. For a time the two friends enjoyed a moderate celebrity. The achievement had gathered potency and clout, closing another chapter of Everest exploration. It had been more than just "a good day out," as Brice had referred to it; it had been epic, empowering, life-changing.

"It was a big effort," Taylor recalled. "I think for Russell and I it was the biggest thing we'd accomplished, before or since. It was the climb that put us on the map."

. The '88 expedition also introduced the pair to a figure who would bear a large influence on the rest of their lives: Loel Guinness, aspiring alpinist, adventure benefactor, and scion of the Guinness banking and brewing family.

A year after the Pinnacles climb, Guinness contacted Taylor and offered him a climber's dream job: Plan and pull off big, bold adventures in big, bold mountains and send Guinness the bill. By then Taylor was living in Chamonix, the epicenter of all things extreme, where he was honing his paragliding skills with the idea of one day flying off Everest. With the go-ahead from Guinness, Taylor promptly recruited Russell Brice, now back in New Zealand.

These were halcyon days for the two friends. They set themselves up in a scenic mountain town with an ample population of beautiful girls, had a wealthy patron eager to fund their adventures, and traveled regularly to the Himalayas to climb and paraglide. For Brice, the move to Chamonix established his trajectory for the next twenty years and beyond. He was thirty-seven, still single, with an increasingly impressive climbing résumé. More important, at least in terms of his professional life, he had merged his skills as an engineer with his yen for big adventure. His future as a guide and expedition leader had taken hold.

CHAPTER 2

THE NORTH SIDE

At the turn of the twentieth century, long before Brice would build his modest mountain empire, it seemed that Everest's north side—not the south—would be first to be conquered and commercialized. Some of the first Westerners to glimpse the mountain had noted that the Northeast Ridge, rising gently and in striking relief above the other massive peaks, appeared to be the most obvious line to the summit. What lay below the lofty ridge in the distance was anyone's guess, but a growing corps of explorers, adventurers, diplomats, and feverishly obsessed iconoclasts were determined to find out.

In the spring of 1913, a British army captain named John Noel traveled north through Sikkim, toward Tibet. Noel was all of twenty-three, with a smooth complexion, chiseled features, and ambitions for a long, distinguished military career. He had a facile grasp of the languages spoken by the hill tribes of the eastern Himalayas, and when he neared the border he smeared his face with a dark balm and fitted himself with a black pageboy wig and the clothes of a Muslim pilgrim. Beneath his robes, he had concealed a compass, a crude map, and a spyglass. Accompanied by three natives with whom he'd developed a trusted friendship, Noel made his way illegally into Tibet, where he hoped to discover a viable approach to Mount Everest.

The primary passes were heavily guarded, so Noel veered east, trekking up through the arboreal midlands until he had reached Chorten Nyima La, a steep notch that he hoped would reveal a river valley leading to the mountain. Instead, he encountered an impenetrable topography of cliffs and ravines—and soldiers who were less than enthusiastic once they discovered his identity. Before he was chased away, Noel stood on the pass as the clouds surrounding the high peaks parted to reveal a dazzling sight. "Directly over the crest of Taringban appeared a sharp spire peak," Noel wrote. "This, through its magnetic bearing by my compass, proved itself to be none other than Mount Everest. A thousand feet of the summit was visible."

Noel stood forty miles from the mountain, closer than any Anglo before him.

The Raj had a keen, if not always committed, interest in Everest. Tibet resided strategically close to China, India, and Russia, Asia's three burgeoning powers, each intent on expanding its reign—an occasionally violent territorial imbroglio that came to be called the Great Game. Exploration in general and mountaineering in particular were inextricably linked to cartography, and since the 1860s the Raj had been quietly dispatching specially trained "pundits," a corps of "Tibetan-looking Indians," to scout the region. The pundits were taught to track mileage by counting their own steps and using a Tibetan rosary as an abacus. They hid notes in their prayer wheels and thermometers in their staffs. They calculated altitude by the boiling point of water. They returned from their trips loaded with information, but much of the Himalayas remained terra incognito—one of the last great unmapped regions on earth.

Noel's mission was unique in that it had brought a sahib so close to the great peak. Perhaps more significantly, his speech to the Royal Geographic Society in 1919, when he recounted his surreptitious journey, later galvanized enough support to set a bona fide climbing expedition in motion. By 1921, the first English Everest reconnaissance party had boarded a steamship bound for Calcutta, the first leg of its long journey into country yet unseen by Western eyes.

Nothing about Everest was easy; even finding it had taken nearly fifty years and the cumulative efforts of one of the greatest feats of scientific inquiry in the history of the human race: the Great Trigonometrical Survey of India. It's hard to imagine an era when cartographers lacked a comprehensive bird's-eye view of a given town, nation, or continent, but this was certainly the case in 1802, when the survey began in Madras, India, at the Madras Observatory, one of the few places in the region with well-established geographic coordinates.

The Great Arc, as some called the project, was headed by William Lambton, a lieutenant in the British army who had a personal obsession with, and knack for, a growing field of science that focused on the earth's curvature, called geodesy. Lambton's elaborate calculus allowed him to establish the latitude, longitude, and elevation of a given point on land by triangulating from two established reference points. When Lambton died, in 1823, he had succeeded in mapping more than seven hundred linear miles of the Great Arc—roughly the distance from Washington, D.C., to Chicago.

After his death, Lambton's modest project fell to George Everest, his deputy, who succeeded Lambton as surveyor general. Everest was thirty-two when he took the job. He had a midsized frame with an outsized head covered by a full beard and wavy hair the color of sand. He was a stickler for accuracy and he rode his staff hard, pushing them through the

Indian jungles with bellicose intensity, despite a steady onslaught of illness, accidents, and fatalities. His crew—highly trained surveyors, engineers, porters, cooks, camp staff, and translators—contracted malaria, dysentery, and mysterious fevers. They drowned in rivers. They fell from scaffolds erected above the jungle canopy. A few were eaten by tigers. Everest himself endured fevers and bouts of blindness. More than once he was formally diagnosed as mentally ill.

None of the problems prevented the survey from extending north of Delhi and east along the Himalayas by the time he retired, in 1843. Nor, apparently, did his reputation as "the most cantankerous sahib in India" curtail his career or his legacy. He went on to serve as a vice president of the Royal Geographic Society, and was knighted in 1861.

Everest—who pronounced his name "Eev-rest" rather than the more commonly heard "Evah-rest"—not only never saw the mountain that bears his name but was disdainful of mountain climbing altogether. "Bagging mountain peaks was not his business," wrote historian John Keay in *The Great Arc*. "For those who pursued the subject, often with inferior instruments and speculative observations, he felt only contempt."

Nor did he have much say in naming the peak. The appellation was bestowed by his successor, Andrew Waugh, who had pushed the survey north into the Himalayas. It wasn't until the mid-eighteenth century that Waugh's field agents began reporting a strikingly tall mountain near the center of the range, calling it variously Peak B, Sharp Peak H, and Peak Gamma. Waugh had already measured several mountains that had usurped previous height records—including Kangchenjunga and Nanda Devi, now known to be the third- and seventeenth-highest peaks in the world. Waugh identified this new finding as "Peak XV," and it looked so impressively massive that he assigned the final analysis to Radhanath Sickdhar, his most brilliant mathematician. Sickdhar concluded that, indeed, Peak XV was higher than any other point yet discovered on earth. Waugh finally went public with his discovery in 1856, adding, "I have determined to name this noble peak of the Himalayas Mont [*sic*] Everest."

Everest had been identified and measured with as much accuracy as possible at the time, but it would be nearly seventy years before a serious effort to climb it took place. Until the end of the nineteenth century, mountaineering as a discrete pursuit was just coming into its own. The "Golden Age of Alpinism," as it was called, reached its zenith in 1865, when the British climber Edward Whymper made his historic ascent of the Matterhorn, near Zermatt, Switzerland. It was his eighth attempt, punctuated by tragedy when four of his teammates slipped and fell to their deaths. Tainted as it was, the accomplishment was a watershed moment and would later prompt Whymper to pen what, in one form or another, would become a long-standing mountaineer's credo. "There have been joys too great to be described in words," he wrote, "and there have been griefs upon which I have not dared to dwell; and with these in mind I say: Climb if you will, but remember that courage and strength are nought without prudence, and that a momentary negligence may destroy the happiness of a lifetime. Do nothing in haste; look well to each step; and from the beginning think what may be the end."

As mountaineering developed, it began to feed scientific interests beyond cartography, including the investigation of high-altitude physiology. For the select few who fantasized about climbing the world's highest peaks, the news didn't appear very promising. Altitude's debilitating and, in some cases, lethal effects had become well known by the late 1800s, if not necessarily well understood. Mountain sickness had been noted as early as 1590 by missionaries clomping around in the Andes. "When I came to . . . the top of this mountain . . . I was suddenly surprized with so mortall and strange a pang that I was ready to fall from the top to the ground," wrote the Jesuit priest and explorer

José de Acosta after climbing 18,752-foot Tullujuto in Peru. "I was surprised with such pangs of straining and casting as I thought to cast up my heart too: for having cast up meate, fleugme, and choller, both yellow and greene, in the end I cast up blood with the straining of my stomach. To conclude, if this had continued, I should undoubtedly have died."

Since the 1770s, scientists had known that air was composed of gases—primarily oxygen (originally called "phlogiston" and thought to be a fifth elemental substance, along with air, water, fire, and earth), nitrogen, carbon dioxide, and water vapor—and that these elements grew scant at altitude. They were beginning to understand *what* happened to humans as they climbed into the sky, they just didn't know *why*. Even by the late nineteenth century, altitude illness remained so poorly understood that a primary treatment involved slicing the victim's forehead open with a sharp knife.

Some of the most significant breakthroughs in altitude science came from a French physiologist named Paul Bert, who, in 1878, published his landmark work—*La Pression Barométrique*—effectively introducing the world to the relationship between atmospheric pressure and blood oxygen levels. Bert's work had been inspired by the legendary Italian Evangelista Torricelli, the inventor of the barometer and the namesake of the torr, the measurement unit still in use today. It was Torricelli who initially suggested that humans live at the bottom of an ocean of air, and that the higher we rise in it, the lower the atmospheric density. As oxygen molecules disperse in the thin air of high altitude, blood oxygen saturation begins to fall at roughly corresponding levels.

Paul Bert studied this connection between altitude and blood oxygen extensively, sacrificing more than a few sparrows, guinea pigs, and frogs along the way. Almost all of his work was laboratory-based; he was one of the first scientists to use hypobaric chambers large enough for human subjects. Soon some of Bert's peers were indulging their own professional curiosity about altitude—and they weren't shy about using themselves as subjects.

At the time, those who were traveling the highest above sea level weren't climbers but balloonists. During Bert's time, the existing balloon altitude record—in fact, the highest a human had ever traveled—had been set in 1862 by James Glaisher, a meteorologist, and Henry Tracey Coxwell, a dentist. On September 5 of that year, the pair soared to 36,000 feet. Near the apex of their flight, as Glaisher would later describe it, "Mr. Coxwell noticed that my legs projected and my arms hung down by my side, and that my countenance was serene and placid . . . it struck him that I was insensible." About to succumb to the same fate, Coxwell clambered up through the basket ring to release the balloon valve. His hands were too cold to be of much use, so "he seized the cord with his teeth, and dipped his head two or three times, until the balloon took a decided turn downward."

In 1875, Paul Bert consulted with a team of balloonists who were hoping to set a new altitude record in a craft they had dubbed the *Zenith*. The crew—three French aeronauts named Gaston Tissandier, Joseph Croce-Spinelli, and Théodore Sivel—were better prepared than Glaisher and Coxwell had been, at least in theory. Both Croce-Spinelli and Sivel knew Bert and had visited his lab in Paris, where the physiologist had spoken with them at length about barometric pressure at altitude. He'd placed them in his decompression chamber and lowered the pressure until they had attained a virtual height of 23,000 feet, at which point the pilots had begun to experience hearing loss and mental impairment. Bert had then fed them concentrated oxygen through a tube in the chamber. Almost immediately it had ameliorated the physical effects of altitude. When the *Zenith* launched on April 15, 1875, it became the first trip to extreme altitude using bottled oxygen.

Bert, however, worried that the crew had not outfitted themselves with enough oxygen to last the flight. He dashed off a last-minute note to his friends, but it arrived too late. Once airborne, the hardware aboard the *Zenith* set up to deliver the oxygen—thin straws piped through a wash bottle to mask the foul odor—failed miserably. As the *Zenith* approached 26,000 feet, Tissandier drifted into a hypoxic reverie.

"About the height of 25,000 ft. the condition of stupefaction which ensues is extraordinary," he wrote. "The mind and the body weaken by degrees, and imperceptibly, without consciousness of it. No suffering is then experienced; on the contrary, an inner joy is felt like an irradiation from the surrounding flood of light. One becomes indifferent. One thinks no more of the perilous position or of danger. One ascends, and is happy to ascend. The vertigo of the upper regions is not an idle word; but, so far as I can judge from my personal impression, vertigo appears at the last moment; it immediately precedes annihilation, sudden, unexpected, and irresistible."

In the midst of Tissandier's observation, all three men in the craft's wicker cockpit fell unconscious. By the time Tissandier came to, the *Zenith* was plummeting earthward in a barely controlled fall; it crashed in a field about two hundred miles southwest of Paris. Croce-Spinelli and Sivel were dead even before the impact. Tissandier pulled their bodies from the wreckage and staggered to a nearby farmhouse to find help.

The news devastated Paul Bert, who refused to be involved in any more manned flights to high altitude. The accident made headlines around the globe, prompting outrage and indignity over the unreasonable risks and senseless deaths. There wouldn't be another trip that high for the next twenty years.

By the turn of the century, climbing Everest was still a pipe dream, but it was a uniquely British pipe dream and one that the nation didn't casually let go. The pundits of the Raj had provided a valuable, if spotty, body of knowledge about the Himalayas. But their cumulative effort may ultimately have made less progress toward Everest than the swift, blunt force applied in 1904, when a young colonel named Francis Younghusband, acting under George Nathaniel Curzon, then viceroy of India, brought more than ten thousand soldiers into Tibet on a nine-month incursion that would take him all the way to Lhasa and send the Dalai Lama fleeing to Mongolia.

What had started as a "diplomatic" mission quickly became a brutal massacre. Younghusband's well-trained troops were armed with rifles and machine guns, confronting disorganized monks wielding hoes, swords, and flintlocks. Some accounts estimated that more than five thousand Tibetans were killed during the campaign, while the total number of British casualties was about five.

When Younghusband reached Lhasa, he was greeted by hordes of clapping Tibetans. He took it as a gesture of welcome, not realizing that clapping was a traditional way of warding off evil spirits, and he promptly drafted a unilateral treaty granting free trade between Tibet and the Raj. Since the Dalai Lama was now in exile, Younghusband brought the treaty to the acting Rinpoche and a hastily scrabbled together government counsel, who signed their agreement without pause. The troops were withdrawn from the country, but the siege would become an infamous chapter in the history of the British Empire. Younghusband would be remembered as the "last great imperial adventurer," and soon after he returned to England would become *Sir* Francis Younghusband.

Knighted, but suffering a bitter hangover from the 1904 invasion, Younghusband moved on to become the director of the Royal Geographic Society in 1919. Prompted in part by John Noel's lecture about Everest, combined with his long interest in the mountain, he renewed his efforts to stage a climb. His treaty in Lhasa had, presciently, included language that permitted British teams to visit the Himalayas for "science and fact-finding expeditions." Now he needed to gather public support—and the capital to finance an expedition.

Other events conspired to help. The North and South Poles had been reached—dramatically—in 1909 and 1911, by an American and a Norwegian, respectively. Everest, which some referred to as the "third pole," was arguably the last great objective of terrestrial exploration. The British had found it, named it, and now they wanted to be the first to climb it. Increasingly, though, purely pragmatic arguments for an expedition fell flat. Staging such a difficult, dangerous, and expensive project seemed frivolous for the purposes of science, and "will not put a pound in anyone's pocket," as Younghusband said, though "it will take a great many pounds out."

What was to be gained, exactly? "If I am asked what is the use of climbing this highest mountain? I reply, No use at all," Younghusband said during his presidential address to the Royal Geographic Society in 1920, "no more use than kicking a football about, or dancing, or playing the piano, or writing a poem, or painting a picture. . . . But the accomplishment of such a feat will elevate the human spirit. . . . As long as we impotently creep about at the foot of these mighty mountains and gaze on their summits without attempting to ascend them, we entertain towards them a too excessive feeling of awe. . . . But as soon as we have stood on their summit we feel that we dominate them—that we, the spiritual, have ascendancy over them, the material."

A few years later, during a lecture tour to drum up additional support for the early Everest expeditions, George Mallory took his cue from Younghusband and echoed a similar opinion. The final argument, it seemed, was a metaphysical one. Mallory had found himself so badgered by reporters about his justification for climbing Everest that he began his lectures with a preemptive strike: "So, if you cannot understand that there is something in man which responds to the challenge of this mountain and goes out to meet it, that the struggle is the struggle of life itself, upward and forever upward, then you won't see why we go. What we get from this adventure is just sheer joy. And joy is, after all, the end of life. We do not live to eat and make money. We eat and make money to be able to enjoy life. That is what life means and what life is for."

That George Herbert Leigh Mallory, a schoolteacher from Godalming, England, would find himself immortalized by Everest is one of those curious historical eddies that sometimes thrust unlikely characters into the public spotlight. When he was recruited to the reconnaissance team in 1921, he had distinguished himself as a good, though not necessarily great, climber. Mallory himself was initially ambivalent about the project, but World War I had decimated the ranks of his climbing contemporaries and Mallory was one of the few able-bodied talents still standing. At a lunch meeting with Younghusband, expedition leader Harold Raeburn, and Alpine Club secretary Percy Farrar, Mallory accepted their formal invitation "without visible emotion." But clearly, this was the chance of a lifetime. Mallory had grown disenchanted with teaching, and the uncertainties about his professional future were only exacerbated by a festering domestic ennui. "It seems a rather momentous occasion, with a new job to find when I come back," he wrote to his friend Geoffrey Young, "but it will not be a bad thing to give up the settled ease of this present life."

When Mallory shipped out for India on April 8, 1921, at age thirty-four, he was certainly fit and, by now, enthusiastic, but it was obvious that he didn't come from quite the same stock as his older, more hirsute expedition companions. He was more like a uniquely suited performer, willowy and attractive, dexterous on rock and resilient at altitude. Mallory was certainly bright enough, but he was spacey and preoccupied during the expeditions, exasperating those around him. During the trips, Mallory would often forget his boots, luggage, or some other important piece of equipment. In one of his most famous gaffes, he and Guy Bullock, his friend from the Winchester Ice Club, burned through numerous costly film plates, which they had inserted into the camera backward, trying to photograph potential routes on the mountain. "The failure of Bullock and Mallory to photograph anything is deplorable," groused Arthur Hinks, the irascible secretary of the Royal Geographic Society's Everest Committee. "They must be singularly unintelligent people not to be able to learn the elements of the thing in a day or two."

Mallory didn't lack for tramontane outings—the climbing trips and new routes he'd pioneered with friends in the Pen y Pass climbing club in Charterhouse were largely the reason he'd been invited to Everest in the first place—but his experience on big mountains was limited. The highest he had climbed was 15,781-foot Mont Blanc, near Chamonix, and the 1921 expedition was his first trip to Asia. Tibet was particularly removed and rustic, and Mallory swung wildly between adoration and disdain for the country and its people.

It wasn't until the climbing began in earnest that Mallory emerged as a figure the rest of the world would come to know—a driven and tenacious mountaineer, externally romantic, internally conflicted, perpetually under Everest's spell. When the reconnaissance team pulled up to the Rongbuk Monastery that May, his anxiety was almost palpable.

"I wish some folk at home could see the precipice from this side—a grim spectacle most unlike the long gentle slopes suggested by photos," Mallory wrote. "Amusing to think how one's vision of the last effort has changed; it looked like crawling half-blind up easy snow, an even slope all the way up from a camp on a flat snow shoulder; but it won't be that sort of a grind; we'll want for climbers and not half-dazed ones; a tougher job than I bargained for, sanguine as usual. E. is a rock mountain."

Mallory traveled to Everest three times—to reconnoiter potential routes in 1921, and in '22 and '24 when he attempted to reach the top. Mallory groused, complained, and nearly bailed out on each of his Everest trips. But the mountain was insidious and it had wormed its way into his psyche to a degree that even he couldn't fully appreciate. Everest was defining him, even as he was defining it. In 1924, on his third visit, Mallory came to regard Everest as the grail that would deliver him from the professional and financial uncertainties looming in his future. Everest had given him a taste of something greater, more expansive than the mundane routine of teaching students and raising a family. He had flirted with fame after the previous expeditions, but if he could pull it off this time, if he could get to the top and back again, he would secure his place in the pantheon of legendary explorers.

Ruth Mallory, George's wife, felt hinky about a third expedition—she'd had premonitions, she told her husband before he left. The 1922 expedition had ended abruptly when Mallory and sixteen others were caught below the North Col in an avalanche that killed seven Sherpas. Mallory had tasted the risks; he knew how easily Ruth could be left a widow and his children without a father. But Everest was unfinished business that, in the end, he simply couldn't hand off to someone else, a fact Ruth came to accept. "[She] was always proud of what he had done, how he had done what he thought was the best thing possible," recalled their daughter Clare. "In a very honourable sense, he had done what he thought was right."

Mallory departed high camp on June 8, partnered with Andrew "Sandy" Irvine, a twenty-two-year-old engineer and stand-out collegiate rower from Birkenhead, England, who had almost no previous climbing experience. Irvine was, however, extraordinarily fit and a sturdy, mechanically gifted worker—he had essentially rebuilt the oxygen apparatus that he and Mallory now carried on their backs. If Mallory had emerged from relative obscurity, Irvine was even more of a wild card, and they were now poised a few thousand feet from becoming the first men to stand on Everest's summit.

Four days earlier, their teammate Edward Norton had climbed to within 900 feet of the top without gas, and though he had wound up snow-blind and desperately weak, he believed that a strong team should have no problems, especially with oxygen. Mallory and Irvine ascended into a promising, relatively mild morning. Noel Odell, the expedition photographer, could see the climbers from a rocky perch near the North Ridge, although intermittent clouds swept across the upper mountain and periodically obscured his view. Around one P.M. Odell observed a "tiny black spot silhouetted . . . in the ridge; the black dot moved. Another black dot . . . moved up the snow to join the other on the crest. The first then approached the great rock-step and shortly emerged at the top; the second did likewise. Then the whole fascinating vision vanished, enveloped in cloud once more." They would never be seen alive again.

After their disappearance, heated speculation swirled around whether Mallory and Irvine had actually made it to the top—still one of the great unsolved mysteries in the history of exploration. When Mallory's body was discovered seventy-five years later, during the spring of 1999, by American Conrad Anker during the Mallory and Irvine Research Expedition, it seemed the question might be settled once and for all. The corpse was lying facedown below the ridge at 26,750 feet, nearly perfectly preserved in the sterile air, though the clothes were shredded, bleach-white limbs exposed, like those of a mannequin made of alabaster. Anker and his teammates knew Mallory had been carrying a camera—a small Kodak Vestpocket; no doubt it would contain the case-closing summit photos, or lack thereof—but after carefully searching the body they could find no such item.

Why did it matter, in the end, if Mallory and Irvine had reached the top or not in 1924? Didn't summits count only if you returned from them? As Ed Viesturs, the first American to climb all fourteen 8,000-meter peaks without oxygen, would say years later, "Getting to the top is optional; getting down is mandatory."

Over the years, as the tale acquired mythic dimensions, knowing the truth gradually became less a matter of historical record than of public infatuation. Mallory, the idealist, and Irvine, his loyal, broad-shouldered companion, grew larger than life, their story told, retold, and analyzed under a thousand varied lights. The 1924 ascent, successful or not, became the ur-climb—a seminal event that reified the most commonly held ideas about Everest: that it was every bit as massive, difficult, and dangerous as it seemed.

Mallory and Irvine had persevered into the unknown, in hobnailed boots and wool trousers, inventing the business of climbing Everest as they went. They deserved to get to the top; many believe that they did. The clues were circumstantial, but the most serious scholars point not to what was found—for instance, Mallory's goggles, stuffed in his pocket, suggesting that it was night when he fell—but what *wasn't*. Mallory had been vocal about intending to leave a photo of Ruth at the summit. When Anker and the others discovered the body, they found a satchel containing letters from friends, the most likely place for such a picture. No photo of Mallory's wife was ever found.

That the first British expeditions had ended tragically only served to fan Everest's mystique at a time when many in the West were becoming intoxicated with Tibet in general and the Himalayas in particular. *The Epic of Everest* emerged in 1924, a documentary about the ill-fated Mallory expedition earlier that year, made by former master of disguise John Noel and introducing Western audiences to life on the Tibetan Plateau. But public relations with Tibet had become so tense that even ostensibly innocuous film projects had to be spun and censored. In *The Epic of Everest,* a scene showing a Tibetan man plucking and eating a nit from a child's scalp was deleted because of its crude overtones. The delicate relationship between

British India and Tibet was hardly improved in the wake of the early expeditions, with climbers roving around and leaving bodies behind on Tibet's most sacred mountain. The Dalai Lama was so irritated, he denied permission for another Everest expedition for nearly ten years.

If the cursed climb of 1924 slowed further Everest exploration, it hardly dimmed interest in it. In 1933, the same year the next British Everest expedition finally got under way, James Hilton published *Lost Horizon,* a novel about a small group of English expats whose plane crashes in a Himalayan mountain pass and who subsequently stumble upon a pastoral utopia of peace-loving monks. Hilton dubbed his mystical valley Shangri-La, a slight spin on Shambhala, a name derived from Sanskrit meaning a "pure land" of enlightened residents. At the time, Tibetan Buddhism was still such a curiosity that one of the novel's characters, a priggish missionary named Miss Brinklow, seems to speak for her entire society when she puzzles over the monks' daily ritual of meditation and contemplation. "But they aren't doing anything," she says to the head lama. "Then, madam," the lama replies, "they do nothing."

The book and, later, the Frank Capra film addressed an increasing attraction to the East as an antidote to a modernizing West, a growing awareness of the tension between material prosperity and spiritual enrichment—between *inner* and *outer.* Mountains as Mecca were an ongoing motif in art, literature, film, and poetry throughout the century, though more nefarious associations with the Himalayas also emerged at the time. Adolf Hitler considered Tibet the potential home to ancestors of an Aryan master race believed to occupy subterranean cities and to command a psychokinetic energy force called Vril. During the 1930s, he dispatched discreet archaeological expeditions to Tibet (the basis, years later, for certain characters in Steven Spielberg's *Indiana Jones* films) to suss out the cultish theories. Even the swastika, the emblematic "hooked cross" of Nazi infamy, originated in south-eastern Asia as a symbol of good luck.

The more expansive the mythology around Mount Everest, the more it seemed to inspire ever more audacious attempts to climb it. Among the most infamous was the solo effort made in 1934 by Maurice Wilson, a former lieutenant in the British army who, after the war, worked as a farmer, "restorative medicine" salesman, and women's dress shop owner. Wilson had served a brief but remarkable tour during the First World War. During an intense skirmish at the Fourth Battle of Ypres, in Belgium, his entire regiment was gunned down during a German charge while he defended the line, unscathed—a feat that earned him decorations and public accolades. A few months later, Wilson returned to the same battlefield, where he was shot in the chest and arm, nearly dying in the mud before he was evacuated on a stretcher.

After the war Wilson was plagued by a restless anxiety. He quit jobs, bought into and cashed out of small businesses, and spontaneously bolted from England to travel the world. He felt that he was looking for something—a direction, a purpose—but he didn't quite know what. When he finally returned to England, he befriended a group of yogis he'd met during a long steamship ride. He was riveted by their philosophy and practice, with its emphasis on "the purification of mind and body, concentration on a single object and the generation of supernatural powers."

Back in London, however, he once again drifted into despondency. He grew sickly, plagued by rheumy eyes and a hacking cough. Strung out and rudderless, Wilson finally went to see a faith healer, though he would never identify the person by name and even close friends were suspicious of his story. Whatever the case, when his friends saw him again he looked remarkably healthy—the result, he claimed, of thirty-five days of fasting and meditation. During his recovery he had had a major epiphany: He was going to show the world what faith could accomplish by flying a plane to Tibet and climbing Mount Everest, by himself. Little matter that Wilson had no experience as a mountaineer or a pilot; within a year he had purchased a Gipsy Moth biplane, painted "Ever-Wrest" on the nose, and enrolled in flight school at Stag Lane airfield in London.

On April 23, 1933, the night before his planned flight to India, Wilson took off in the *Ever-Wrest* from Stag Lane. His destination: Bradford, where his mother lived. En route, though, he stalled the craft in midair, clipped a hedge trying to glide to a landing, and flipped upside down on a country lane. Before he'd unclipped himself and spilled out of the cockpit, photographers were on the scene, documenting the first leg of the incredible journey of Maurice Wilson.

A month later, Wilson did in fact fly all the way, and illegally, from London to Purnea, in northeastern India, near the Nepalese border—an extraordinary trip in itself. His plan was to continue on to the mountain aboard the *Ever-Wrest,* where he would crash-land the plane and commence his climb.

By now Wilson was a minor celebrity—the media were tracking him zealously—but officials in Purnea curtailed his flight by impounding the *Ever-Wrest,* forcing him to take a train to Darjeeling and, from there, walk into Tibet, adopting the old pundit trick of dressing up in Chinese robes and posing as a holy man. Before he left Darjeeling, Wilson hired three Sherpas who had been part of the British Everest expedition the previous spring. By early April 1934, they had trekked all the way to the Rongbuk Monastery, near the base of the mountain, where the head lama, impressed by Wilson's fortitude, invited him to dinner.

Per his plan, Wilson spent the next week fasting and meditating, and on April 16 he set out on his own toward the peak. He would return in six days, he told his Sherpas, but after nine days there was no sign of him. The concerned Sherpas were about to head up the trail in search of their companion when they saw a figure stumbling toward the monastery: Wilson. They barely recognized him. He was shockingly gaunt, his appearance made even more distressed by his edema-swollen face. He was also nearly blind and suffering from intense pain in his left arm. The mountain had been deserted, with no obvious trail, and Wilson had gotten pitifully lost, reaching only midway up the East Rongbuk Glacier, not even within sight of the North Col. He lay in bed for the next three days, sleeping and eating ravenously. It would take another two weeks of convalescing at the monastery until he felt well enough to try again.

On May 12, he lit out for a second try. "Faith," he had written in his journal during his recuperation, "is not faith that wavers when its prayers remain unanswered." This time he brought two of his Sherpas, Tenzing and Rinzing, who knew the route. It took them only three days to reach what is now Advanced Base Camp, at 21,000 feet. Here they discovered a food cache left behind by the Brits the year before, and they gorged themselves on plum jam, anchovy paste, chocolate, and Ovaltine. Despite the unexpected feast, they were all suffering—Wilson most of all, wracked by skull-splitting headaches, weakness, and sleeplessness.

They spent a week in camp before Wilson attempted to climb the North Col. Rinzing showed him the way before returning to camp at dusk. The Briton was hoping, if not expecting, to find a route, complete with chopped steps and fixed rope, left behind from the previous season's expedition. But when he reached the base of the 1,500-foot ice wall there was nothing but a blank canvas of ice and snow, gouged with dark fracture lines. No route. No ropes.

Wilson didn't know how to use the ice ax he'd brought, or crampons, which he hadn't (he had found a pair at the British camp but had tossed them aside, not knowing what they were for); nevertheless, he managed to scrape a few hundred yards up the headwall before being defeated by a steep slope. He spent that night in his sleeping bag, wedged in the snow at a thirty-five-degree angle. The next day he descended clumsily, lucky to make it back alive. "Did two sheer drop rolls down the face of the ice, but fortunately without any effect," he wrote in his diary. "Ribs sore but not much."

Back at camp, the Sherpas urged him to return with them to the monastery. Wilson ignored them, alone in his shelter, fading into quiet repose. He rested for three days, eating little and hardly speaking, before setting out again on May 29, looking weary, bent, and dreadfully thin. He made it just half a mile above camp before setting up his tent and crawling inside. "This will be the last effort," he had written that morning. "Have pulled out my flag of friendship and it feels quite cheering. Strange, but I feel there is someone with me in the tent all the time."

A year later Charles Warren, a doctor from a 1935 British expedition, discovered Wilson's body just a short distance from his last camp, lying on its side in the snow, knees to the chest, a tent and sleeping bag in shreds nearby, stripped away by the wind. A pair of boots were scattered some distance farther. That afternoon, Warren and his teammates collected what they could, wrapped the corpse in the remains of the tent, and slipped it into a crevasse on the East Rongbuk. Future expeditions crossing the glacier would report finding swatches of clothing clinging to bits of Wilson's bones.

In the decades that followed, no Everest attempt would garner the enduring admiration of Mallory's or attain the infamy of Wilson's, but not for lack of effort. In 1947, Earl Denman, a Canadian-born Brit, made a Wilsonesque climb by sneaking into Tibet disguised as a native, though a few notable differences characterized Denman's trip: (1) not a word was written about him until after the trip; (2) he intended to go to the summit with two Sherpas, one of whom was Tenzing Norgay, who would later be immortalized after making the first Everest summit with Edmund Hillary; and (3) though Denman climbed only about as high as Wilson, he lived.

Denman's attempt would be one of the last before the boot heel of Communist China bore down on Tibet in 1950, curtailing the last of the limited access to Everest's north side. Serendipitously, the closure coincided with relaxed access in Nepal. While the early north-side attempts had spanned three decades, the south side "went" in a mere three years. In 1953, after an important reconnaissance in 1951, a British expedition led by John Hunt, and including Hillary, Tenzing, and a platoon of twenty handpicked Sherpas, plodded up the South Col route. On May 26, two British team members, Tom Bourdillon and Charles Evans, climbed to 28,750 feet, less than 300 feet from the summit. But it was already one P.M., and they would not have enough oxygen to last the descent if they kept going.

The next day, Hillary and Tenzing arrived at the same spot by nine A.M., Tenzing wearing the red balaclava Denman had given him a few years before. Two and a half hours later, he and Hillary became the first men to reach the top of Everest, an occasion more than thirty years in the making. "Mixed with relief was a vague sense of astonishment that I should have been the lucky one to attain the ambition of so many brave and determined climbers," Hillary said. "It seemed difficult at first to grasp that we'd got there. I was too tired and too conscious of the long way down to safety really to feel any great elation."

With the top finally tagged, and the South Col route now established as the best way to get there, attention turned back to the north side. By the late 1950s, the Chinese were planning their own military-scale expedition to the Northeast Ridge. In the spring of 1960, a 214-person team traveled overland in a convoy of trucks and jeeps, eventually establishing the largest camp ever seen in the Rongbuk Valley. If Wilson had believed the Northeast Ridge could be climbed on sheer faith, the Chinese were out to demonstrate that it would be con-quered by pure might.

When news emerged that May that two Chinese climbers, Wang Fu-chou and Chu Yin-hua, and a Sherpa named Gonpa had reached the summit from the north side, the climbing community was at first stunned, then impressed, and finally highly skeptical. Inconsistencies and dubious details marred the Chinese account of the climb. Among the most bizarre was the claim that at the Second Step Chu Yin-hua had removed his boots and socks and attempted to scale the cliff barefoot. When that didn't work, the trio had resorted to a human ladder, sur-mounting the step by having one man stand on the shoulders of another. The team had supposedly spent more than thirty hours making their round-trip assault—a fact, some pointed out, that meant they would have been descending on May 26, the day the monsoons arrived. The climbers would have been wasted from their epic effort and descending through violent weather—but it received no mention in their report. In the end, the Chinese were credited with the first ascent, even though the only photographic evidence they could produce was a photo taken earlier in the day, around the Second Step. Their skeptics begrudgingly conceded that the true details had probably been lost in translation.

Ascertaining news was difficult at best once Everest's north side closed to foreigners, hidden now behind the veil of communism and mounting Cold War tensions. Rumors occasionally circulated around the climbing community—a team of Russians had been killed in an avalanche; more Chinese had reached the summit—but the re-ports were impossible to confirm. One attempt, however, flared vividly before the north went entirely dark.

During the spring of 1962, a four-man team made up of three Americans and one Swiss snuck into Tibet from Nepal and managed to reach nearly 26,000 feet on Everest's North Ridge, without support or oxygen. Of course, Everest had now been climbed numerous times via the south side. But the clandestine attempt via the north side would have put the first Americans on the summit.

The expedition leader was Woodrow Wilson Sayre, a gawky blond forty-three-year-old assistant philosophy professor at Tufts University, in Massachusetts, and the grandson of the twenty-eighth American president. Sayre was more an academic than a mountaineer, but he had been consumed with the desire to climb Everest since college, as much to investigate why men were interested in such a pursuit as to try it himself. In his contemplative account *Four Against Everest,* he laments that mountaineers, when writing about their climbs, too often ignored the "internals . . . the hopes, the fears, the despairs, the gladnesses, the numbnesses, the excitements." What better way to explore that inner space, he figured, than climbing toward outer space.

The team included Sayre's friend Norman Hansen, thirty-six, a lawyer from Boston; Roger Hart, a twenty-one-year-old geology student from Tufts; and HansPeter Duttle, twenty-four, a schoolteacher from Switzerland whom the others met by chance in Zermatt on their way to Everest. None of them had much mountaineering experience. Sayre had cragged with friends from the Appalachian Mountain Club; hiked up 14,495-foot Mount Whitney, the tallest peak in the contiguous United States; and successfully summited Mount McKinley with Norm Hansen—the first time either man had used crampons or an ice ax. Hart was a solid rock climber but had spent almost no time at altitude. Duttle claimed he had mountaineering training, but when he and Hart were strolling across a glacier near the Zermatt ski area, discussing the Everest trip, he fell into a crevasse.

Perhaps because of his academic background, Sayre placed an irrational amount of trust in the power of human ingenuity. He and Hansen devised an expedition strategy that was equal parts ambition, idealism, and naïveté, operating on a permit to climb Gyachung Kang, in Nepal, twenty-five land miles southwest of Everest. By May 9 they had established a decoy base camp, sent their porters down-valley, and lit out across the Nup La, into Tibet, headed for Everest's Northeast Ridge.

Whatever notion the team had about its pending journey, it couldn't have predicted the two months of high-altitude punishment that ensued. They lugged 120 pounds of supplies apiece, forcing them to ferry the load in thirds, effectively tripling their daily mileage through a labyrinth of cliffs, over scrabbly moraine, and across fragile snow bridges—all above 17,000 feet. Sayre and Hansen had precalculated their nutritional needs—two pounds of food per person per day—but they had settled on "a no-nonsense diet consisting essentially of sugar and meat-bars," deeming culinary variety "a psychological luxury." They had no maps, nor an established route, and frequently got lost, hallucinated, and fell down cliffs.

On June 5, the day the team reached its high point at around 25,500 feet on the North Face and finally called it quits, they were moving at less than 100 vertical feet per hour. Several weeks later, while Sayre was recuperating at the hospital in Kathmandu, he learned that he had contracted amoebic dysentery, cracked a rib, badly bruised one arm, and lost thirty pounds during the course of the trip.

The Sayre expedition ultimately became a small footnote in Everest's history, but few expeditions better illustrate the emerging anti-establishment, do-it-yourself ethos that came to characterize climbing after World War II. The good professor may not have gotten any closer to understanding why men want to climb mountains than he did to tagging Everest's summit, but it didn't stop him from stepping up to the lectern and putting a fine point on it. "People grow through overcoming dangers and difficulties," he wrote. "They are not better off for being carefully wrapped in cotton batting. Deep within us I think we know that we need challenge and danger, and the risk and hurt that sometimes follow. . . . Men climb mountains because they are not satisfied to exist, they want to live—climbing the heights is one way."

CHAPTER 3

BASE CAMP: TIBET

Russell Brice was anything but idle after his move to Chamonix in the late '80s. He promptly began to rack up mileage on 8,000-meter peaks like Cho Oyu, Shishapangma, and Kangchenjunga. In June 1989, he guided his first Himalayan commercial expedition, to 24,738-foot Himalchuli West, successfully summitting in May. He would go on to run dozens more commercial trips, while also logging a handful of impressive personal accomplishments, including, in 1990, making a three-man paraglider flight off of Cho Oyu, located on the Tibet-Nepal border twenty miles northwest of Everest, with Harry Taylor and a Swiss climber named Andrea Kuhn. The next spring, he made another oxygenless attempt on Everest, during which he and Taylor turned back in bitterly cold weather.

He was also developing his logistical skills by running, among other things, the 1991 Balloons Over Everest Expedition, during which an Aussie and three Brits became the first to fly a pair of hot-air balloons over Everest's summit. The seven-story crafts skirted the top with barely a thousand feet to spare, before crashing on the Tibetan Plateau. Brice spent the fateful 1996 year running spring and fall trips to Cho Oyu, during which he set a speed record on Cho by climbing from Camp One to the summit and back in eleven hours, a trip that typically takes three days.

By 2000, Brice was the go-to guy for anyone interested in staging complicated projects in the Himalayas and for special-needs climbers pursuing big peaks. In 2004, he helped the double amputee Mark Inglis reach the summit of Cho Oyu. And in 2005, his eleventh Everest expedition included a forty-two-year-old Australian named Paul Hockey, the first one-armed man to climb the Northeast Ridge.

When Brice arrived at Everest Base Camp in April 2006, the site resembled a Himalayan military redoubt. Trucks, buses, and the ubiquitous Toyota Land Cruisers employed by the Chinese Tibet Mountaineering Association rumbled across the gravel flats in a swirl of dust, disgorging climbers and supplies. Yak caravans trundled up the valley. Clusters of pitch-roofed tents materialized, stovepipes poking through the sagging canvas canopies, furling smoke.

In 1994, when Brice brought his first commercial expedition here, approximately one hundred individuals had gathered on Everest's north side; this year conservative estimates put the number at nearly five hundred climbers, spread across the two-mile-wide glacial basin like nomadic tribes. The teams included big players like Brice's Himex team and Alex Abramov's 7 Summits Club. Nearby were another sixty or so small to midsized expeditions, including Basques, Brazilians, Bahrainis, Brits, Turks, Japanese, Spaniards, Malaysians, Swedish and Norwegian skiers, a large Chinese group, and "Mr. Pak's Korean Expedition."

Climbers came to the north side for several reasons. Least tangible but hardly irrelevant was the opportunity to ascend a classic route

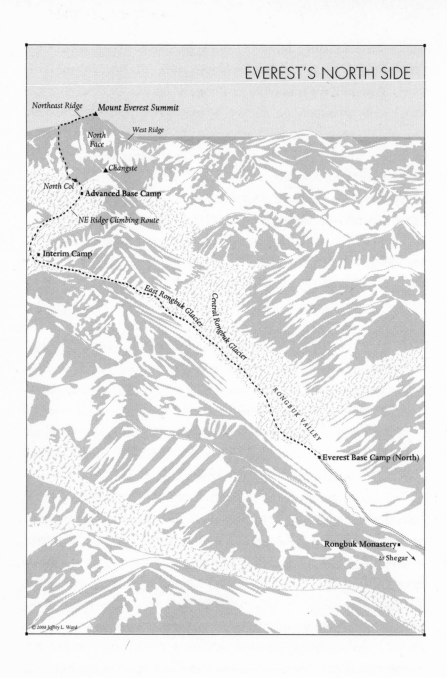

EVEREST'S NORTH SIDE

Northeast Ridge   **Mount Everest Summit**

North Face   *West Ridge*

▲*Changste*

North Col   ■ **Advanced Base Camp**

NE Ridge Climbing Route

■ **Interim Camp**

East Rongbuk Glacier

Central Rongbuk Glacier

RONGBUK VALLEY

■**Everest Base Camp (North)**

Rongbuk Monastery ■

to Shegar ↖

© 2008 Jeffrey L. Ward

with a storied history, following the hobnailed bootsteps of George Mallory, Sandy Irvine, and other Everest pioneers. Climbing from the north also took the south side's Khumbu Icefall—a lethal maze of man-eating crevasses and teetering seracs—completely out of play. But the single most appealing aspect of climbing this side of the mountain was undoubtedly the price. The Chinese charged about $25,000 per team; authorities in Nepal charged $70,000.

How a given commercial operator defrayed its costs and established its fee depended on the outfit, but the range was considerable. Himex, the priciest of the north-side operators, offered a fully supported trip for $40,000 per climber; similar trips on the south side ran about $65,000 per person. At the lowest end, several outfitters offered bare-bones north-side expeditions for around $7,000, which included little more than transportation from Kathmandu to the mountain and back, and a cook and mess tent at Base Camp and ABC. Everything else was à la carte.

All things being equal, climbing on the north side is a tedious affair in which the misery begins almost from the moment you depart Kathmandu. Climb from the south and you arrive in Base Camp on foot, after a short flight and long trek through the Solu-Khumbu, a verdant Shangri-La in northeast Nepal where cleft valleys thrum with the sounds of swollen rivers and frothing cascades. Climb from the north and you arrive by vehicle after a dusty drive across the Tibetan Plateau. Cash-flush expeditions like Himex begin the road trip in Lhasa, after an hour-and-a-half flight from Kathmandu. Most teams, however, travel overland, along the Friendship Highway, a precarious, potholed ribbon of dirt contouring gorges so steep that, in places, you can drop a rupee from the car window straight down into the roiling Bhote Khosi River, a thousand feet below. The Friendship Highway climbs out of Nepal's lush hillsides, through the gritty border towns of Kodari and Zhangmu, rising up and over the Lalung La before dropping down into the Tibetan desert and buttonhooking back to Everest. The views from the pass are grand—the 8,000-meter massifs of Cho Oyu,

Shishapangma, and Lhotse hulking above the lesser mountains—but soon the horizon flattens and bleaches into an arid expanse of auburn hills and austere windswept plains. By the time you arrive in Base Camp, after a four-day trip, there isn't a tree within thirty miles.

The bleak environs are livened up by a few man-made attractions: the Rongbuk Monastery, the highest temple of its kind in the world, and "Shanty Town," a natty strip of temporary shelters where visitors can buy junk jewelry, a beer, a bed, or a prostitute for the night, not necessarily in that order. Mostly, though, teams tend to ensconce themselves in camp, resting, reading, worrying. A typical expedition spends nearly two months on the mountain; only about ten days involve actual climbing.

In clear weather, it's hard not to simply stand around staring at Everest's massive North Face, towering above the glacier like a tsunami of rock and ice. Few views in the world rival the sheer dazzling scale of this one. Nearly 13,000 feet above Base Camp, the Northeast Ridge cuts clean against the southern skyline. Despite the distance, it is close enough that a visitor to Base Camp can distinguish the three technical steps interrupting its nearly horizontal pitch. The light at that altitude takes on a phosphorescent quality, and the upper mountain and adjacent slopes shimmer above the foreground peaks like the surface of another planet rising in its orbit. It might be beautiful were it not for the unsettling fact that the ridge is the single most dangerous place on Everest, having claimed 41 percent of the seventy deaths on the mountain since 1996. Worse is the realization that this mile-long catwalk littered with bodies and looming at the edge of the troposphere is the final, unavoidable obstacle between the summit and those now gathered nervously beneath it.

Most climbers make the trip from Base Camp to ABC in two days, laying over at Interim Camp for at least a night. The hike spans fourteen miles and 4,000 vertical feet one way, tracing the edges of the Central and East Rongbuk glaciers. Viewed from above, the Rongbuk is shaped like a giant trident, its three prongs extending down from Everest's north side before merging into one wide flow that terminates at the gravel flats above the monastery. The trail, well established after years of yak traffic, begins innocuously enough, climbing slowly along Central Rongbuk before doglegging left onto its eastern branch and gradually wrapping around toward the North Col. The hiking might be enjoyable were it not quite so long, desolate, and dismally high. As if that's not enough, the prevailing winds sweep in from the south, raking down over the glaciers in a constant, grating headwind. Hike in a group, as most do, and each of your companions' footfalls kicks up a cloud of dust that swirls into your face like belches of auto exhaust.

From the East Rongbuk the trail ascends more steeply, undulating over the glacier, though the ice itself is hidden beneath a thick layer of pulverized gneiss and swales of ankle-wrenching till. After a couple of miles the path drops into a ravine, crosses a thick stream of milky meltwater, then zeds steeply onto what some climbers call the "whale's back," the debris-blackened crown of the East Rongbuk. Just on the other side of the glacier is Interim Camp, a spartan cluster of tents nestled among 100-foot-high pinnacles of wind-sculpted ice. At a distance the translucent fins look unimposing, but in camp they are huge and phantasmagoric, a dreamscape of turquoise and white.

Interim Camp sits at approximately 19,000 feet, and it is somewhere shortly above this point that the altitude becomes not just uncomfortable but nearly intolerable. Pass through 20,000 feet, where the amount of oxygen in the atmosphere is about half what it is at sea level, and it's akin to running into the ocean. Even fit climbers grind to a sluggish plod, gulping air at every rise in the trail. It seems as though it should be easier—you share the path with yak trains, teenaged

Tibetans, and an occasional dog—but the final switchbacks into ABC are brutal: Five steps. Rest. Psych up. Repeat.

Below Advanced Base Camp, the climb involves little more than high-altitude trekking. It's just above ABC where the real climbing begins. The route rises gradually out of camp toward a wide cirque, arriving at the edge of a glacial plateau: Crampon Point, where climbers pull on harnesses, crampons, and whatever additional gear they'll need for the rest of the ascent. Across the glacier awaits the ice wall leading up to the North Col—the saddle between Everest's North Ridge and neighboring 24,803-foot Changtse. Here a climber usually ascends a fixed rope aided by a jumar, a clamplike device with a built-in handle. Jumars have angled teeth that bite the rope when you pull down but slide easily forward as you ascend. The device works as a self-belay, preventing you from sailing down the slope should you slip, trip, or stumble, but also providing extra leverage while you're climbing. Ascending the rope is strenuous and, in places, awkward, requiring a duck walk—the Everest Shuffle, some call it: feet splayed, one hand guiding the jumar. Step-step-slide. Step-step-slide.

Above the North Col—also called Camp One—are two successive tent sites: locations vary slightly from year to year and team to team, but generally Camp Two sits at around 25,000 feet and Camp Three another two thousand feet above. Himex utilizes a fourth camp at a little above 27,000 feet, the highest camp on earth. This adds more time on the upper mountain but slightly shortens the summit day. Barring bad weather or other problems, climbers spend a night at each camp on the way up and descend as far as possible on the way down.

Everest mucks with plenty of sensations, but above all it distorts your sense of scale. From the col, the top appears tantalizingly close, yet it is still more than a vertical mile above, and three days away. Camp Two is in plain view at the top of a snow ridge, but it takes

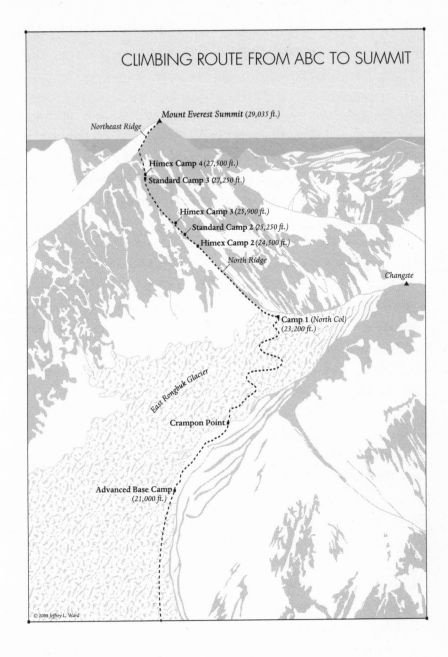

CLIMBING ROUTE FROM ABC TO SUMMIT

Mount Everest Summit *(29,035 ft.)*

Northeast Ridge

Himex Camp 4 *(27,500 ft.)*
Standard Camp 3 *(27,250 ft.)*

Himex Camp 3 *(25,900 ft.)*
Standard Camp 2 *(25,250 ft.)*
Himex Camp 2 *(24,500 ft.)*

North Ridge

Changste

Camp 1 *(North Col)*
(23,200 ft.)

East Rongbuk Glacier

Crampon Point

Advanced Base Camp
(21,000 ft.)

© 2008 Jeffrey L. Ward

climbers as long to ascend this moderate pitch as the trip from Crampon Point to the col. It's another deceptively long and strenuous slog to Camp Three, perched on a cramped ledge of rock and snow, where the route begins to veer off the North Ridge onto the North Face. Ditto Himex's Camp Four. Above this final way station, climbers scramble through a section of shattered rock steps, threading a series of chutes called the Exit Cracks. From the top of the Exit Cracks, you turn right onto the Northeast Ridge and begin the final traverse.

The ridge rises about 1,000 vertical feet over its final mile, an average grade that is a little more than the slope of a suburban driveway. From below, it appears deceptively easy. The footing along the ridge can be forgiving, even easy, but in places the path constricts to just a few inches, over ice and loose rocks angled downward like roof tiles, exposed to the emptiness below. You walk this vertiginous stretch bundled in a bulky down suit, stepping gingerly along in crampons, hemmed in by a harness, oxygen mask, and ski goggles, running on little food and zero sleep. The ridge's moderate angle seems relatively benign until you begin the precarious traverse, reduced to two points of contact—your boots—rather than the three or four of steeper terrain, where you can use your hands and ice ax. And you negotiate all of this when you are at your most exhausted, in the thinnest air and the most severe weather.

Of the three technical features on the ridge, the First, Second, and Third Steps, two are negligible—moderate hiccups of rock, snow, and ice. The Second Step is the crux of the climb. It thrusts up abruptly, like the side of an office building, 100 feet high, more than twice the size of the infamous Hillary Step on the Southeast Ridge. "If it had been daylight on the way up and I had seen what was involved, I would have turned around right there," said 7 Summits Club client Kirk Wheatley. Without the ladder originally bolted to the rock courtesy of a Chinese team in 1975, and improved in 2004 when Himex placed a longer one beside it, few climbers would be able to complete the route.

Tricky as the traverse can be, it is not the technical difficulty that makes it so lethal; it's the altitude. On the Northeast Ridge, you grind along above 28,000 feet for more than nine hours. To a height already at the limits of survivability, add wind, snow, cold, fatigue, dehydration, and fear. Successfully navigating the ridge ranks as one of the most formidable accomplishments in the annals of human endurance. "I never feel euphoric or elated when I'm up there," said veteran guide and expedition leader Eric Simonson. "Just anxious. It's like swimming as far out into the ocean as you can, then turning around and wondering if you can make it back."

Himex had set up its Base Camp in the usual location: near the center of the basin, at the foot of a barren hillock—"the Mound," as it was sometimes called—decorated with a dozen or so stone memorials honoring Everest's dead. Most of the bodies remained on the slopes above. The Mound was a graveyard by proxy.

Some climbers avoided the Mound altogether. "Bad mojo," as one mountaineer said. Others felt compelled to pay their respects, wandering among the markers and observing the names scratched crudely on flat shards of shale: Sandy Irvine (Mallory had his own special marker about a mile away), Peter Boardman, Joe Tasker, among others.

In 2006, no one needed any special reminders. The carnage began even before Brice arrived in Base Camp on April 5. The previous day, one of the young Sherpas in his employ, a kitchen boy named Tuk Bahadur who had been helping ferry loads up the mountain, had died from a bout of pulmonary edema. According to reports, Tuk had fallen ill and died so quickly that some speculated he'd had some condition that had predisposed him for illness on the mountain. It would never be known; in the Sherpa tradition, Tuk was cremated at the Rongbuk Monastery by the end of the next day.

The only other person who had died on a Himex Everest trip had been Marco Siffredi, a big-mountain snowboarder from Chamonix who had disappeared in 2002 while attempting a descent of the Hornbein Couloir. Siffredi had been a friend, not just a paying client. It was his third Himex trip, and on the first two he'd successfully snowboarded both Cho Oyu and Everest. Brice had been perfectly willing to support his climb, but the snowboarder was on his own for the descent, and Brice felt his death shouldn't reflect on Himex's sterling safety record. "Technically," he said, "Marco's contract expired at the top."

The somber mood that followed Tuk's passing was soon offset by the double amputee Mark Inglis, who had brought a set of prosthetics with the intent of fitting them on a local Tibetan yak herder named Tilly who had lost his legs twenty years earlier after falling into a crevasse while attempting to cross a high pass. Inglis had met Tilly during the fall of 2004, when Inglis was climbing Cho Oyu. The Tibetan had heard about a sahib with magic legs and had offered him a case of beer in exchange for them. Now, at last, Cowboy and Inglis were bent over the man, fitting a new pair onto the yak herder.

Finally set up on his fiberglass prosthetics, Tilly rose shakily to his synthetic feet, clad in a pair of running shoes. For two decades he had crabbed along on the ground, sentenced to a dismal legless purgatory, employing pieces of car tires lashed to his stumps as skid plates. Now he stood almost as tall as the climbers who crowded around him. Inglis helped him take his first few tentative steps forward, both of their faces streaked with tears.

All the early drama made Brice uneasy, but it delighted the documentary filmmakers. Most of the climbers were happy to cooperate with the project—it meant valuable exposure for the sponsored team members. A few, however, like Himex guide Bill Crouse, were less than eager to participate. Crouse was a seasoned mountain athlete, fit, opinionated, and intense—the kind of guy who rode his bike 150 miles at a stretch and got out of bed at four A.M. to lift weights. He had been climbing and guiding in the Himalayas since 1991, and this was his sixth trip to Mount Everest. The filmmakers attempted to win him over by arguing that the TV exposure could make him famous, but Crouse was experienced and savvy enough to understand how many contingencies were involved in any given season. He'd seen the fallout from a big media event in the wake of 1996, when several of his friends had stopped guiding Everest altogether, horrified at the misperceptions created during the frenzy of attention.

Back in Kathmandu, at the beginning of the expedition, Dick Colthurst, an executive producer for Tigress Productions, the film company from Bristol, England, that was shooting the Everest series for Discovery, had addressed the group at the Hotel Tibet. "We're here to observe, not interfere," Crouse recalls Colthurst telling them. "If at any time you're unhappy, tell Russell or the guides or the film crew, and we'll resolve the issue." Of course, resolving the issue generally meant trying to persuade the climbers to relax and cooperate. A number of those present felt that the producers and directors were eager to see personal story lines emerge during the expedition—tensions, rivalries, love affairs, whatever, so long as it provided good footage.

One afternoon during the five-day trip from Lhasa to Base Camp the team had gone for an acclimatization hike to Shegar Dzong, an ancient fortress above the village of Shegar. During the hike, client Brett Merrell and guide Shaun Hutson appeared to strike up a bit of testosterone-fueled competition. One of the cinematographers approached Crouse and thrust a camera in his face: "I see that Hutson and Brett are really kind of pushing each other today," she said. "Is this how you see things shaking out? Is this just going to be a race up the mountain?"

"There ain't no fuckin' drama this early in the trip," Crouse growled. "People are going for a day hike. Get real."

"We had some conflicts, definitely, in the beginning, where they were trying to develop a little more drama than was there," Crouse said later. "But I was very clear with them that I was not interested in being part of a reality Everest program."

Big Boss found himself in the unenviable position of fielding concerns on both sides. This wasn't the first time a film crew had been aboard a Himex expedition. Brice had been working with cameras nearly as long as he'd been on Everest. As recently as 2003, the Outdoor Life Network (now called Versus) had produced a *Survivor*-inspired flop called *Global Extremes,* a kind of outdoor game show in which contestants competed in mountain sports in exotic locales, vying for a chance to climb Everest in the final episode. But *Global Extremes* had relied on a modest six-person team for the Everest segment; in 2006, the filmmakers outnumbered the clients.

Brice had plenty to gain from the documentary project—money, for starters; his contract with Discovery was said to be worth several million dollars. Filming in such an extreme environment also entailed the kind of complex logistical and engineering work he relished. Furthermore, the show was setting up to portray him in a favorable light—noting the thoroughness of his operation and underscoring his decades of experience—and the prospect of laudatory coverage was not unwelcome. Though many of his peers held Brice in high regard, public relations was not his forte, and he had taken his licks in the press over the years.

Brice had developed a particularly contentious relationship with Everest's emerging cybermedia, specifically EverestNews.com and, a few years later, a rival site called ExplorersWeb, a.k.a. ExWeb. Everest-News had been started by George Martin, a Web manager based in Granville, Ohio. Martin wasn't a climber, and had never been to the Himalayas, let alone to Mount Everest, but he was passionate about the culture of mountaineering, particularly on the big peaks. It was Martin's Internet wizardry and shrewd timing, more than his point of view, that turned EverestNews into such a hit. Still, plenty of climbers were eager to contribute, and it became a popular clearing-house for expedition updates and breaking news. Martin had created the first electronic forum devoted exclusively to the 8,000-meter climbing community.

The advent of dedicated Everest Web sites, more reliable technology, and speedier communication was a mixed blessing. On one hand, it allowed unprecedented access and close to real-time reportage directly from the mountain. On the other hand . . . it allowed unprecedented access and nearly instantaneous reportage directly from the mountain. In 1996, Internet "journalism" was in its infancy; by 2006 it was ubiquitous. Any climber with a satellite phone and a laptop could be in business, and many were—reporting on blogs, personal Web sites, or widely read portals like EverestNews and ExWeb, feeding the rapacious public appetite for all things Everest.

Brice's rift with the Web sites began in 1998, when EverestNews reported the death of Roger Buick, a Kiwi from Sydney, Australia, who owned an adventure travel company. Brice's account of the climber's demise seemed to grow more colorful with each telling. Buick had lobbied Brice to join a Himex Everest trip on several occasions, but the most Brice would allow was for Buick to buy onto the Himex permit and climb independently. "He kept trying to put his things in my camp," Brice recalled, "and I kept throwing them out."

Late in the season, as Brice was coming down from the summit, he passed Buick heading up, on his own. Brice informed Buick that the high camps were being taken down and that everyone was clearing off the hill, but Buick was resolved to continue upward. The next day, at ABC, Brice saw a figure on the North Ridge above the col, lying catatonic in the rocks. Brice climbed back up to find Buick still clipped to line, facing uphill and clutching a thermos with the bottom broken out of it, his mouth a frozen grimace. Brice unhooked him, dragged the body off the route, collected Buick's backpack, and made his way back to ABC. In Buick's tent, he found surprisingly few belongings, little more than a folder with a lawyer's phone number inside. By the time he had reached the lawyer in Sydney, word was circulating on Everest-News about the death, picked up from the mountain's radio traffic.

Buick's death haunted Brice. He had found only "a ball of string" in the recovered backpack. "No food. Nothing," he recalled. Later, he said, he heard from Buick's acquaintances that while cleaning out his house, they had found a map of Everest on the wall, marked with a cross at approximately 24,280 feet, the same elevation where Brice had found Buick's body. "I've done a lot of possum poisoning in my day," Brice said, "and they get that same grimace from cyanide. And why is the bottom out of his flask? So someone else doesn't come by and take it."

Whatever basis there might or might not be for Brice's speculation, the incident signaled a new reality: He had little control over the information leaking off the mountain—even when it involved him. Sure, there was plenty of good news to report, but Brice learned quickly enough that good news doesn't make headlines.

As big as EverestNews became, it was soon shouldered aside by ExplorersWeb—a more sophisticated and comprehensive site launched by bona fide Everest climbers. The site was started in 1999 by Tom and Tina Sjogren, a Swedish couple who had recently immigrated to New York. The pair had met in 1979, when they were both twenty. Tina had been born in Czechoslovakia, but she, her mother, and her brother had fled the country in 1968, during the Russian invasion, leaving their father, a Communist, behind. Tom had grown up in Sweden and had become a professional figure skater and sailor. The two were married in 1984, and two years later they started a business called

Easy-shop, a toilet-paper home-delivery service. The company made them rich, freeing them to pursue their real dreams: hard-boiled adventures around the world. Everest was up first. They tried for four consecutive years, beginning in 1996 and finally succeeding on May 26, 1999. It was Tina's fortieth birthday.

While each of their attempts had had its issues, none quite compared to the Sjogrens' introduction to Everest in '96. The couple had signed up with a commercial expedition helmed by Henry Todd, a charmingly garrulous Scotsman who had started running trekking and climbing expeditions on Everest's south side the previous year. Before his climbing career, Todd was best known in connection with Operation Julie, the 1977 drug bust that recovered around six million tabs of LSD—the largest sting of its kind in English history. His subsequent conviction for trafficking narcotics throughout Europe and Australia netted him seven years in prison.

During his tenure in the Himalayas, Todd made more headlines. He was banned from climbing on the Nepal side for two years after reportedly beating up an American journalist in Base Camp in 2000. In 2002, Todd was named in a lawsuit after a twenty-two-year-old British climber named Michael Matthews vanished on Everest's Southeast Ridge. Todd had provided an oxygen system that combined Russian regulators with British canisters—an unorthodox setup that the family claimed had contributed to their son's death. When the case came to trial in 2006, Todd was cleared of all wrongdoing, but he could not shake the stigma attached to his past. Some still referred to him as the "Toddfather."

In 1996, the Sjogrens simply knew Todd as a cheerful voice on the phone offering them a last-minute, attractively discounted opportunity to join his expedition. They jumped but soon wished they hadn't. During the approach, camping equipment lagged behind the climbing party. Food supplies fell short. Team members got sick. Eventually, Tom and Tina pushed ahead more or less on their own. They reasoned that if they had any chance at all, it would only improve the farther they got from the group.

By May 10 they had reached Camp Two in the Western Cwm, at 21,000 feet, and had hunkered down, listening to the radio and catching bits of news about the climbers trapped in the storm on the upper mountain. Two days later, the survivors came limping past the Sjogrens' camp. "They looked like they were coming off a battlefield," Tina recalled. "It was really grim."

Many climbers were so rattled by the havoc caused by the storm that they simply pulled up stakes and left. The Sjogrens debated going home as well, but they had come this far and were still feeling strong. From Camp Two on the Nepal side, the summit was just three days away. They decided to go for it, but they couldn't move any higher until Todd sent up oxygen and an extra mask.

"I can get it to you tomorrow," Todd promised when they radioed down to him.

The next day an exhausted Sherpa trundled into their camp hauling oxygen and an additional mask. When they inspected the equipment, they were horrified to discover that the mask was covered in dried blood.

"It works just fine," Todd reassured them over the radio. "I was able to recover some of the gear from the climbers who just came down. It's Beck Weathers's mask. Just clean it out with some snow."

The Sjogrens were too disturbed to continue, and they bailed from the climb the next day.

"Henry did what he said he would—he got me oxygen and a mask," Tina recalled later. "But Beck Weathers's nose was still in it."

The virtual collision between the Sjogrens and Russell Brice seemed inevitable—the die-hard independents versus commercial climbing's Big Boss—even though they had never met in person. The

Sjogrens' troubled attempt in 1996, combined with success in 1999 while managing their own expedition, had galvanized their defense of do-it-yourself climbing while fanning their disdain toward big-budget operators and their pampered clientele. The Sjogrens felt qualified to opine. In 2002, with Everest under their belt, they had skied, unsupported, to both poles, back to back. By 2006, they were contemplating an ascent of K2. By 2014, they insist with complete seriousness, they intend to pull off the first manned spaceflight to Mars.

Why the Sjogrens seemed to have it in for Brice, he could only guess. On ExWeb, they waxed on about the "Himex conveyor-belt," championing instead those who went at it alone, tackled alternative routes, or climbed sans oxygen and support—high risk but, in their opinion, real mountaineering. They certainly had more climbing credibility than EverestNews's George Martin, but they were so cynical about the entire commercial enterprise on Everest, and their reports so error-riddled, that Brice had a hard time taking them seriously.

The irony, of course, was that ExWeb itself was becoming a big business. The site was smart and attractive, and its daily posts had gathered a large, regular following. The Sjogrens had also started a sister company, HumanEdgeTech, that sold bundled hardware, including satellite phones, handheld PCs, and solar chargers—pretty much everything a climber needed to have a fully functional mobile office anywhere in the world. Their wares also included a proprietary software program called Contact that allowed climbers and other adventurers to post dispatches, photos, and low-resolution video directly on ExWeb or other sites. Mountaineers and adventurers could even find "how-to" information on the site: oxygen guidelines, expedition logistics, weather reports, route maps.

Within a few years, ExWeb had become one of the most influential voices in the adventure community, though its editorial bias tended to spin the overall Everest story in a way that was rarely favorable to the commercial crowd. The Sjogrens described Brice alternately as a "dictator," a "bully," and "Tony Soprano." They lambasted him over a dustup in 2004 regarding fixed ropes. And in the early fall of 2006, a week before the Discovery Channel series ran, they labeled Brice's actions that season the "most shameful act in the history of mountaineering."

Brice contended that he didn't pay attention to these Web sites, but word always seemed to get back to him, and he was hardly immune to the criticism. "Many people only understand one thing about Russell—that he is a tough boy, he's very direct, he likes to get things done," said his wife, Caroline, a journalist from Paris. "He's the boss. That's what they call him on Everest—the Big Boss. On the other hand, though, he is very sensitive. He likes people, and he wants people to like him. He can be too sensitive, I think, for his business. When he watches a film on TV, you know, he cries. We say in French, he is *fleur de peau*—sensitive to everything that touches his skin."

On April 9, Brice convened a multiteam meeting in Base Camp to discuss rope fixing that season—arguably the most important, contentious, and expensive task required on the mountain. Rope fixing entails stringing nearly three and a half miles of polypropylene cord along the route, stitched intermittently to rock and ice with screws, pitons, and slings. The ropes started 1,500 feet below the North Col, at the foot of the steep headwall, and ran continuously to the summit, aiding climbers through the technical sections, but primarily functioning as the world's longest safety line.

Some veterans scoffed at using so much rope on such moderate terrain; while the exposure, particularly on the summit ridge, could be spine-tingling, most of the route simply wasn't that steep or technical. The commercial operators, however, hardly questioned the value of fixing it. Strong climbers in optimal conditions might have little need for ropes, but guided clients with limited experience—now unavoidable on Everest—were a different situation altogether. "You look at accidents in the past and you say, Why did that happen?" said Brice. "I mean, why do they not put a piece of four-millimeter cord from the tents at the South Col to the Balcony? They still don't. Just put your carabiner on the line and walk right to the camp. [The fatalities in] 1996 were a bit needless. Lesson learned."

The rope meeting took place at the Chinese camp, led by Brice and supervised by Nima Tshering, the sirdar, or head Sherpa, of the Chinese team. The attendees included 7 Summits Club leader Alex Abramov; Dan Mazur, owner of the U.S.-based outfitter SummitClimb; the Indian expedition leader Harbhajan Singh; and a handful of others. For the last couple of years, Brice and the Himex Sherpas had shouldered a large percentage of the rope-fixing job; few other teams had the resources or manpower to handle it efficiently. Brice wasn't thrilled by the responsibility—it was a huge, expensive pain in his ass, but handling the job himself was logistically easier and helped ensure consistent quality.

In 2004, the teams had attempted to divide the rope duties among themselves—a complicated affair that resulted in some bad blood. Brice, annoyed with the process, had pulled his ropes as his team had left the mountain after their climb, a move that sparked outrage by those still at the high camps. "Our climbers were fully loaded with artifacts, tents and supplies coming down," reported EverestNews, which was sponsoring a team on the north side that year. "Fortunately for all involved Dan Mazur had a group at 7,500m and they were able to carry rope down to the col in order for our climbers to secure safe passage for themselves and others down to ABC! Our afternoon radio contact from 7,500m projected our climbers back at ABC around 3:00 pm. . . . At 9:30 pm, exhausted and furious, the climbers arrived at ABC. All they could say (well what all they said that we can print) was 'what happened to the rope . . . this is wrong! we fixed much rope up high and now Russell Brice takes it away . . . in the dangerous sections around the Col???' Dan Mazur and his team continued to fix more ropes."

Brice's solution to the rope conundrum was simple: Let his team fix the entire route, and charge teams $100 per climber, excluding Sherpas, to offset his costs. This system worked admirably on Everest's south side, at least on the lower mountain, where an independent team of Sherpas nicknamed the Ice Doctors fixed ropes through the Khumbu Icefall each season.

If nothing else, by 2006 the north-side team leaders were at least willing to discuss the job in the spirit of cooperation. "There will never be a year where everyone is totally satisfied," Brice told the group that afternoon. "But if someone thinks they can do a better job than we can, it's all yours."

"What if we're ready before the ropes are up?" said Dan Mazur, who had sounded the alarm about the rope issues in 2004. "We'd be willing to put the ropes up on the summit ridge."

"Fine by me," said Brice. "But you should take our ropes, since the color will match and everyone will know which line to use."

Dan Mazur was a congenial climbing guide, lecturer, and building designer based in Olympia, Washington. He had grown up in the Chicago suburbs, then migrated west to attend the University of Montana in Missoula in 1978. Mazur first climbed Everest "by accident," as he says, back in 1991. He had been hanging out in Asia, a slackpacking thirty-year-old, climbing a series of 7,000-meter peaks (no costly permits required) and sniffing around to see if he could shoehorn into a bigger expedition. One day, while loitering at a climbing shop in Kathmandu, he struck up a conversation with a Russian climber who mentioned that he was on his way to Everest. Twenty-four hours later, Mazur was headed for the mountain's south side, in Nepal, part of a tough team of ten that included the late Kazakh climber Anatoli Boukreev.

The Russians partnered Mazur with a forty-year-old team member named Roman Giutachvilli. As a boy, Giutachvilli had lost the use of one of his lungs after a bout of tuberculosis—a small bit of personal history that the team neglected to share with Mazur. No one expected much from a novice Yank and a handicapped Russian, but on October 10, Mazur and Giutachvilli reached the summit together, surprising everyone, including themselves. Getting to the top was relatively trouble-free, but Giutachvilli collapsed on the way down, exhausted, still an hour above the South Col. It was now after eight P.M. and dark, the wind whipping up a ground blizzard. Mazur was too wasted to be of much help, so he dug a snow hole, set Giutachvilli in it with the rest of their oxygen, marked the spot with a ski pole, and stumbled down to camp, nearly passing out by his tent door when he arrived.

Fearing the worst, Giutachvilli's teammates scrambled up through the darkness to find their climber ailing but alive, and managed to rouse him enough to get him back down to camp. For the next week, Mazur and the others helped Giutachvilli off the mountain and back to Kathmandu, but that's where their contact ended. "I never heard from Roman again," Mazur wrote later. "However, sometimes when I am climbing in the Himalaya, I meet Georgians, and when I introduce myself, they all seem to know my name already!"

Mazur went on to amass a world-class climbing résumé that included K2, Lhotse, Makalu, and three other 8,000-meter peaks. He traveled often and for extended periods, adding several technical first ascents involving steep, dangerous lines to his checklist. He came home with ever more wild and entertaining stories. In 2000, while attempting a new route on Muztagata, a 24,757-foot peak in central Asia's Pamir Mountains, he was blitzed by cerebral edema and took a spectacular fall as they were moving their camp up the mountain.

"I hurried to the edge . . . to see Dan go over a steep ice-snow cliff, cartwheeling with one bag in each arm," recalled Walter Keller, Mazur's climbing partner. "Head over heels he went, disappearing briefly before reappearing on the steep snow slope below, spinning about a center axis with one bag still wrapped around each arm. Stopping three hundred feet below his high point, he did not move."

Astonishingly, Mazur got up, brushed himself off, and eventually carried on. He rejoined Keller only to run out of daylight after they'd topped out and were making their descent. He, Keller, and a third teammate, Jon Otto, were forced to bivouac in a tent belonging to a Slovenian climber who'd been killed earlier that season. Mazur later described Muztagata as "the world's easiest 7,500-meter peak."

In 2004, Mazur returned to Everest, this time to guide the Northeast Ridge. He was then forty-two, his hair receded to a light-brown garland, but he was still mountain-fit and enthusiastic, having discovered his business niche: serving an ever-increasing population of mountaineers who were neither interested in nor could afford the premium Himalayan expeditions. SummitClimb offered two categories of Everest trips. A "full-service" climb, for about $19,000, included, among other things, a trip leader, transportation from Kathmandu, Sherpas, tents and cooks at Base Camp and ABC, "plenty of hot drinks," and "comfortable tables and chairs." Following the bargain-basement lead of Nepal-based outfitter Asian Trekking, Mazur's $7,000 "basic climb" covered little more than permits and transportation to the mountain.

"Why are the prices of these trips so low?" the SummitClimb Web site read. "We are dedicated to a philosophy of encouraging mountaineering by keeping costs to a minimum and welcome team members who are willing to share in achieving our objectives. . . . *THIS IS NOT A LUXURY EXPEDITION.*"

Mazur wasn't oblivious to risk—he gave a safety talk to his clients at the beginning of every expedition and held training sessions on the mountain—but he ran his trips with a laissez-faire approach that had rankled some other mountaineers. "He's a gifted climber who acclimatizes quickly, but he doesn't understand that other people aren't like him," said Michael Brown, a Boulder, Colorado, filmmaker who was on Mazur's 2004 Everest trip. During that climb, a thirty-three-year-old American client named Ryan Bendixen had to be evacuated after suffering pulmonary edema. "Ryan's bleeding out of his mouth, and he's about to get on a jeep and just disappear out into the Tibetan Plateau," recalled Brown. "We're still pretty high up, and it's no-man's-land out there, and Mazur is just freaked that he has to give up a bottle of oxygen. I saw him throw a crate of oxygen bottles in frustration. That's when I thought, Holy shit, this guy's a menace."

The next season hit SummitClimb hard. Mazur was leading two Himalayan expeditions that spring—a March trip to Pumori, a 23,494-foot peak adjacent to Everest, and a south-side Everest trip during April and May. While descending Pumori, two SummitClimb team members—Alex Chen, a thirty-five-year-old pearl seller from Panama, and a twenty-five-year-old Sherpa named Phurba Tamang—slipped and fell down a forty-five-degree slope near the summit. Mazur was just a little way below them, with another client. Phurba, who was roped to Chen, screamed at Mazur as he sailed by, "Help me! Please, help me!" They were fifty feet away, so Mazur could only scream back: "Ice ax! Dig in your ax!" The pair could not arrest the slide before they disappeared over a cliff.

A little more than a month later, on Everest's south side, Mazur lost a third team member—a thirty-nine-year-old bartender from Seattle named Mike O'Brien. The accident occurred in the Khumbu Icefall when Mike and his brother Chris were descending from Camp One through the frozen labyrinth. They were moving through an exposed section when Mike stumbled and fell into a crevasse. Why he hadn't clipped into the fixed line along the track was never clear. Chris O'Brien, Mazur, and teammate Arnold Coster were nearby and made their way down to their injured teammate. They performed CPR for more than an hour, but Mike soon died in his brother's arms.

Few outfitters had the resources or initiative to emulate the expedition gold standard that Brice had established, but at least a few tried—chief among them, the 7 Summits Club, run by Russian Alex Abramov. Abramov was a forty-two-year-old mountain guide with thinning black hair mowed down to a skullcap and a wide jaw that appeared stubbly no matter how often he shaved. He specialized in outfitting trips to the highest point on each of the seven continents. When he wasn't off on a climb, he lived in Moscow with his wife, Ludmila Korobeshko, a blond, broad-shouldered mountaineer almost as tall as Abramov who often accompanied him on expeditions. They were both favored with placid dispositions and spoke passable English—two qualities that made them well suited to run commercial climbing trips.

Abramov had summited Everest himself in 2004, and had completed the Seven Summits by 2005, but he was perhaps best known for driving a Land Rover to the 18,510-foot summit of Mount Elbrus, the highest peak in Europe. It was the first—and only—time a vehicle had been driven to that elevation, let alone to the top of one of the Seven Summits. Abramov and a ten-man team slid, skidded, and fishtailed to the top on September 13, 1997, but while driving back down over the ice and snow the rig caromed out of control. The driver dove out the door before the Land Rover crashed into a pile of rocks at 17,716 feet, where it was eventually abandoned.

Abramov had dodged his share of mishaps, not all of them on mountains. His own climbing career had nearly come to an abrupt halt in the spring of 2005 when he had attempted to depart Kathmandu, bound for the Friendship Highway and Mount Everest, in the middle of a *banda,* one of the public strikes frequently declared by leaders of Nepal's then ten-year-old Maoist insurrection. Abramov, his teammate Sergey Kalmschnikov, and their Nepali driver had made it only a few miles outside of town, puttering along in a small taxi, the roads eerily devoid of other cars, when armed soldiers ambushed them from the roadside brambles. The guerrillas hurled homemade pipe bombs that bounced off the car's roof and hood with loud metallic thunks until one of the devices crashed through a side window and landed on the floor in the back. The detonation shredded Sergey's left foot and blasted shrapnel into the back of Abramov's seat. The Maoists sprinted after the car as it sputtered to the top of a hill, where the Russians and their driver narrowly escaped over the top and returned to Kathmandu in time to save Sergey's foot, not to mention his life.

Whether determined, ambitious, damned lucky, or some combination thereof, Abramov's 7 Summits Club expeditions had endured long enough to earn a reputation as one of the best values in commercial mountaineering. The advertised price for his 2006 Everest trip—a full-service climb via the Northeast Ridge—was $20,000. By the time the full 7 Summits Club team had gathered at Base Camp, it was not only the largest trip Abramov had staged, it was the largest commercial group on the mountain.

The 7 Summits Club had established its Base Camp a short walk south of Himex's, tucked up against a wall of silt and debris spilling down from the terminus of the Central Rongbuk. Abramov had shown up this year with a proud new forty-foot-long Quonset-style "chess and mess" tent that bisected the campsite like a giant yellow caterpillar. He had further pimped out their home base with a sauna, a dartboard, a Ping-Pong table, and an entertainment lounge with a stereo, two TV sets, and a stack of DVDs purchased in Kathmandu. The team also had the welcome luxury of a dedicated medic named Andrey Selivanov, enough climbing Sherpas to pair one with each of the client, and more than one hundred bottles of oxygen. Whatever

Abramov lacked in Everest experience, he made up for in services and support.

The 7 Summits Club didn't simply attract budget-conscious climbers; it also drew individuals seeking a certain level of autonomy. Abramov was happy to accommodate them, at least within the parameters of his acclimatization schedule. The large group and expedition infrastructure also added an extra degree of safety.

"The bigger the team, the more clout they're going to carry on the mountain," said Kirk Wheatley, a commercial diver from Brighton, England, and a 7 Summits Club client in 2006 who had climbed six of the Seven Summits. "Generally, more people mean more Sherpas, more food, more oxygen, and more help if you get into a problem."

Abramov had initially intended to split the expedition management in 2006 with a Dutch climber named Harry Kikstra, a thirty-five-year-old mountain guide and photographer who had climbed the Northeast Ridge with Abramov's group the year before. Some felt Kikstra was an odd choice to be coleader. He'd almost died on the ridge during his '05 climb after summiting late and running out of oxygen during the descent. He might well not have made it off the ridge had it not been for the sustained efforts of Lakcha Sherpa, who had assisted Kikstra back to high camp.

Kikstra's role as coleader of the 2006 trip ended up being a moot point. He was still planning to participate in the climb, but as a private guide for a forty-one-year-old German financial manager named Thomas Weber—a decision that struck some as even more bizarre, since Weber suffered from a vision disability that was exacerbated at altitude. Kikstra was a personable, seasoned guided, but his experience above 8,000 meters was limited to his near-fatal ordeal on the ridge the season before. Now he was signing on to guide a climber who was likely to become blind during the ascent, on a route that had claimed dozens of lives.

Thomas Weber had queried other operators, including Russell Brice, about the possibility of climbing with them, but he either had been rejected as too much of a liability or hadn't received the kind of enthusiastic response that he sought. Kikstra had been the only one who had "engaged him in a dialogue," and within a few weeks they'd begun talking price and planning their schedule. Before the team had departed Kathmandu, Abramov had stressed that Kikstra and Weber, plus a two-man film team and their Sherpas, would be accompanying the expedition but would be climbing as an independent entity managed by the Dutch guide.

All together, the 7 Summits Club roster rivaled Himex's for its wide range of experience and ability. Plenty of preexpedition hype had percolated around fifteen-year-old Christopher Harris, from Leonay, Australia, a shy, gangly teen with a buzz cut who was hoping to become the youngest person to climb all Seven Summits. Christopher had revealed himself to be a climbing prodigy as early as age three, when he had scrambled up Mount Wareng, in Australia's Blue Mountains, "with some assistance" from his father, Richard. By age eight, Christopher and his dad had climbed an alpine route on Mount Kosciusko, the highest point on mainland Australia; by age eleven, he had bivouacked in a snow cave. At age twelve, he became the youngest person to summit New Zealand's Mount Cook, via a technical route.

Richard Harris prided himself on being Christopher's climbing partner, but he had also become his son's agent, promoting Christopher's endeavors while simultaneously encouraging him to tackle bigger, more ambitious goals. By the spring of 2006, they had summited Kilimanjaro and Elbrus and had had near misses on Aconcagua and Mount McKinley. Some of Richard Harris's Everest teammates described the elder Harris as a "handful," though they agreed that his intentions were in the right place. "He was your typical burping, farting, cursing outback-type bushman kind of guy," Kirk Wheatley said, "but on the whole I found him quite enjoyable."

Given the magnitude of their objective, Richard Harris had invited two seasoned Australian climbers to join them: filmmaker Michael Dillon and Dillon's good friend Lincoln Hall, who would handle the high-altitude footage. The two men had a long history together—most notably, they had both participated in the first Australian expedition to Mount Everest, in 1984. Dillon had stayed in Base Camp filming while Hall had climbed to 26,700 feet before being forced to turn around due to the cold and the late hour.

When Dillon had e-mailed Hall in February to let him know that "Christopher's Climb," as Richard Harris had dubbed it, was a go, Hall hesitated. His fitness had slipped after a football injury in December. What's more, he was now a husband, father, and full-time magazine editor. He hadn't been on an 8,000-meter peak in more than six years, and he would have less than two months to train for this trip. His deliberation didn't last long. By early April he was dusting off his crampons and ice ax and packing his duffel for Everest.

The Harrises were delighted. They now had a highly competent cameraman who could handle the rigors of high-altitude cinematography. But they were kidding themselves if they considered that the real reason to have Hall on board. Yes, it had been a while since he'd climbed such a serious peak, but his pedigree was world-class, the kind of experience you could hardly find anymore. Hall was, in no uncertain terms, a ringer.

The rest of the 7 Summits Club group was composed of a Ukrainian, a Dane, a South American, two Norwegians, three Brits, eight Russians, and four Americans, including David Lien, a credit examiner from Colorado Springs, and Slate Stern, an ex-marine turned attorney from Santa Fe, New Mexico—about as diverse an international ensemble as you would find in the Himalayas. The group arrived in Base Camp on April 18, after the four-day trip along the Friendship Highway, pulling up to the mountain in a driving snowstorm.

The next morning they woke to nearly a foot of fresh powder. It rarely snowed so heavily at Base Camp, and some wondered if 2006 wasn't setting up to be one of those dismal weather years that deny the summit to pretty much everyone. The team members passed the time listening to the BBC on shortwave radio, playing Jenga, and discussing pressing matters like Tom Cruise's sexual orientation. They tried to make the best of their time, but it was obvious that morale was already slipping.

"Weather remains bad—snow falls down," Abramov wrote dourly on the 7 Summits Club Web site shortly after their arrival. "We have not seen Everest yet. Our [Web] master Sergey Chistjakov promises to adjust internet in couple days. . . . The altitude, certainly, has an effect. At some members have appeared easy attributes of mountain illness. The doctor, Andrey Selivanov, already began active reception of patients."

As for Himex and the other teams, they weren't going to let a little inclement weather spoil their acclimatization schedules. The day 7 Summits Club pulled into Base Camp, the Himex climbers were spending their second day at Advanced Base Camp, 4,000 vertical feet above. The high winds and snow hammering the upper mountain were just an inconvenience, not an interruption. After a few days of rest at ABC, the plan involved making a few forays higher—to the North Col and even a little above—briefly exposing the climbers to more severe altitude. After that, they would return all the way to Base Camp for a week, enjoy a thorough rest and recovery, and then push back up for their shot at the top.

CHAPTER 4

ADVANCED BASE CAMP

ABC occupies a narrow gully running between the northern edge of the East Rongbuk Glacier and the soaring southeast face of Everest's northern neighbor, Changtse. By mid-April 2006, the site had become wall-to-wall tents, propped on terraces and rock platforms, spreading along half a mile of talus. Himex had erected its camp near the top of the site, closer to the North Col; at this altitude, even a quarter mile made a difference. Compared with the expansive elbow room at Base Camp, ABC was the equivalent of high-altitude tenement housing. The climbers and guides all had private dome tents, but they were packed as close together as space allowed, the camp webbed by a series of narrow footpaths. Privacy was a low-elevation luxury.

If Base Camp appeared busy, ABC's high-density environs revealed the full extent of the crowds. Brice knew that most of the teams would be converging on the ridge during the last two weeks of May—the optimal climbing window during springtime in the Himalayas, weather permitting. He had decent rapport with most of the commercial operators on the north side, but it was simply impossible to know who would be going where when. Conceivably, Himex could be among the first groups ready to ascend, but an early summit push was contingent on myriad factors, including route conditions and client health—hardly a sure thing considering that the group included a double amputee, an aging climber just back from cancer surgery, and a lumbering giant with half a dozen screws in his body.

Acclimatization has long been both a science and a kind of art. George Mallory once remarked that the first principle of mountaineering was to stay as comfortable as possible for as long as possible, and this wasn't simply an excuse for the British expeditions of the early 1920s to pack along champagne and tinned quail. Even then they understood that comfort meant less stress, and therefore more effective acclimatization and better odds on getting to the summit.

The body compensates for low-oxygen environments by ramping up red-blood-cell production, a process that kicks in even at the modest altitude of, say, Denver, Colorado, elevation 5,280 feet. At extreme altitudes, like 16,000-foot Everest Base Camp and above, the process intensifies until the blood is so thick it courses like sludge. The increased viscosity can lead to heart attacks, strokes, and pulmonary and cerebral edema. To help thin their blood, mountaineers hydrate obsessively, and some munch aspirin as if they're Altoids.

Even with unlimited time, few Westerners would ever fully acclimatize at ABC. You expend so much energy staying warm, fueling your muscles, and maintaining your basic body functions that it's difficult, if not impossible, to regain your metabolic equilibrium. At this altitude, your body begins to eat itself, first burning up whatever glucose your blood can provide, then gnawing away on protein—muscle tissue—which is more easily converted to energy than fat is. As your appetite dwindles, you lose weight, slowly and reliably, but remain strangely flabby. The running joke about an Everest fat farm concludes with the same sad punch line: You'll still have to exercise and diet when you get back to sea level.

The speed at which an individual acclimatizes varies from person to person, and sometimes from trip to trip, subject to the particulars of personal health, fitness, weather, and diet. The first week at ABC seemed less than promising for the Himex team. Mark Inglis had been stricken with laryngitis, his voice, already scratchy in the dry air, becoming a painful rasp. Brett Merrell, the L.A. fireman, staggered woozily around camp, his face ghostly under a thick layer of sunscreen. Medvetz caught a chest cold.

Such suffering was neither unusual nor problematic—at least, not yet. The only glaring concern at this point was Medvetz. On the first trip to the North Col, during which the climbers intended only to tag the saddle and then return to ABC, Medvetz fell immediately behind the pack, arriving at Crampon Point, less than a mile from ABC, more than an hour off the pace. Brice and his guides used the North Col climb as a kind of litmus test to assess their clients' fitness and ability. Brice himself could still stomp up the thing in an impressive two and a half hours with a full pack, faster than most Sherpas. But that was Brice. He allowed his clients a generous five hours to reach the top. Take longer than that, he told them, and their chances of eventually making the summit were slim.

Medvetz had taken nearly two hours to reach Crampon Point, less than a third of the way to the Col, and not nearly as steep as the headwall dead ahead. His size was working against him. It was hard enough pushing his mass uphill, but his ankle had grown sore and his backpack grated against the titanium cage wrapping his lower spine. He strapped on his crampons at the edge of the glacier and walked across the snowfield to the fixed ropes. He needed a break before tackling this formidable stretch, so he set his pack in the snow, lay down on top of it, and drifted into a deep sleep.

Brice was dismayed. "You have no business being on this expedition," he told Medvetz after the guides had finally turned him around and sent him back to camp.

"I just needed a break," he told Big Boss. "I'll do better next time."

Brice understood that once things began to unravel up high, they unraveled fast. Everest was dangerous, but it needn't be deadly, and his strategy attempted to eliminate as many variables as possible. As a final fail-safe, he partnered each client with a Sherpa, most of whom had already been to the summit at least once.

For the ascent above ABC, Brice planned to divide the expedition into two summit teams. Big Boss would remain at the North Col, where he would help direct the show, tracking each climber's pace, oxygen supply, and even rest breaks. This allowed him to gauge— hopefully, well in advance—who was going to make the top and descend before their gas ran out. He knew that most climbers, especially Western clients, were barely compos mentis by that point, and his job was to act as a surrogate brain. If Brice determined that a client wasn't moving fast enough to complete the trip, he would order him to turn around—and the decision wasn't up for debate. "You might reach the summit," he'd remind such a client, "but you won't make it back down."

Brice's anxiety was understandable; he was concerned about the welfare of his climbers. Already their acclimatization sorties had encountered long queues forming on the fixed ropes up to the col—ten, twenty, at times thirty or more people stacking up like dominoes, all relying on a few small anchors for protection. What's more, should an accident occur, the cameras were never far away.

* * *

Life at ABC was generally a colder, more hypoxic version of life at Base Camp; climbers spent a lot of time just sitting around, waiting for their bodies to acclimatize, trying to find ways to beat back the boredom. One afternoon at ABC, around the third week of April, a tall, cattail-thin climber named David Sharp, seeking a little face time with old pals, strolled into a nearby camp to visit his friend Jamie McGuinness. McGuinness was a forty-year-old New Zealand expat who ran an outfitter called Project Himalaya. The two had known each other since climbing Cho Oyu in 2002. "I think he just wanted to get out of his camp and not feel on edge," McGuinness recalled. "I got the impression that meals were pretty quiet over there."

On paper, Sharp belonged to a group dubbed the International Everest Expedition I, an ensemble of thirteen mostly independent climbers from the United States, the United Kingdom, Brazil, Austria, Malaysia, and Ecuador. In reality, he might as well have been alone on the mountain. Some climbers came to Everest with all the support that money could buy; Sharp had come in high Messnerian style, with almost none at all. He had access to the community mess tents in Base Camp and ABC, but otherwise he was on his own. Minimal oxygen, no Sherpas, no guide.

Misfit expeditions like Sharp's were becoming increasingly popular, in part because they were now so easily possible. The International Expedition to which he belonged had been coordinated by Asian Trekking, the Kathmandu-based outfitter owned and managed by Ang Tshering Sherpa, who, in addition to his many business interests, also directed the Nepal Mountaineering Association. Some referred to Tshering as a "Sherpa Brahman," given his unusual stature near the top of the social hierarchy. Asian Trekking provided soup-to-nuts support for large groups like Alex Abramov's 7 Summits Club, but the outfitter specialized in catering to small teams and solo mountaineers who had neither the resources, the need, nor the desire for a big-budget trip.

Sharp had already been to Everest twice before, in 2003 and 2004, both times to climb via the Northeast Ridge. He knew the drill well enough already, and he'd shopped around for an outfitter who could provide him only what he needed, at a price he could afford. When Sharp had walked into the Asian Trekking offices in Kathmandu, a modest room with a scattering of steel desks and a ceiling fan spinning slowly above them, it was simply to pay the balance for his $7,000 trip, collect his oxygen, and find out when the group's bus would be departing for Everest. "Basically, the fee covers services from Kathmandu to ABC," said Dawa Sherpa, Asian Trekking's expedition manager. "But above ABC, the climbers are on their own."

David Sharp was thirty-four, an engineer from Guisborough, England, a town of 7,400 people bordering the moors on England's northeast coast. He and his older brother, Paul, were products of proper English stock—a quiet, conservative, cerebral family. His father, John, had worked as an analyst at a chemical company. His mother, Linda, had been a lab assistant. They were both now retired. John and Paul were serious birders; they even looked vaguely avian, with angular noses and wiry limbs.

Before his climbing life had taken hold, Sharp distinguished himself in mathematics. He accelerated briskly through the Laurence Jackson School in Guisborough, and at sixteen he enrolled in nearby Prior Pursglove College. "I remember him as a bit of a loner, even in the classroom," Steve Hunnisett, a physics teacher and assistant principal at Pursglove, told Charlie Gillis, a writer for *Maclean's*, in 2006. "He was determined to find the best solution, not wishing to rely on others. He would often seek out extra challenges with additional reading, then push my intellectual limits by discussing them. David was one of the ablest students I've ever taught."

Sharp graduated with honors from Pursglove and promptly enrolled at the University of Nottingham to pursue a degree in engineering. At Nottingham, he joined the school's mountaineering club, working out on the school's indoor climbing wall and signing up for field trips to the Alps and Mount Kilimanjaro. With his tall frame and broad wingspan, Sharp was a natural rock climber, but his real ambitions skewed toward the big peaks and ambitious objectives. His intellectual drive spilled into his growing infatuation with mountains. He read climbing literature, particularly the history of Mallory and the early British expeditions. His fixation on one day climbing Everest began brewing.

In 2002, Sharp climbed Cho Oyu, his first 8,000-meter peak. Cho is a rite of passage for many climbers. At 26,906 feet, it is the sixth-highest mountain in the world, but it is widely considered one of the easiest of the fourteen 8,000-meter giants. The trade route, a low-angle slog up the mountain's northwest ridge, presents few technical challenges beyond one steep ice wall and a few rock bands, generally draped with fixed ropes to help climbers cheat past the hardest parts.

Sharp had signed up to climb Cho with Jamie McGuinness's Project Himalaya. McGuinness ran a low-key outfit for budget-minded clients looking for a Western operator with a positive attitude. "Why book with us?" went the sales pitch on the Project Himalaya Web site. "We . . . try harder than anyone to make sure you have the best experience. . . . We will be totally honest with you. . . . We enjoy what we are doing!"

These were not minor promises, considering that Nepal had been in a political tailspin since King Birendra, his wife, and seven other members of the royal family had been massacred in 2001 by the king's deranged son—an event that further destabilized the country, then in the sixth year of a violent Maoist uprising. The upshot was an increasing number of U.S. State Department warnings cautioning tourists about traveling in this part of the world, which was already beginning to suffer a dramatic slump in tourism. The only people who weren't steering clear, it seemed, were climbers—admittedly, a relatively small piece of the economic pie, but a piece that plenty of businesses wanted a bite of.

The 2002 Cho climb went brilliantly, or at least brightly, given that McGuinness had lured just two clients, Sharp and an Australian businessman named Tony Bragg. "We said we would run a guided expedition no matter how many bookings we got," McGuinness wrote later on the Project Himalaya site. "We ran this expedition with only two bookings. If we say we are going, we will!" Unfortunately, Bragg got sick and dropped out of the trip midway, but McGuinness, Sharp, and their cook, Tshering, summited on May 14.

It was obvious from the outset that Sharp had what it took to be a solid, maybe even outstanding, high-altitude mountaineer. He was steady and strong, but more important, perhaps, he was willing to suffer the risks and discomforts of a big climb better than most. At Camp Three, on the morning of May 14, perched at 24,800 feet, they climbed out of the tent to assess their summit chances. They had no electronic weather forecasts, so their decision whether or not to climb that day would be based on the age-old technique of looking around and making their best guess. McGuinness could see a massive cloud bank on the horizon. Lightning flashed inside the column of gray and bright white bolts fired out the bottom and down to the ground. McGuinness was inclined to wait or bail altogether, but Sharp was game to try a summit push.

"Let's go for it," he said to McGuinness. "We can always turn round if necessary."

There were two routes out of high camp, one veering left to a more gradual traverse and one leading straight up, a more direct line that crossed a rock band a little ways above their tents. When Sharp reached the obstacle, the fixed ropes looked questionable, so he free-climbed the rock, using just his hands and the points of his crampons, protected only by a "cow's tail," a short leash cinched to his harness and clipped to the ropes with a single carabiner. McGuinness watched with admiration as his client lizarded up the wall, then opted to use the ropes and his jumar. He was experienced enough to trust the anchors, and too exhausted to have a choice.

McGuinness and Sharp summited around noon, knackered but reveling in their accomplishment. Cho Oyu's summit is a large plateau, as flat as a football field. They dug bucket seats in the snow and sat down, enjoying a snack, gazing east at one of the most impressive views anywhere in the Himalayas, Everest itself just a few miles away. Before they left, they pulled out their cameras and McGuinness snapped a shot of Sharp in the classic mountaineer's pose, both arms raised, ice ax thrust skyward like a sword, a sea of whitecapped peaks spread across the horizon in the background.

Sharp had bagged his first 8,000-meter peak. Everest was next.

McGuinness and Sharp formed a casual but lasting friendship. Despite Sharp's idiosyncracies, McGuinness had come away from the Cho Oyu trip with a high regard and genuine fondness for his client. "At first, he really came across like a bit of a geek," McGuinness said later. "He was very science-oriented in his thinking, very meticulous. He was concerned about how we secured our tents, because he had lost his down suit on a previous expedition when his tent had blown away. But he was just a very nice guy to be around, really a great expedition companion. He could be philosophical at times, but he never tried to force his opinions on anyone."

In the fall of 2002, McGuinness informed Sharp of an Everest expedition he was helping organize for a Northern Ireland team for the following spring. The team was led by a twenty-six-year-old engineering instructor named Richard Dougan. Both McGuinness and Sharp had met Dougan on Cho Oyu, when the Northern Ireland team was struck by trouble—a close friend and teammate of Dougan's had been killed when he fell into a crevasse, and two others nearly met a similar fate in a separate incident. McGuinness ended up assisting two of the climbers and, later, helped carry the body of the dead man off the mountain.

Despite the problems on Cho, Dougan was planning a private, small-scale Everest climb, and McGuinness seemed like just the guy to help him do it. He contracted with Explore Himalaya, Project Himalaya's sister company in Nepal, to help with logistics and hired McGuinness as a "climbing Sherpa," an ideal arrangement as far as McGuinness was concerned because it removed him from any guiding responsibilities but still allowed him a try at the summit. Sharp, too, would benefit, since he could join up at cost—far less than the retail price of a commercial trip. And so in the spring of 2003, Sharp and McGuinness found themselves in a bus, rambling along the Friendship Highway on their way to Everest Base Camp in Tibet with Dougan and a climber named Terry "Banjo" Bannon, illustrious members of the First Northern Ireland Everest Expedition.

The climb wasn't as troubled as the Cho Oyu trip, but it had its problems. None of the team members, including McGuinness, had attempted Everest before, and they got a stern introduction to the mountain's potent altitude and volatility. At Base Camp, the expedition medical team left for home when one doctor was afflicted with cerebral edema. Later, Dougan was forced to descend all the way to Base Camp when he came down with acute tonsillitis while attempting to haul a load to the North Col. A windstorm ravaged camp at the col and ABC, destroying several tents. At last, though, Sharp, McGuinness, Bannon, and Dougan were positioned at ABC, ready to make their summit bid. Dougan and Sharp would make the first attempt, as a pair, and Bannon and McGuinness would try during the next available weather window.

Dougan and Sharp left their high camp on May 22, a little after midnight, in marginal conditions. The wind bit hard, and light snow spun around them. Still, they managed to climb to the Northeast Ridge and trudge to the base of the Second Step. Sharp was having some issues with his oxygen system, and when he took off his mask at the bottom of the step Dougan noticed the telltale ashen blotches of frostbite on his cheeks. They would only be more exposed to the wind and cold above the step, so Sharp decided to turn around and head down, urging Dougan to keep climbing toward the top. It was his expedition, after all, and they were so close. But at the top of the step the wind grew even worse, so Dougan bailed as well, catching up with Sharp on the descent. At Camp Two, where they would spend that night, they removed their gloves and boots to discover the flesh on their fingers and toes blistered and turning purple. They did their best to treat it as they moved down through the camps, while McGuinness and Bannon made their run at the top a few days later, both summiting on May 31.

At the end of that summer, Sharp e-mailed McGuinness:

28 August: sadly, I'm still in England—I had to have surgery to remove about two thirds of my left big toe, and about a fifth of the second toe on my right foot. I put off having the operation until after my best mate's wedding, by which time the big toe was on the way to amputating itself, so I had surgery on the 28th July. Everything went OK, but in order to keep as much of the big toe as possible, the surgeon just took off the dead tissue, leaving an open wound, and this takes longer to heal than if he'd removed more, and then sewn a flap of skin across. The smaller toe is well on the way to recovery, but it's going to be a while before the big toe is in good enough shape for me to travel—at the moment, it needs dressing every two days, due to the fluid oozing out of it. Looking on the bright side, when it has healed I won't have any problems walking,

but at the moment I don't want to roll any weight onto that toe. Fortunately, cycling is OK, and the weather here is still excellent, so I'm gradually building my fitness up on the bike.

Everest had drawn first blood, but the injury hardly quelled Sharp's ambition. If anything, his near miss had stoked his desire even more. He began to consider another attempt, this time without oxygen. Since they'd met, he and McGuinness had shared numerous conversations about oxygen—how much a climber really needed; what it would take to survive a night out up high, if it came to that. The oxygen he'd used during the Northern Ireland expedition had been faulty and frustrating—perhaps the reason Sharp had failed on that attempt. If he went without oxygen, it would be an accomplishment that would place him in a very exclusive club, distinguishing him from the parade of amateurs who managed to scrape their way to the top. Since Messner and Habeler's historic climb in 1978, only 113 people had pulled off an oxygenless ascent. Three of these climbs had been disputed. Twenty-three others had died trying.

Sharp returned to Everest's north side the next season, in spring 2004. This time he had joined an independent commercial group organized by Thamserku Trekking, an operator based in Kathmandu. The group was composed of a four-woman Spanish team, a couple from France, Sharp, and another solo climber, James Milne, a sixty-one-year-old math professor from New Zealand who now lived and taught in the United States. The others had all hired Sherpas—Milne had engaged two—but Sharp was attempting the climb alone, without oxygen and without a Sherpa. This meant he would be hauling his own gear, cooking his own meals at the high camps, and generally looking after himself for the duration of the two-month expedition.

Solo climbs are excruciatingly difficult. You must carry and cache gear and provisions on the upper mountain in preparation for the final summit assault, since it's not feasible to haul everything at once, in true alpine style. There's a good reason Everest climbers have long relied on the support of Sherpas. For many, it would be impossible to do all the work necessary, in the time required, to reach the top and get back down again. Sharp was pragmatic; he sought only the support he needed, but no more. Thamserku provided tents, food, and a cook at Base Camp and ABC. And he split the cost of yak rental with Milne and the French couple, conceding to let the animals ferry his equipment up to ABC.

Sharp spent the first week making short forays above Base Camp, reading Shakespeare, and laying low to allow his body to adjust to the new heights. By May 8, he had spent a couple of weeks at ABC and had made multiple trips to the high camps above the North Col, stashing gear as high as Camp Two. He was ready for his summit push.

Timing is critical on an Everest ascent, and because it typically takes four to five days to summit from ABC, and much longer to appropriately acclimatize, jumping on a weather window can be challenging at best. Climbing without oxygen only complicates matters further. You're not simply out of breath; you move more slowly, are more susceptible to cold, and typically lose what little coordination you have left at extreme altitude. Sharp departed Camp Three around midnight on May 17, but he turned around at the start of the ridge proper when, again, he began to suffer from frostbite. He hoped to descend, recover, and try a second time, but the damage, though not permanent, was severe enough that a second attempt was impossible.

It was a valiant effort. Reaching the ridge had placed him higher than almost any other point on earth. Granted, it was still more than a horizontal mile farther along the ridge to the top—another six hours or more—but each attempt came more knowledge and experience, if also with a fair bit of disappointment. Later, Sharp commiserated with Milne, who had turned around at 28,000 feet when the weather appeared to be deteriorating. Back in Base Camp, before they shipped out,

Milne had found himself trying to explain to some "do-or-diers" why he hadn't done either, and why that was okay. But it was Sharp who put a fine point on it. That's what makes you a mountaineer, he said.

That summer, Sharp e-mailed his friend Tony Bragg, the Australian who had been on the Cho Oyu trip with him two years earlier. "It was a really strong performance," he wrote, referring to his recent Everest attempt. "Don't think I'll be back to the big E, as, with O$_2$ and good weather, I have no doubt that I can reach the top." Of course, he *would* come back, and by the time he arrived at Everest in the spring of 2006, he was resolved that it was going to be his last attempt.

Certainly Sharp wanted, even needed, to get Everest out of his system, but other factors were complicating the process, not the least of which was his evolving career. Before the 2006 trip, he had quit his job at QinetiQ, a global defense and security firm based near London, and completed a postgraduate certificate in education. He had lined up a teaching position that promised a more soulful and ultimately satisfying occupation than working for the defense industry, even if, as a profession, it would be far less tolerant of six-month climbing sabbaticals. Sharp needed to get Everest out of his system, and soon.

By some accounts, the 2006 International Everest Expedition I was an altogether bleak affair in which the participants spent little time together, toiling along in their own private suffering. Not that the expedition was entirely without interaction; it shared Base Camp with five other groups, including two teams attempting the coveted Fantasy Ridge route, what some considered the last great unclimbed line on Everest. One of those teams was led by George Dijmarescu, a controversial forty-four-year-old mountaineer of Romanian descent who lived in Hartford, Connecticut.

Dijmarescu had a caterpillar mustache, stringy dark hair that he combed straight back, and eyebrows that formed a menacing chevron. Despite his impressive climbing résumé—he had summited Everest the past seven years in a row—he was infamous among certain climbers for a dispute he had with his Sherpani wife, Lhakpa, at the north-side Everest Base Camp in 2004; with one punch he had knocked her out cold. In 2006, some climbers considered Dijmarescu Asian Trekking's de facto liaison and leader, given his experience on the mountain. But those inside the expedition argued differently. "There was no leader," said Dave Watson, a thirty-year-old mountain guide and ski patroller from Burlington, Vermont, and Dijmarescu's teammate on the Fantasy Ridge climb. "Everybody was on their own agenda. It was really just a bunch of people working in the same place."

Watson and Sharp struck up a friendship during the trip, tenting near each other at the lower camps and chatting in the Asian Trekking mess tent. They listened to music—often Bob Marley, one of Sharp's favorites—and swapped stories, their discussions ranging from previous climbs to Sharp's "interesting encounters" with English soccer hooligans. "He was a funny guy," recalled Watson. "Not the kind of guy who could crack you up all the time, but he was a good storyteller, and he could make you laugh really hard."

At a time when Base Camp was replete with iPods, portable DVD players, and laptop computers, Sharp prided himself on being something of a Luddite. He climbed with a weathered old Berghaus backpack and the same down parka he'd used on the previous two Everest trips—though he'd splurged this year and set himself up with a new pair of Millet high-altitude boots. Usually, he kept to himself, immersed in one of the only two books he'd brought: the Bible and the collected works of Shakespeare, his expedition staple.

By the end of April, Russell Brice had begun to commit to an early summit attempt. Though the weather had been inauspicious earlier in the month, the pattern had begun to stabilize, and the long-range forecasts showed fair weather moving in by mid-May. This was earlier than usual but not atypical. The spring Everest season revolves around what is typically a two- to three-week summit window that materializes sometime in May, as daylight increases and temperatures wax, and then closes by early June, when the monsoons arrive.

Brice received his weather information from Meteotest, a Swiss company that provided state-of-the-art meteorological data for expeditions around the world. Himex gathered updates several times a day, and Brice relied heavily on these forecasts to plan his summit strategy. The service wasn't cheap; Meteotest charged about three thousand dollars to service an expedition, and Brice was protective, even proprietary, with the information. It wasn't that he wanted to jeopardize others' safety, or to gain an unfair advantage for his team. Rather, he hoped to provide his clients with the best opportunity for a safe climb. Given the growing crowds converging on the narrow ridge, this often required a bit of brinkmanship.

While Brice finalized his summit plans, the film crew milled around, shooting more interviews, landscape scenery, irreverent tent tours, and heartfelt video letters to family and friends back home—a little atmosphere from life at ABC. Once the climbing proper commenced, the team would have precious little time or energy for anything but the task at hand.

Whatever pre-expedition concerns the filmmakers might have had about a dearth of drama during the expedition were assuaged quickly enough. It started in BC, with Tuk Bahadur's death, and picked up again on April 25, during the team's first acclimatization hike to the North Col. At the saddle, the Himex climbers encountered an Indian expedition with a climber who had fallen unconscious, stricken by high-altitude cerebral edema, lying in the snow, bloody sputum coating his lips and chin. Terry O'Connor, an American ER physician working as the Himex team doctor, and Himex guide Shaun Hutson started field

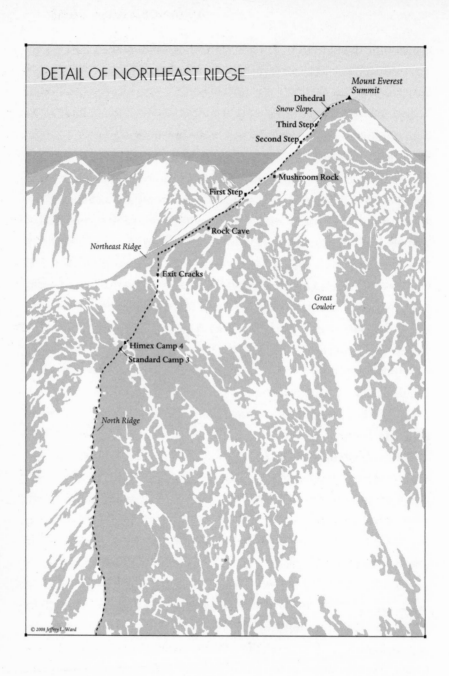

DETAIL OF NORTHEAST RIDGE

Mount Everest Summit

Dihedral

Snow Slope

Third Step

Second Step

Mushroom Rock

First Step

Rock Cave

Northeast Ridge

Exit Cracks

Great Couloir

Himex Camp 4

Standard Camp 3

North Ridge

© 2008 Jeffrey L. Ward

triage and rigged a litter from a coil of rope. Once they had set up a system for evacuation, the Indians, Himex climbers, and several Sherpas carefully lowered the man down from the col. O'Connor helped stabilize him at ABC, and then a Sherpa hauled him piggyback fourteen miles down to Base Camp, where he eventually recovered.

Some kind of incident seemed to flare up every few days. On April 28, Mark Inglis was descending from the col when an anchor for one of the fixed lines ripped out of the ice, sending the double amputee rocketing toward the bottom, upside down. Inglis arrested the slide, saving himself from injury or worse, but discovered that during the fall the foot had snapped off his right carbon-fiber prosthesis. He radioed down to Brice, his voice a barely audible rasp. "Broke me leg," he told Big Boss. "Gonna need a spare." Soon a Sherpa was on his way with a replacement limb while Inglis bound his foot back together with electrical tape. In a while, he was continuing down the lines, the filmmakers rushing up to meet him.

Around six A.M. on April 30, Phurba Tashi and five other Himex Sherpas left high camp carrying nearly 4,000 feet of coiled line between them—enough to string along most of the upper Northeast Ridge to the summit. Following the rope-fixing meeting a few weeks earlier, Brice had taken responsibility for the job this year. Even if it was likely to cost him yet more money, at least this way he knew that the job was in capable hands.

Phurba Tashi was Big Boss's lead climbing Sherpa and trusted expedition lieutenant. Phurba came from the village of Khumjung, in Nepal. He was thirty-four years old and, at six feet tall, a specimen among Sherpas—taller and broader than most of his friends. He had smooth, symmetrical features, a helmet of obsidian-colored hair, and widely spaced almond-shaped eyes that belied his Tibetan ancestry. During the early weeks of the expedition, he had entertained himself by observing the season's fresh crop of sahibs; they always brought trouble and opportunity, often at the same time. Phurba wasn't suspicious, exactly, but he was watchful, and cautious. On a silk string around his neck dangled an ancient Tibetan *dzi* bead, a millennia-old chunk of etched agate worth thousands of dollars to antiquities collectors in the West, and believed to protect the wearer and bestow good fortune on him. So far, Phurba's luck had held; by 2006 he had been to the top of Everest seven times.

Brice had plucked Phurba from dishwashing obscurity during an expedition on Shishapangma back in 1995. He'd taught him the basics—how to use crampons and an ice ax, how to ascend a rope—and then set him to work ferrying supplies to the high camps. In 1999, after Phurba reached Everest's summit for the first time, he returned to ABC looking as if he'd just strolled across camp. "It's not really like I am climbing mountain," he said later. "I am just walking with clients."

Phurba's strength and endurance became the stuff of legend around Everest. He had helped a number of climbers over the years, none quite as dramatically as in 2001. That spring, he and another Himex Sherpa, Lobsang Temba, climbed from Camp Three to the Second Step, nearly 4,000 vertical feet, to help rescue Himex client Jaime Viñals and his guide Andy Lapkass, despite the fact that the Sherpas had just summited the day before. No climbers in Everest history had ever gone so far, so fast.

Lapkass and Viñals were in dire shape. They had been too slow getting off the ridge the day before and had been forced to spend the night at 28,500 feet, near the Third Step. That morning they were too exhausted and hypothermic to move. Brice had spent the night organizing a rescue, and the two men certainly would have perished on the ridge where they were stranded had it not been for the Sherpas and three other American climbers who came to their aid: Dave Hahn, Tap Richards, and Jason Tanguay, members of an International Mountain Guides team who were also at high camp. The IMG climbers were the first to reach the two men. Richards and Tanguay helped Lapkass down, while Hahn worked on Viñals, managing, with great effort, to prod him to the Second Step; there Viñals rappelled to within ten feet of the bottom before becoming hopelessly snared in the spaghetti of ropes draped down the rock. Hahn, below, was so spent that he could only look up and scratch his head; he was certain he was going to watch Viñals die before his eyes.

"I really thought we weren't going to make it," Hahn recalled. "Then Phurba arrived . . . and jumped up past me, placed his own goggles, mask, and oxygen on Jaime and untangled him from the ropes in about two minutes flat."

Later that year, Phurba, Lobsang, and four IMG guides (another IMG climber, Andy Politz, had brought extra oxygen up to the rescuers) received the American Alpine Club's David A. Sowles award for "going to the assistance of fellow climbers imperiled in the mountains, with unselfish devotion at personal risk or sacrifice of a major objective." It was the first and, to date, only time the award had ever been given to Sherpas.

With each season, Phurba's responsibility on the ridge expanded a little more. Not that he would ever think of it in those terms; his Buddhist upbringing had taught him that Chomolungma, as Tibetans call Everest, allowed him to climb and work there only because he paid the mountain due respect, a deeply instilled reverence and trepidation that most Westerners could never fully understand or appreciate. To the Sherpas, all climbers are trespassers. When white men died up high, a skill at which they seemed to excell, Phurba and the others would quietly remove the bodies from the ridge and drop them down Everest's North or East Face—usually at the request of the families, and followed by generous compensation.

Removing bodies is odious work, not only because of the nature and location of the task but because most Sherpas are deeply superstitious. They believe that until the souls of the deceased are properly guided to the afterlife, they are easily agitated and can bear down on the living in ways that fill many Sherpas with dread. Usually only lamas are permitted to handle corpses, but Sherpas can no more bring a lama to the bodies than the bodies to a lama. Phurba, as he put it, had a "special understanding" when it came to conducting the mountain's dirty work. Guiding might have been the glamorous part of his job, but Phurba and his crew were also Everest's custodians and undertakers.

"For Sherpa, if we can help someone in life, it is very, very good for our religion," he said. "But to move body is always hard, very hardest thing I have to do."

Around three P.M. on April 30, Brice got the call he'd been waiting for, Phurba's voice coming over the receiver: "ABC, ABC, Big Boss. We are all six Sherpas summit now together." It was the earliest the route had ever been fixed all the way to the top. Far above, Phurba anchored his coil of rope at the summit and then, in an uncharacteristically proud move, tossed the remaining hunk of it down the Southeast Ridge, a welcome mat for the south-side climbers he knew would be arriving in a few weeks.

Fixing the route was a significant accomplishment, but it marked a season that was beginning to take an ominous turn. At Base Camp, Himex had already lost Tuk Bahadur to pulmonary edema. Then, on April 20, three Sherpas had been killed on the south side in the Khumbu Icefall. The Sherpas were part of two different expeditions, but they were traveling together, carrying equipment to the upper camps, when twin seracs groaned and gave way, knocking down a section of ice and burying six men from the team, three of them permanently.

Accidents still gave most climbers pause, but since 1970 the mountain had averaged five deaths per season. By May, the news about the Sherpas was already fading. Not that it had much affected the north-side teams anyway. With the ropes in on the Northeast Ridge, attention was now focused on the summit. At the Himex camp, Brice and guide Bill Crouse discussed the details—winds aloft, precipitation, temperature—of the forecast for the coming weeks. A particularly enticing weather window appeared to be arriving around May 11. The temperatures looked like they would remain cold—minus 30s and 40s—but the winds seemed calm and the skies clear. Crouse nodded. With the exception of Medvetz, who had returned to Base Camp stricken with bronchitis, the team was in pretty solid shape. The guide believed the clients would be ready for an early summit bid. Initial preparations had begun, but it would be several more days before he or Brice breathed a word of it to anyone.

With Himex's plan in motion, there was little to do now but try to rest at ABC, waiting for Brice's signal to start heading up. The first of May was Russia's Labor Day, and Alex Abramov invited Brice, Crouse, and the other guides to celebrate with his team in the 7 Summits Club camp. Earlier that day, Himex clients Marcel Bach, Kurt Hefti, and Gerard Bourrat had arrived at ABC. By May 7, even Medvetz had returned, now fully recovered from his bronchitis. Himex was fully intact again and ready to go.

On May 8, Brice gathered his climbers and informed them they would be departing on their summit push the next day, Team 1 ascending ahead of the second group by a day. The following morning the climbers began to trickle discreetly out of ABC, careful not to call too much attention to their movements for fear of prompting a stampede toward the ridge.

After the long, idle weeks, the action would accelerate quickly now. To describe a summit attempt as an assault seems a throwback to the days of mountaineering yore, but the term is apt on Everest. The climbers had to storm the upper mountain as quickly as possibly, since the physical attrition would soon become intolerable. Because Himex utilized three camps above the col, rather than the standard two camps, it was even more critical that things progress swiftly and smoothly. The teams would spend a night at each camp, some climbers hitching to oxygen as soon as the col. Any mistakes now could bring disaster later.

On May 10, as Himex moved up from the North Col, the difficulty of the upper mountain became all too apparent. Brett Merrell, the L.A. fireman, had started out for Camp Two that morning "feeling like a million bucks," but two-thirds of the way to camp suddenly felt all his energy evaporate. He soon ground to a halt and sat down in the snow. It was midafternoon, and the wind and snow had picked up. Now engulfed in a whiteout, Merrell tried to find his breath. He had been out of radio contact for more than two hours, and he finally called down to ABC and spoke with Brice.

"I've got nothing left," Merrell wheezed. "I'm too knackered to make it down to the col right now, way too knackered."

Brice encouraged him to come down as soon as possible, and Merrell eventually gathered enough strength to descend, reaching the col that afternoon through worsening weather. Everyone else from Team 1 had continued on up.

The next day, May 11, a few climbers who had set out even earlier than Himex began to summit from the north side, including George Dijmarescu and Dave Watson of the Fantasy Ridge team (though they had altered their route at the last minute due to conditions). When Watson returned to the col, he met another climber he knew well: David Sharp, who was now also on his way up, chasing an early summit attempt. The two men spoke briefly, exchanging the common Everest repartee about route conditions, how the climb had gone, and so on. It was one of the last conversations anyone would have with Sharp.

"When I saw him, he seemed fine, anxious to go up," Watson recalled. "Because we made it, everybody started getting antsy. He was going to go up the same day as Russell Brice's main team, on the fourteenth. He was a good observer, just a little bold on strategy. He didn't have a weather report, but he had the experience to know that if Brice was going, it was going to be a good summit day."

Brice was unconcerned about the small teams and independent climbers shadowing Himex; it was the large expeditions that worried him. He estimated that the ridge could accommodate as many as sixty climbers on a given day, but it required careful planning and a diligent kind of air-traffic control in order to avoid deadly bottlenecks. Many of the teams remained below at ABC, or even Base Camp. But there were dozens of climbers moving into position on the upper mountain who could get in Himex's way.

The three upper camps Himex used on the North Ridge were slotted above and below the two sites commonly used by other teams. Brice placed his second camp at the top of a long snow ridge, at around 24,500 feet; Camp Three a little higher on the ridge, at 25,900 feet; and their last camp out on the upper aspect of the North Face at around 27,100 feet. With so many sites in use, you were lucky to identify your own teammates. Climbers—now morphed into alpine spacemen with their thick down suits, goggles, and oxygen masks—got strung out all along the North Ridge. Who was going where, and when, was almost impossible to determine.

May 12 brought Team 1 to Camp Three, but the winds had picked up again, blowing so hard that Brice had to reconsider his summit plan. He reviewed his weather forecasts. The slight meteorological hiccup looked like it would subside in the next twenty-four hours, but that meant his team would have to hunker down for a day at a grueling 25,900 feet. Still, Brice made the call to hold for a day; the fourteenth now looked like a much better option.

On May 13, the mountain derailed another Himex climber. When Team 1 rolled out of Camp Three headed for high camp, Mogens Jensen, the Danish triathlete climbing without oxygen, trailed just behind his companions. After forty-five minutes, Jensen flopped against a rock wall, unable to walk any farther. Supplemental oxygen lessens the debilitating effects of altitude but it doesn't completely eliminate them. By now, Jensen wasn't just physically wasted—to be expected at such heights—he was in trouble. He had a ballistic headache. His speech was slurred, and his lips were turning a pale shade of blue. The horizon was doing flip-flops, as if he were drunk, a frightening early warning sign of cerebral edema. Over the radio, he alerted Brice, who urged him to retreat and hook up to oxygen as quickly as possible. Back at Camp Three it took Jensen several hours to become coherent again, and at least he stumbled the four hours back to the col—kaput.

Without Jensen and Merrell, Team 1 had been whittled down to five Westerners—lead guide Bill Crouse, cameraman Ken Sauls, team doctor Terry O'Connor, and clients Kurt Hefti and Marcel Bach—plus their Sherpas. On the afternoon of May 13, they tumbled into the high-camp tents to rest and refuel before they left for the summit just a few hours later. Below them, Team 2 had moved into Camp Three with few problems. The weather had stabilized again; there was only a light wind and a sprinkling of snow—a good thing since the Team 1 climbers were extraordinarily, terrifyingly high now, and the clock was running.

Now that the team had ground its way up to Camp Four and positioned itself within feasible striking range of the summit, the next few hours would go something like this: Gag down some lukewarm liquids; rest for a short while; pull on frozen boots; and stumble out into one of the darkest, coldest, windiest, and most lifeless stretches of ground on earth. Aim your barely animated body toward the top and try not to stop, no matter what.

Everyone felt the pressure to perform come summit day. It wasn't just the toughest day of the trip—it was the culmination of months, even years of planning and preparation, tens of thousands of dollars, and, for many climbers, unhealthy amounts of anxiety and emotional strife. Mistakes and mishaps had a way of compounding themselves at any point during the two-month expedition, but above 26,000 feet the margin of error shriveled to zero.

It's fashionable to talk about terrain at this altitude, the mystical 8,000-meter mark, as the "death zone," and it's true that death is imminent for humans here, even with oxygen, fluids, and warm clothes. It's around this elevation that oxygen intake becomes so compromised that your system can't sustain basic metabolic functions. But the hypoxic impact varies among individuals; there isn't a specific threshold where everyone expires at once. The speed at which a given climber wilts is often unpredictable, undetectable, and slow. It can be eerily similar to falling asleep, and it can take hours, or days.

Most climbers depart for the summit with two bottles of oxygen. The cylinders weigh a little less than eight pounds each and, at an average flow rate of two liters per minute, last up to eight hours apiece. A common tactic is to run off one bottle to a bulbous landmark on the ridge called Mushroom Rock, at about 28,200 feet, stash the half-used bottle, suck off a second full bottle on the way to the summit and back to Mushroom Rock, and then finish the descent on the original bottle. Climbers tend to carry little else—maybe extra gloves, a vial or two of dexamethasone (a powerful steroid to help revive someone in an emergency), some food, and a thermos of tea. No one wants more weight than is absolutely necessary. An old mountaineering saying goes something like, "Prepare for a bivouac and you will."

Bill Crouse crawled out of his sleeping bag at around eleven P.M. on May 13. He was tenting with Terry O'Connor, who still lay quietly in his bag. The team wouldn't depart until one A.M., which seemed prudent enough, even given the crowds, but Crouse wanted to check the weather and ensure that he had plenty of time to assemble his guide's pack. There'd be ample opportunity to sleep when they were done.

Even the simplest tasks were an exercise in hypoxic tedium. It took Crouse thirty minutes just to lace up his boots and get his gear together. When he finally emerged from the tent, the first thing he noticed was the cold, which was shocking, even for Everest. Ambient temperatures hovered around minus 40. It was overcast with a light breeze, and Crouse looked down the route, toward the neighboring camp below. More than a dozen headlamps were already bobbing toward him.

"Shit," he mumbled. He had no way of knowing who the teams were, but one thing was certain: Himex was about to be behind them.

During the next hour, a steady parade of climbers clomped past the Himex tents. Crouse and O'Connor could hear them crunching over the snow and rocks on the other side of the tent walls.

Team 1 was organized and rolling just after one A.M., as planned. They pulled out with Crouse in the lead, followed closely by Sauls, O'-Connor, Hefti, Bach, and the Sherpas. The climbers cranked up their oxygen to the maximum four liters per minute to help jump-start their climb. Once you were warmed up and moving steadily you could dial back to two liters per minute for much of the ascent.

The route angled steeply across the North Face, toward the Exit Cracks, the top of which merged with the Northeast Ridge. On average it took about two hours to reach the ridge from high camp, but on this morning progress had gridlocked almost immediately. There were at least two large teams ahead of Crouse and company: a group of Indians and a second comprised of Chinese. Crouse tried to communicate with the Chinese climbers, just in front of him, but they didn't speak English and had no Sherpas with them to interpret. It was too difficult to pass anyone on such steep terrain, and the others up ahead were either oblivious or unwilling to step aside and let the quicker climbers play through.

As they shuffled up the route, Crouse and Sauls passed one man who was slumped off to the side. He didn't appear to be using oxygen—neither would recall seeing a mask. Sauls thought some-thing was off.

"He didn't look right," Sauls remembered. "I couldn't say exactly what it was about the guy, but it just struck me."

"People asked me, how do you know someone's not in trouble," Crouse said later. "And I'm like, it's summit day, *everyone's* tired. People are always stopping, taking a break, sitting to the side. You can't know, and you can't check on each person."

So much congestion so early in the day did not bode well for Himex. A few mechanical complications were also beginning to crop up. Terry O'Connor's oxygen regulator had jammed shortly after he'd left camp. Without the gas, he immediately grew dizzy and lethargic, but he radioed Crouse, just ahead, and they were able to remedy the problem, clearing the rime that had crusted O'Connor's regulator.

The climbing was stop and go. Crouse, stuck in the line, con-stantly kicked his feet in the snow to try to keep his circulation flow-ing. By the time Team 1 reached the ridge, they were more than half an hour behind schedule.

Nearly a mile below, Brice was burrowed in his sleeping bag at the North Col, propped on one elbow so he could speak on the radio—not conversation, exactly, just brief, perfunctory bits of information. He would be awake pretty much continuously for the next forty-eight hours while his two teams negotiated the ridge, so he did his best to maintain a modicum of comfort while tracking the climbers' progress. He logged each radio exchange by hand in a spiral notebook. He also recorded the time of arrival at various checkpoints—Exit Cracks, First Step, Mushroom Rock. The data helped him chart his clients' move-ment but, more important, he was also able to make quick calculations to see how much oxygen remained.

By five A.M., Team 1 had pushed up the ridge and was beginning to approach the Second Step. They had passed a few more of the slower climbers, some of whom were peeling off and turning around altogether, but there were still many individuals ahead of them. It was light now, a predawn ambience that bathed everything in a murky, monochromatic gray. Spindrift gusted over the ridge. Crouse and the others could see the wagon train of down suits in front of them, moving at a snail's pace.

Sauls had skirted ahead, trying to work his way out in front of the team so he could do some filming, but the word from farther up the route remained deflating. The large group ahead of Himex was just pulling up to the base of the Second Step—the hardest, slowest part of the climb. Crouse was becoming more pessimistic with each passing minute. At this pace, there was no way they were going to make it; Team 1 would be forced to abort the climb. He started barking angrily at the climbers ahead: "Let's go! Get the fuck outta the way!" But they just ignored him.

Brice had become agitated as well. He radioed down to ABC and dispatched a Sherpa to the Chinese camp. Brice needed to speak with their sirdar, Nima Tshering, whom he knew from previous years on the mountain. A few minutes later Nima's voice came over the receiver.

"You need to tell your team to move aside and let us pass," Brice told him.

"Yes, yes. I understand," Nima radioed back. "I will do my best."

Whatever exchange took place between Nima and the Chinese climbers, it had little effect. When Himex arrived at the foot of the Second Step, the Chinese team was splayed out along the ropes, flailing at the difficult features. The Second Step has several distinct sections, including a series of lower ledges that require some awkward scrambling over snow and rock. The final pitch entails ascending a sixteen-foot vertical rock face aided by an aluminum ladder.

Climbers ascend Everest's North Ridge on their way to Camp Two, near the top of the prominent snow ridge in the foreground. The route merges with the Northeast Ridge, visible along the skyline to the right. The jagged spires along the left-center of the skyline are the Pinnacles, first crossed by Russell Brice and Harry Taylor in 1988.

Everest's towering North Face, as seen from near Base Camp in Tibet. The Northeast Ridge follows the left skyline. The West Ridge traces the right-hand skyline. The peak just in front of Everest is Changtse, with an elevation of 24,803 feet.

Russell Brice and lead guide Bill Crouse check out climbers on the route above Advanced Base Camp. Brice monitors activity on the mountain throughout the climbing season.

In 2006, British climber David Sharp was making his third attempt on Everest—alone, without Sherpa support, and with as little oxygen as he thought feasible.

AP Images/Jamie McGuinness/Project Himalaya

Slate Stern

From Advanced Base Camp the route threads a steep ice wall. Teams and climbers often stack up here as slower climbers impede progress along ropes fixed to the ice. Camp One on the North Col is hidden at the top of this picture.

Camp Two is perched on the North Ridge at about 25,000 feet. Camp One, on the saddle at the North Col, is just visible far below in the center of the image. Changste rises out of the frame in the background.

Shaun Hutson treats his frostbitten toes at Advanced Base Camp after returning from his summit bid in May 2006.

New Zealand climber Mark Inglis arrives at the North Col. In 2006, Inglis was attempting to become the first double-amputee ever to reach the summit of Everest.

American Chris Klinke makes his way along the uppermost section of Everest's Northeast Ridge. The East Rongbuk Glacier stretches away from Everest, far below, in the lower left corner of the photo. Advanced Base Camp can be seen along the edge of the glacier.

Los Angeles biker Tim Medvetz was hoping to summit Everest in 2006. In 2001, he had nearly been killed in a motorcycle accident; five years later, he was climbing with metal hardware embedded in his ankle, knee, back, and skull.

Brett Merrell

Dawa Gelgie

Members of the Project Himalaya team descend the Second Step. This photo was taken shortly after German Thomas Weber's collapse. A few climbers can be seen tending to him near the bottom of the steep rock face.

Dawa Gelgie

A climber negotiates one of the two ladders used to surmount the most difficult section of the Second Step. The shorter ladder was originally placed here by a Chinese team in 1975. The second ladder was installed a few decades later by Himalayan Experience.

Australian Lincoln Hall was part of the legendary first Australian ascent of Everest in 1984, though Hall turned around just short of the summit. He returned in 2006 to see if he could reach the top and finally realize his dream

Thomas Weber, a German financial planner, suffered from a vision disability. During his 2006 Everest attempt he was hoping to raise funds for a nonprofit organization that helped cure cataract blindness in Nepal and other developing nations.

Climbers ascend the last section of the Northeast Ridge. The Third Step is visible in the center of the photo, and, just above it, the steep Snow Slope. Everest's summit is just out of sight, behind the highest point visible in this photo.

A climber takes the final steps up the Northeast Ridge to the summit. The prayer flags in the foreground—called *lung ta* (meaning wind horse) in Tibetan—decorate the Himalayas' most sacred places.

Russell Brice and Phurba Tashi, in Base Camp at the end of the 2006 season. Each season, Brice relies heavily on Phurba, his lead climbing Sherpa and a ten-time Everest summiter, who helps install the fixed ropes and leads clients to the top of the mountain.

At sea level, the Second Step would easily be within the ability of novice climbers; add the ladder and it would be a joke. At 28,200 feet, however, it is strenuous and intimidating, and the Chinese were making a good mess of it. One climber was draped over a rock outcropping, his leg stemmed out, trying to haul himself over the top as if he were clambering back into a rubber raft. Another spun on the rope, dangling beside the ladder's rungs like a circus performer. Crouse was incredulous. He had witnessed some pitiful mountaineering but this was the most egregious display of inexperience he'd ever seen. It took two hours for the Himex team to make its way from the base of the step to the top of the ladder.

Given the disappointingly slow progress, Brice nearly pulled the plug and turned his team around, but when they'd all reached the top of the step they still had sufficient oxygen—barely.

"If you motor, I think we can still do this," Brice told Crouse over the radio.

Just past the Second Step, Himex was able to move past more of the Chinese, and while there were still many people in front of them the traffic jam was easing up.

They needed to get moving anyway; the cold was exquisite. Even the sunlight, which typically brought moderating temperatures, provided little relief. Everything was coated in a silvery layer of rime, the moisture frozen out of the intermittent clouds. The zippers on Crouse's parka were so cold that when he tried to get into a pocket to fetch his camera the pull tab sheared off in his hand.

There was still more than an hour of climbing left, and they plodded past the Third Step, barely a minor inconvenience compared with the lung-busting demands of the obstacle they'd just surmounted. They advanced up a snow slope and around an exposed, blocky ledge to a short rock dihedral. Finally, they reached the last section of ridge and a flat snow-crusted boot track, the homestretch. They were just twenty feet below the top when they ground to a standstill once again. A line of climbers in front of them waited for their turn on the small summit plateau.

At last they took their final steps onto a tabletop of snow, stamped flat by the dozens of boots that had arrived ahead of them. It was fully daylight now, the skies clear, the perspective so vast that the climbers could see the horizon's curve. Far to the north stretched Tibet's alluvial plains, falling away from the mountains; to the south lay the lush lowlands of Nepal. The Himalayas themselves extended east and west, a vast jagged spine, the topography buckling, folding, then sharpening toward the crest of the range, the high peaks glinting like platinum.

Crouse radioed Big Boss to let him know the team was on top. It was too cold to linger for long, but Brice didn't want them there for more than thirty minutes regardless. They were already cutting it close. Sauls filmed what he could: the crowds; the scenery; a poignant monologue from O'Connor, holding a photo of his father, who had died almost two years earlier.

Twenty minutes.

The climbers took the requisite summit shots. Crouse pulled his mask down to speak into the video camera, but his nose promptly turned white, the beginnings of frostbite. His regulator froze, and when he beat on it with a carabiner he broke the valve clean away. Terrific. Now he would get to know what it was like to descend without oxygen.

Ten.

Brice congratulated the team, then reminded them that the top was only halfway; they still had a long day ahead of them. The climbers and Sherpas took a last sip of tea, packed up, and checked their gas. Some crossed themselves; some sprinkled a handful of rice on the tattered prayer flags tied to a post. Some did both.

Five.

Then it was over and they were moving again. Descending now, after weeks of up, the icy line gliding through their gloved hands, the snow crunching like Styrofoam underfoot.

Down is deadly, as most climbers know. Eighty percent of Everest fatalities have occurred during the descent. There are a few obvious reasons. Your balance is off and the footholds precarious, sloping away, unexpectedly fragile, primed for a slip. Worse, you face away from the mountain, forced to stare at the terrifying emptiness below. Particularly debilitating is the energy crash. As adrenaline—more technically, the hormone epinephrine—wanes, fatigue and disorientation come crashing down like a wave set. Plenty of climbers have plunged to their deaths on Everest, but dozens of others have simply sat down and faded away.

Brice preached the 25 Percent Rule: Save 25 percent of your energy for the descent. He meant not just oxygen, liquids, food, and other fuel but the more ephemeral idea of gumption, get-up-and-go, whatever you wanted to call it. Blowing your reserves on the way up might get you to the summit, but it might leave you there, too. The question, of course, was, How did you know? How did you know what you had to begin with, or how much would remain after reaching the top? How long could you keep moving, even as your body began to shut down and blink out?

It was around eleven A.M. by the time the Himex team stumbled back to the Third Step. There were still several climbers on the ropes, most of them moving down now. The wind was beginning to pick up slightly, and the deep cold continued. O'Connor had lost feeling in four fingertips. His goggles were icing up, but he was afraid to take his hands out of his mittens for fear of doing further damage. He was a doctor, after all; his hands were his livelihood. It would prove to be a prescient decision. Down the ridge, just out of view, a long queue was already beginning to stack up at the top of the Second Step. The real wait had just begun.

Crouse hiked at the back of the pack, since it was easier to reach someone in distress from this position. The group weaved through a sequence of modest rock obstacles, and at the bottom he noticed his team trying to avoid a climber parked in the middle of the route. Coming off the final ledge of the Third Step, Crouse almost landed on the guy.

"I was like, 'Hey, watch out!'" Crouse recalled. "He's clipped to the fixed line and not very responsive. But it's Everest. We're at 28,000 feet. It's the middle of the day. I thought it might be one of the Indian climbers. He's in a mask and goggles, you know, he looks like a climber. So I get past him and my focus is to get the fuck down, and get everyone on the team down. We're in a tight group. I'm like, 'Let's keep going, let's get to the Second Step, that's where the bottleneck is going to happen.'"

It was a relatively easy cruise across a snow ridge to reach the top of the Second Step, but when they arrived Crouse's fears were confirmed. A long line of climbers stood there, stamping their feet to keep warm, waiting their turn. Brice had a clear view of the step, and he watched as those in front of his group flailed on the ropes and ladder. Twenty-three climbers stood in a queue ahead of his team. "I'm sorry, guys," Brice sighed into the radio. "I'm sorry for the pathetic standard of mountaineering in front of you, and I hope they can fucking hear."

Crouse and the others hunkered down, turning their backs to the wind, which was picking up again. They dropped their oxygen flow as low as was prudent. Crouse was at the back of the crowd, sitting next to Sauls. He could see back up the slope now and noticed that the climber they had passed at the bottom of the Third Step was on the move again, inching slowly up the moderately angled snow slope. It was the last pitch of any real grade before the final run-up to the summit. "That guy's heading up pretty late," Crouse said to Sauls. The cameraman looked up the slope, too, and nodded.

After two hours, they were able to get on the ladder and start descending again. Crouse was the last to go, shivering almost uncontrollably. *Bad,* he thought. *This is bad.* A dodgy little move to get onto the ladder required him to turn and face the slope. He looked up the route again as he clipped into the rope. More climbers had gathered near him and were waiting for their turn on the ladder, but up above the Third Step he saw the man he'd almost stepped on, still grinding his way up the snow slope. He'd moved only a hundred yards or so during the last two hours. At his current pace, he'd be lucky to reach the top by dark.

Crouse barely had time to make note of that fact before he lowered over the edge and disappeared behind the rock. The other Himex climbers were all below him now, marching resolutely down the ridge—thank God. Crouse's busted regulator was taking its toll. He wasn't sure if he had enough energy to help anyone else at this point. It was hard enough just to keep himself moving.

CHAPTER 5

THE NORTHEAST RIDGE

By three-thirty on May 14, Bill Crouse was back at Himex's Camp Four, hunched by a narrow blue cylinder, sucking in deep lungfuls of sweet supplemental oxygen. Terry O'Connor sat nearby, inspecting his frostnipped fingers. In another hour or so, they would collect themselves enough to stand again and continue their wobbly journey down to the North Col, where they could safely stay the night. Considering the traffic jams earlier in the day, they'd gotten off lucky.

Team 2 had now also arrived at Camp Four, and the talk revolved around the crowds on the ridge. The climbers all carried radios and had overheard the tense exchange between Brice and the other team members that morning. More teams were moving into position a short distance below the Himex camp, and Brice was adamant that Team 2 be on the move by eleven that night. That was two hours earlier than a typical start, but better to be moving through extra hours of darkness than standing still at dawn.

Brice had placed Mark Woodward in charge of Team 2. Woody was from Queenstown, New Zealand, where he had a wife and three kids. He was forty-two but looked younger, with a thatch of short blond hair, blue eyes, and a narrow face that resembled Ed Hillary's in his early days. He could be all business when he needed to, especially during the summit push, but mostly Woody was a jocular, chronically courteous Kiwi who was popular with the clients. If all went well, this would be Woody's third summit in as many years. His first, in 2004, had been almost a fluke. He'd been leading a North Col trip when another Himex guide had bailed out of the climb. Woody stepped in and quickly found that he had a penchant for performing at altitude. It wasn't long before he had a job taking clients to the top.

Team 2's climbers included Cowboy, Inglis, Medvetz, Gerard Bourrat, the Aussie Bob Killip, and Max Chaya, from Lebanon. The group also included cameraman Mark Whetu, Phurba Tashi, nine other Sherpas, and a second Himex guide, Shaun Hutson, from Chamonix. Whetu was hauling two video cameras, while Phurba Tashi and another Sherpa, Tashi Phinjo, had been set up with high-altitude helmet cams.

As Brice had predicted, the weather had held to May 15. The temperature remained alarmingly low, but as long as his team kept moving it would be manageable. As daylight drained from the sky, the climbers retired two to a tent, where they melted water for the next day's drinks, heated soup-in-a-bag, and sorted gear. Some changed into their last remaining pair of unsoiled socks, carefully preserved for just this occasion. Then, fed and hydrated, and mostly dressed for the next day, the climbers had little left to do but burrow into their bags and stare at the inside of the tent, their breath glazing the walls with ice crystals, the chill cinching slowly around them like a noose.

That afternoon, as Himex's first team had descended, David Sharp had continued to scrape his way toward the top. He passed a few stragglers from the Indian team, but soon he would have been alone on the upper ridge, bitter wind cutting in from the north, cirrus clouds curling across a sky turned a shade of adamantine blue rarely seen from earth.

Had Sharp been able to savor the circumstances—which, considering that he had been climbing for more than fifteen hours, was unlikely—he might have appreciated what he'd already achieved: Few climbers had stood alone this close to the summit of Everest. And Sharp had accomplished it with virtually no help at all.

It may never be known for certain whether he reached the top of the mountain that day. What can be known is that at around two P.M. on May 14 he was still making progress up the snow slope, as Bill Crouse and Ken Sauls had witnessed toward the penultimate traverse. Normally, climbers would cover that ground in a little more than an hour. Given Sharp's pace, he would have taken at least twice as long.

Two scenarios could have played out that day. In the first, somewhere between the snow slope and the summit, Sharp had the wherewithal to turn himself around. Perhaps he was physically defeated by the dihedral just below the final ridge, lacking the strength even to make a few simple, if strenuous, steps and lug his body weight along on his own two feet. Or perhaps somewhere around this location his oxygen apparatus froze, failed, or just fizzled out; he may well have taken his final sip of gas and decided he could go no higher without it. Or perhaps, alone now, without a radio or a companion or backup of any kind, Sharp had a flash of clarity, or fear, or some combination thereof; he ran the numbers and recognized that his only shot at survival entailed reversing course and hurrying down.

In the alternate scenario, Sharp continued his slow, resolute plod to the top. And while this path was certainly the more difficult, was it not also the most likely? After all, this was his third try; he had declared to Jamie McGuinness that this was "his final (final) attempt"; and he had told Dave Watson that he "was willing to lose more fingers and toes to do it." Twice before he'd been to the ridge, and twice before he'd been driven back. Now, closer than ever, there was little room for prudence.

Within the next hour Sharp would have climbed the last dihedral, cresting a gently sloping corniced ridge, the summit straight ahead. If crossing the last section of ridgeline appeared difficult—and what didn't at such altitude?—even more difficult would be returning to the world below with this business unfinished. The summit wasn't the end of the journey, but it was its culmination—the cure for the thing that had gnawed inside him for so long. What folly to think that anyone climbs Everest for the views, or the thrills, or the bragging rights, or, vaguest of all, because it's there. What's there is this: the chance to be worthy of your own dreams.

Imagine now that he crossed the final section of ridge, following the well-beaten boot path, the last of the fixed line. It was late—too late—but that no longer mattered. He was prepared to sleep on the ridge if it came to that, which it would. He was all in, as the poker players say, and there was nothing to do now but carry on and close the loop. Perhaps in those last few steps there was a surge of something like joy, maybe even bemusement that he couldn't spring up to the plateau but still had to pause at each step, breathe deep, stumble into the next one.

And then suddenly, finally, it was done.

Mountaintops have earned a reputation as euphoric destinations, and deservedly so, for the most part. Climbers shed tears here, as much from relief as joy, an understanding that the job, if not quite complete, can at least now *be* completed. Like other holy sites in the Himalayas, this one was dressed up with yellow and white ceremonial scarves and strings of prayer flags—*lung ta,* the Tibetans call them, *wind horse*—thick braids of colored squares lashed to a metal post, frayed and faded, galloping madly. The summit was a sacred place, the tallest anywhere, but it was also just another frozen perch littered with human detritus and urine-speckled snow. In the end, standing here, did it mean anything at all?

The sun hung low in its arc, the late-afternoon rays strafing the ridge. There would be light for a couple of hours yet, still plenty of time for the requisite self-portrait, a sip of water, a much-needed rest. And then, the summit snows reddening in the alpenglow, David Sharp would have turned toward the route and begun the long, difficult descent home.

By eleven P.M., Woody and most of the other Himex climbers had gathered outside their tents at Camp Four, lashing on crampons, adjusting their regulators, making the final preparations for the ascent. Overhead, a silver spray of stars filled a velvet sky. Waiting for the others, Woody couldn't shake one overriding impression: *Fucking cold*. He had powered up his electric boot heaters, stuffed hand warmers inside his gloves, and cinched his parka snug around him. Still, the night was piercing; they couldn't stand around for long.

"Tim!" Woody yelled at Medvetz's tent.

"Hold up!" Medvetz called from inside.

The guides had unofficial roles for the day: Woody would stick close to Inglis. Phurba would shadow Bourrat and Big Tim. Hutson would sweep from the back.

Woody and Whetu had hoped to dash out ahead of the others so Whetu could get some footage of Inglis coming up the ropes, but, by the time they were ready to go, Inglis, Cowboy, and Bob Killip had already started up the route. Max Chaya and his Sherpa, Dorje, were even farther ahead. Woody could see headlights approaching from the neighboring camp, so the Kiwis hustled off to catch the others. Hutson and Phurba were still in camp, waiting for the last two clients.

The snake of lights approaching from the camp below was a team that included eight Sherpas and eleven members of a Turkish expedition, including three women vying to be the first females from their country on the summit, and two men, Bora Mavis and Serhan Pocan, attempting to be the first of their nationality to climb Everest without oxygen. They weren't inexperienced. Several members of the team had climbed 26,360-foot Gasherbrum II in 2005, and the entire group had made winter ascents of Turkey's Mount Ararat and Mount Hasan, technical climbs in challenging conditions.

Behind the Turks came Vladimir Lande and his Sherpa, from Alex Abramov's 7 Summits Club expedition. Behind them trailed an independent mountaineer from the Philippines named Dale Abenojar, who was accompanied by two Sherpas. Abenojar was a self-described mountain guide, even though his résumé featured only two peaks, Mount Pinatubo and 9,690-foot Mount Apo, his country's tallest—a tree-covered volcano with a dirt path leading to a crater lake at the top. Abenojar was hoping to become the first Filipino to summit Everest, but the race was on. Two other expeditions from the Philippines, backed by rival TV stations, were on the south side of the mountain at that moment trying to beat Abenojar—and each other—to the top.

Tim Medvetz was en route by 11:20 P.M. Overcoming inertia at this hour and in these conditions was challenging enough, but for Medvetz more than most. His damaged left foot was painfully stiff; he had been up almost the entire night trying to restore feeling to it after it had gone numb in his tent. When he finally ambled out of camp, he could see Inglis up ahead—the Kiwi had placed a flashing red bicycle light on his backpack to make himself more visible—but Inglis was a ways up the route, and now the Turks and other climbers had nipped in front of Medvetz.

Himex's Max Chaya and Dorje flew up through the Exit Cracks—Chaya "always felt great on oxygen," he said later. Woody and the second pod of Himex climbers trailed fifteen minutes or so behind, moving briskly, quickly darting past one of the Turkish women and her Sherpa.

"You're not going to make the summit at that pace, love," Woody told the woman as he scooted around her, but she didn't respond.

When Himex arrived at the Exit Cracks, the route ahead was clear—a great relief. Woody had just stepped up onto the first ledge when he heard Cowboy yelp behind him.

"You kicked me!"

Woody hadn't felt a thing, but Cowboy had caught the heel of the guide's boot barely an inch above his eye, opening a bloody gash. Within a few minutes, an impressive-looking egg protruded from Cowboy's head, but it was so cold, and the climber's blood was running so thick at this altitude, that the pain was minimal and the bleeding clotted almost immediately. Woody inspected the grizzly laceration in the light of his headlamp. It seemed there was little that could be done for it at the moment, so they shrugged and clambered on.

Down at the col, Big Boss was pleased that most of his group had got away ahead of the other teams. Medvetz and Bourrat were just going to have to do the best they could; he had his reservations about them anyway. Maybe better that they were at the back. He settled into his down bag and made a note in his log. He hoped not to hear from the team again until they were through the Exit Cracks and moving up the ridge. Brice had slept about two hours of the last thirty-six, and a little uninterrupted rest would be welcome. The thermometer in his tent read minus 20. *Christ,* he thought, *must be brutal up there.*

Max Chaya and Dorje emerged from the top of the Exit Cracks a little after twelve-thirty A.M., the Northeast Ridge rising gently to their right. With the grade easing, they paused to dial back their flow rate, then quickly resumed their march. You couldn't stop for more than a few minutes before the cold crept in with unsettling alacrity.

Woody, Inglis, and the others arrived on the ridge a half hour behind Chaya and radioed their position down to Brice. The morning was going according to plan, with an open road in front of them up the ridge. After a short break, Woody and his group began making their way along the traverse, climbing steadily along a sidehill that brought them to the ridge's first real landmark—the Rock Cave containing the body of Tsewang Paljor.

"I was about to turn to Cowboy and tell him, 'Here's where Green Boots is,'" Woody recalled. "And then I do a double take because there is another pair of boots there."

The boots were made by Millet, a French company specializing in high-end climbing gear, with bright-red knee-high gaiters for deep snow and warmth at altitude. Wearing them was a man with his back against the alcove, hugging his knees to his chest. He wore black, down-filled salopettes—insulated bib overalls—and a hooded parka. His hands, clad only in thin blue polypropylene glove liners, were knitted together over his knees. He wore a wool hat, but no oxygen mask. On the ground, a few feet away, was the climber Woody had expected to see: Green Boots, lying on his side, partially drifted over with snow.

Whetu, who was just in front of Woody, started yelling at the man sitting there: "Hey! Let's go! Get moving!"

Their headlamps lit up the figure inside the alcove, but he made no response. The man's safety leash was still clipped to the fixed line running along in front of the rocks, but his eyes were closed and his nose was black, as if it had been smeared with charcoal.

The Himex climbers were strung in a line along the route, in front of the cave. Inglis and his Sherpa, Dorje Sonam, were in front, followed by Whetu, Woody, and Cowboy. Bob Killip trailed a little farther back, as did several more Sherpas. Up ahead, Chaya and Dorje had kept moving. Dorje wasn't wearing a headlamp, and Chaya's was emitting only a weak cone of light, so they had glided past the alcove in the darkness, oblivious to the second man there. But Woody and the others stopped, dumbfounded.

"Hello?" Woody said. "Hello?"

Still nothing. Tufts of breath escaped from the man's blue lips, but he did not move or speak or acknowledge the presence of the others. Woody realized he must be a climber from the day before, though he had no idea who he was, or to what team he might belong. No one had been reported missing, and there had been no calls for help—requests that often made their way to Brice. All Woody knew was that the man had been out for a long time, in punishing cold, and now appeared comatose. It seemed amazing that he was still alive at all.

"God, the inhumanity of it," Woody said to Cowboy, who was standing behind him.

Cowboy just nodded. He was stunned. He had been warned about Green Boots, but he could not have been prepared for this—a man in his last hours.

"My feeling was, he was buggered, for lack of a better term," Woody said later. "There was no movement from him, and there was nothing, really, that could be done."

Woody could see the Turks approaching now, just down the route, gaining on them. He and Whetu slid their oxygen masks back in place and began to move up the route with the others. The two were the most experienced climbers of the bunch, and they knew the sad score: At this hour, in his condition, the man was beyond help.

They continued on without another word. "Rest in peace," Cowboy said as he walked by the cave. At the back of the line, Killip saw only one figure as he passed. He wouldn't realize until much later that it could have been someone other than Green Boots.

Down below, Medvetz, Bourrat, Hutson, and Phurba Tashi were still stuck behind the Turks. They had crawled sluggishly up through the Exit Cracks, their pace set by the slowest links in the chain of lights in front of them. It wasn't quite the depressing stop-and-go that had hindered the first Himex team the night before, but it wasn't exactly speedy either. When Medvetz and Bourrat finally made it to the ridge, they were nearly an hour behind Chaya.

Not far ahead of the trailing Himex clients, a few of the Turks had reached the Rock Cave. At least two of them saw the man in the red Millets huddled in the cave. They tried to speak to him but also had no luck rousing the catatonic climber.

"Our team members also passed from the place that this mountaineer, named David Sharp, was at the night of May 14th," the Turks reported later. "Two of the team members, climbing at night, thought that the mountaineer was a climber who stopped for a rest. David was sitting and responded to our friends' warning 'that he has to continue' in a restrained way. After this time David probably fell asleep in the hollow in a motionless way so that the rest of the team that reached to the place approximately 15 minutes later, thought that David was a mountaineer who lost his life in the previous years like the other mountaineer that he was laying next to in that cave."

About a half hour later, Medvetz reached the alcove, where he found his Sherpa, Lhakpa, waiting with his oxygen mask pulled down around his chin.

"Tim, Tim. Look!" Lhakpa said. "Two dead bodies."

Medvetz was so tall that his view was partially blocked by the overhanging rock, but in the light of his headlamp he could make out the second set of boots. Even in such wicked cold, a chill rippled through him.

"It totally freaked me out," Medvetz said later. "I was like, 'Let's just go. This is creepy.' All I could see were four legs, but it added a whole different element to the climb, like, Whoa, there really are dead people up here."

Medvetz didn't know quite what to make of the situation, but he wasn't going to stand around and find out. He was concerned about falling too far behind the lead group, which was increasing the gap ahead of him with each passing hour.

* * *

By four-thirty that morning, the sky was beginning to lighten to a lavender-colored dome. Medvetz had now arrived at the base of the Second Step and, like the day before, there was just enough daylight to reveal a depressing scene. Sixteen climbers were parked in front of him, shifting uncomfortably in line at the foot of the step's lower rock ledges. At the head of the queue, Medvetz saw one of the Turkish women clawing at the rock, dragging herself up to the lip of the first obstacle only to tumble back down repeatedly.

Medvetz stood at the back of the pack, shifting his weight from one foot to the other, kicking the toes of his boots against the snow, clapping his hands together, anything to keep his circulation flowing. "C'mon, let's go! It's fucking freezing down here," he screamed. "I'm going to die of frostbite! It's not funny."

Phurba was annoyed too, but mostly at his own climbers for their slow rollout five hours earlier. "Tim! What I tell you in camp!" Phurba said.

At last, two Sherpas standing at the top of the ledge grabbed the woman's parka and half dragged, half rolled her over it. When Medvetz reached the ledge himself, he scampered up it like a seasoned pro. "I'm not the best mountaineer in the world, but after standing there for so long, and getting that cold—you should have seen me fly up that thing," he said later.

Soon, he arrived at the base of the ladder, where he confronted a scene that made the earlier delay pale in comparison. The Turkish woman who had been struggling on the rock ledge below was now splayed on her back by the bottom of the ladder, unconscious, her legs dangling over Everest's North Face. Two Sherpas were bent over her, pumping on her chest, performing CPR.

Medvetz couldn't believe what he was seeing—was this about to be yet another body on the route? *Maybe the mountain gods are trying to tell you something.* He felt terrible about yelling at her earlier, but what could he do? She had been blowing it for everyone.

The climber, Burcak Pocan, had collapsed while trying to ascend the ladder. Her Sherpas and a few teammates had managed to lower her back to the base of the cliff, where they spent the next hour furiously performing high-altitude triage before they were able to revive her. Several of her teammates continued on their way up, including Eylem Elif Mavis, now poised to become the first Turkish woman to reach the top of Everest.

Far below, at ABC, supporting members of the Turkish expedition were trying to assess the situation on the ridge. Some of the upper Northeast Ridge is visible from ABC, but the Second Step is largely obscured. No one seemed to be quite clear on either the condition or the position of their climbers—Pocan was above the Second Step, they had heard; no, she was below the ladder, and still unconscious; no, she was on her feet and moving down.

The Turks down in camp finally radioed Brice to see if he could tell them more or provide any help. "We have some medicine at top camp at 8,400 meters," Brice told them over the radio from the North Col. "If you can get back to my camp we can give you some dex and some oxygen. Over."

Brice could make out a group of four or five through his scope, descending slowly below the Second Step. Was this their climber? He thought so, but he couldn't be sure; nor could he devote more time to figuring it out. Big Boss was beginning to confront serious problems of his own.

Gerard Bourrat, the Frenchman ascending with Medvetz, Lhakpa, and Phurba Tashi, was experiencing balance problems by the time he reached the top of the Second Step, and he seemed to be growing confused. He had struggled on the ladder, spinning wildly off the rungs at one point, avoiding pinwheeling 10,000 feet down the

North Face only because his jumar was clamped firmly to the fixed line. He was so exhausted at the top of the step that Phurba had to scramble past him on the ladder to help with the dismount.

After a long rest, Bourrat and Medvetz began traversing toward the Third Step, Brice tracking them closely from the col. They were moving neither fast nor well, and stopped frequently. Bourrat could hardly manage a few steps without stumbling and falling over, and Brice got the prickly sensation that he was about to have a dire situation on his hands. Still, they were making forward progress, thanks to much prodding from Phurba Tashi, and Brice was willing, for the moment, to let them roll.

Around six-thirty, the first Himex climbers reached the top. "Summit! Summit! Summit!" Max Chaya blurted enthusiastically over the radio. The other Himex climbers trailed a little behind, just twenty or thirty minutes away.

"Good job, Max and Dorje," Brice said, his voice hoarse from fatigue.

Big Boss peered pensively through his scope. His lead climbers were practically on autopilot, and even the second pod, with the double-amputee Inglis, had made impressive time. He angled his lens down the route to Medvetz, who was now sitting in the snow. Bourrat, just in front of Medvetz, told Phurba that he was snow-blind in one eye and was struggling to make out the rope and the route.

"You can't see?" Phurba said, alarmed. "You go down! Go down!"

"Up!" Bourrat said, yanking on the line and grunting out a few more steps.

Medvetz, meanwhile, had lost feeling in his foot again. He asked Phurba to fish a hand warmer out of his pack and help him stuff it into his overboot.

A little before seven A.M., after watching the troubled efforts, Brice called his lead Sherpa: "Yeah, Phurba, I don't think you're going to have enough time to go to the summit with these two. . . . If you keep going you're going to get into a lot of trouble later. I think you should be coming back."

Phurba relayed Brice's message to the clients: "Russell say go back."

Tim was dazed. Just like that, it was over? He grabbed the mike from Phurba.

"You can't give me a half hour?" he asked Brice.

"No, there's no half hours, Tim. It's now, please."

The year before, Brice had turned back an older Japanese client under eerily similar circumstances, in the same location, when his climber was moving too slowly and running out of oxygen. What Brice couldn't know then was what would happen two years later, during the spring of 2007, when the same climber again attempted to climb the Northeast Ridge, this time with another team. At the Second Step, according to witnesses, he began to show signs of cerebral edema but insisted that he be allowed to continue up, despite the protests of his Sherpa and the expedition leader. At the summit, he reportedly went mad, throwing his gloves over the edge and clubbing himself in the head with his ice ax. His Sherpa managed to force him down a few hundred feet before he collapsed in the snow, where he could not be revived.

Down at ABC now, the other Himex climbers were listening to the escalating problems on the ridge. Mogens Jensen, fully recovered from his ordeal with edema, piped over the radio: "Listen to Russ, Tim. You have to turn around, mate. I know how hard it is, but you have to do the right thing."

A few minutes later Brett Merrell chimed in: "Tim, you're going against everything you've been saying on the trip. C'mon now, you're a stand-up guy, but you're endangering other people's lives. Now turn around and come back down."

Medvetz was creeping along behind Bourrat and believed that if he could just get by him, he could pick up his pace and make the summit in time. They had reached the bottom of the snow slope. At sea level it would have been a joke, like hiking up a beginner's ski run. Medvetz was convinced he could climb it in half an hour, and he pleaded with Brice to give him another thirty minutes—if he wasn't at the top of the snow slope by then, he promised, he would turn around and descend.

Phurba was growing exasperated, but Brice knew his Sherpas were too loyal to leave the clients. He was out of options. He reluctantly conceded, but only after Phurba had lobbied Big Boss to let Medvetz try one more push.

"Once I get around Gerard, you'll see me really move," said Medvetz.

Bourrat had fallen almost completely silent. Down at ABC, Mogens and Merrell were sitting by the radio, listening to the exchange. Mogens turned to his teammate. "What really is chilling is that Gerard hasn't said one word in response to anything," he said. "Tim, we still hear him, he has power in his voice, but Gerard has just been mute. You have no idea what's going on with him."

Up on the ridge, once Brice had given the go-ahead, Medvetz floored it. "I was trying to run up it," he said later, "like Rocky in *Rocky IV*." His effort might have been comical, or at least entertaining, were it not so life-threatening. The snow was softer here, and Medvetz punched and clawed at the boot track with his hands and feet while Brice observed skeptically from below. After twenty minutes, he got back on the radio.

"Phurba, Phurba, I'm not happy with what's happening," Big Boss said. "These guys are just struggling and they aren't gaining anything. They look like a couple of porpoises out of water. You know, Gerard is not strong. And Tim is struggling to take big steps. I'm not happy. I want them to come around."

"I can do nothing with these two member," Phurba told Brice, exasperated. "They just want to go up."

A few minutes later Medvetz called Brice.

"Hey, Russ, you gave me a thirty-minute deadline to the top of the slope—did I make it?"

"You're not at the top of the snow slope," Brice said.

"I'm about thirty steps from the top of this thing."

"Biggest thirty steps I've seen in my life."

"Tell me now, Russ."

"Hey, mister, the top of the snow slope is where you go to the dihedral."

"Your call, man," Medvetz said, breathing hard. "I've climbed real hard to this point."

Brice heard the appeal, but he made no reply.

A little after seven that morning, Woody, Whetu, Inglis, Cowboy, and Killip climbed onto the summit with their five Sherpas. Chaya was just departing with Dorje. It was still bitterly cold, even with the sun bearing down on the ridge. Whetu had carried two cameras to the summit, but they were frozen and inoperable—just extra weight. It was hardly the triumphant affair they had imagined. "We were pretty much like, 'Let's get some summit shots and get the hell out of here,'" Woody said.

Inglis had removed his gloves and held his hands up for Woody to see. Large blisters had risen on five fingers.

"I'll need quite a hand down, Woody," Inglis said. "I've got a bit of frostbite."

After a fifteen-minute rest on the summit, Woody hitched himself to the back of Inglis's harness with a length of nylon webbing. With this system he could trail Inglis down the route, providing a kind of moving belay in case Inglis tripped or fell. Dorje took up a position in front of the client, providing help from below. The others moved out ahead of the trio. Everyone realized Inglis would be coming down slowly.

At the col, Brice had now stopped arguing with Medvetz and Bourrat, but that stratagem didn't seem to be working either. Perhaps the other team members could reason with them as they descended. Chaya had reached the snow slope, but now he sat alongside the route, so exhausted that he could barely speak as Bourrat stomped past him, still pushing upward.

At ABC, Jensen and Merrell alternated turns on the radio, joining the chorus of others trying to turn the two men around. After another half an hour, Cowboy and Whetu arrived at the spot where Bourrat and Medvetz were now sitting in the snow. The pair had apparently stopped moving up, but they weren't descending either.

Cowboy and Whetu were exhausted, cold, and in no mood to haggle with these two, whom they knew had blatantly ignored Brice's orders to turn back. Whetu was already irritable given his camera problems—the reason he was there in the first place.

Whetu was well respected among the expedition members. He was a skilled high-altitude cinematographer and one of the most seasoned veterans on Everest's north side, though his tenure there was marred by an infamous climb back in the spring of 1994. At the time, Whetu had been working as a guide and cameraman for Mike Rheinberger, a fifty-three-year-old electrical engineer from Australia who was making his seventh attempt on Everest. Few climbers had been thwarted as many times as Rheinberger, and during the '94 trip he plodded his way up to the ridge, though it took him until sunset to reach the summit. Whetu had shadowed him the entire way, despite their impending bivouac, which ended up taking place above the Second Step, at a lethal 28,300 feet. The next day, Rheinberger collapsed trying to move farther down the ridge. Whetu tried to get him going until late that afternoon, but he eventually had to abandon the client or risk a second night out. Afterward, Whetu lost all his toes to frostbite. Rheinberger died on the ridge.

Cowboy and Whetu lit into the intractable clients. It was too far to the top, they argued; the men didn't have enough oxygen, and they were going to die on the ridge if they didn't turn around now and descend. Cowboy grabbed Bourrat by the shoulders and shouted into his face: "Gerard, they've been trying to turn you around for an hour! You're going to fucking die up here!"

His urgency seemed to work; the Frenchman nodded, then took

off his gloves and began to take his "summit" photos with his sponsors' banners.

Cowboy, almost completely spent now, radioed the news to Brice. "Gerard and Tim are turning around," he said. "It's fucking suicide. We're all descending. The Sherpas are behind us. The madness has stopped."

"So Tim and Gerard are coming down?" Brice confirmed.

"That's correct," said Cowboy.

Down at ABC, Merrell was hanging on every word of the radio traffic. There was palpable relief around camp; it seemed the worst had been averted. Then, a few hundred yards down the route, Bourrat collapsed in the snow.

"I'm talking to my sister on the sat phone," Merrell recalled, "and I go, 'We just lost a guy.' Gerard's down, they can't get him up. They're screaming at him: 'Get up! Get up! Get up! Get up!' So now, Mark Inglis is in bad shape and Woody's short-roping him. Bob and Cowboy continue down at their speed. They gotta haul ass and get to high camp, you know, 'cause they're gonna run out of O_2. So all in the same breath Shaun comes on the radio and says, 'Russ, hey, it's Shaun. I'm sorry, I got stuck in the queue at the Second Step. I'm working my way up to the third. I'm gonna go for the summit.' And Russ is like, 'Good on ya, mate, go for the summit.'"

Merrell exploded. He couldn't believe Brice was green-lighting a guide to go up when there was a full-blown crisis under way.

"Fuck this guy!" Merrell said, throwing the handset on the table. "This is fucking bullshit." He stormed out of the tent, cameras in tow.

Merrell's outrage seemed at once understandable and overblown. To encourage a guide to pass clients so clearly stricken with problems appeared to be an unforgivable breach of conduct, particularly to someone like Merrell, who was in charge of a fire department back home. As Brice saw it, he already had three Sherpas on the scene, and more on their way down. Given that it was Hutson's first Everest summit, Brice insisted that he wanted to allow his guide every chance to succeed—an accomplishment that would provide a huge career boost.

"Shaun's quite a fit mountain guide, and can move over that terrain pretty fast," Brice said later. "If I've got the support that I need, then I can send a mountain guide to the top, and he can carry on up and catch up later. So that was a clear decision: I think that he can go there and back and catch up and still be of assistance. Which he was."

Once past the jam at the Second Step, Shaun Hutson had made good time to the summit, even though his feet were beginning to feel like blocks of ice. By the time he returned to the clients, the Sherpas had the situation back under control. Bourrat was moving under his own power again. Medvetz, Lhakpa, and a few others had already descended through the Second Step.

Far below, Chaya was feeling better by the hour, and he and Dorje blasted down the ridge with increasing pace. They were comfortably within their time limit, but they were eager to reach Mushroom Rock, where their replacement oxygen bottles awaited.

Around nine-thirty A.M. Chaya reached the Rock Cave, with Dorje close behind. Inside the alcove he saw Sharp, though the climber's identity still remained a mystery. He was no longer clipped to the fixed line but was now lying with his back on the snow inside the shelter, knees up, arms bent but hands in the air, fingers hooked as if he were holding a ball, frozen in place. His eyes were nearly closed, his teeth clenched. Next to him was a depleted oxygen cylinder. Chaya and Dorje were the first to come across Sharp in the daylight, and they could see that the man was shivering.

My God, Chaya thought, *all that trouble above, and now this.* He could feel the tears welling up inside him.

Someone else was talking on the radio. Chaya kept pushing the button on his mouthpiece, trying to break through. After a minute, he raised Brice.

"There's a man here," Chaya said, his voice quavering. "He's not dead, but he's dying. Is there anything we can do?"

Brice told Chaya he could try giving the man some oxygen, but that if he remained unresponsive, he should leave him and continue down. The last thing Brice wanted now was to have one of his clients embroiled in a rescue attempt for a climber who, judging by the information Chaya had provided him, was nearly gone. Whatever team the man belonged to should be tending to him, not Chaya and Dorje.

"He's a huge guy!" Max said through sobs over the radio. "Almost the size of Tim."

Dorje removed his own mask, hunched into the cave, and placed it on Sharp; he spent the next ten minutes attempting to feed the man oxygen. Chaya wouldn't touch him. He was afraid and upset. Brice asked him to search the man's jacket and backpack for I.D., but Chaya refused.

When the oxygen had no effect, Brice became more insistent that Chaya and Dorje continue their descent. They had done what they could, he told them. Chaya was weeping openly now. They certainly couldn't carry the man, or even move him very far—assuming first that Max could muster up the courage. But Chaya couldn't bring himself to leave the man, either. Brice continued to coax him over the radio.

"He tried to understand what the situation was," Chaya said later. "And then when it was clear what state David was in—that he was much closer to death than he was to life—Russ just told me, 'Max, we can't do anything. You have to come back down.' I understand what he was saying now. Russell had an obligation towards me because I'm his client. And he didn't want anyone else to jeopardize their life to try and save someone who's almost dead. I didn't understand it then. I couldn't understand how I could walk past a dying person while being myself in one hundred percent mental and physical condition, without being able to help. But I understand now."

They were only a few hundred vertical feet above Camp Four, but between them and it lay an exposed traverse and the steep, technical chutes threading through the Exit Cracks. Despondent but out of options, Chaya and Dorje began moving down the route again, leaving Sharp still shivering inside the Rock Cave. When Chaya reached his tent at Camp Four, he collapsed inside it and cried for two hours.

Above, the rest of Team 2 continued their progress down the ridge. There wasn't much conversation. Everyone was caught up in his own private misery, Bourrat now short-roped to Phurba Tashi, Medvetz shuffling carefully ahead of them.

Others were also coming off the ridge now, including Dale Abenojar, who would go on to claim victory in the Filipino summit race. The 7 Summits Club's Vladimir Lande and his Sherpa followed, as did the four Turks who had continued up the ridge after the collapse of Burcak Pocan.

The Turks were the next to arrive at the Rock Cave. With them was Dawa Tshiri Sherpa, who co-owned Arun Treks, the outfitter for the Turkish team. Dawa had not only provided logistical support for the Turks but had accompanied them on their ascent. Dawa had seen Sharp early that morning, on the way up. But a Sherpa coming up right behind him had assured him that this was the body of an Indian climber who had died there years ago. Dawa certainly couldn't argue. The Sherpa who informed him had been on the ridge six times before, and this was Dawa's first time. The two had hardly paused on their way past.

Dawa had already spent an additional hour at the Second Step that morning, helping to revive the Turkish woman who'd collapsed. Now he peered into the alcove at another person in dire need of help.

"Where you from?" Dawa shouted. "Which company?" Sharp blinked drowsily but could not reply. Dawa, a second Sherpa, and two of the Turkish climbers tried to move him out of the cave. If they could stand him on his feet, perhaps they could get him walking. But Sharp's arms and legs were frozen at right angles, his hands hooked into claws. They succeeded in shifting him only a few inches. "We tried to carry him, but it was impossible," Dawa recalled. "He was like iron."

The Sherpas looked in the climber's pack and found his mask and regulator. They put it on Sharp and attached one of their own oxygen bottles. It was about all Dawa could do at this point; he was so fatigued that the world seemed to move in slow motion. It was a little after noon; they had been there for almost thirty minutes, and now the wind had returned. Dawa feared that if he stayed any longer he would end up in the cave too, and so he left Sharp to his fate and pressed on.

At the col, Brice puzzled over the identity of the dying man. Chaya had remarked that he thought the man looked eastern European—Russian, perhaps. But Abramov, who typically knew of other Russians on the mountain, hadn't mentioned a missing climber. If the man was with a team at all, Brice had a hunch which one it might be. He'd been by the Asian Trekking camp—by his standard it was a shambles—but he filed the thought and then resumed his position at the telescope.

By noon, most of the Himex climbers had made steady if painful progress down the ridge. Inglis remained near the back of the pack, roped between Woody and Dorje. Bourrat inched along a little ways ahead of them, tethered to Phurba Tashi. Medvetz was moving along in front, now near a Himex Sherpa named Dorje Sonam. The team wasn't yet safe but they had passed the Second Step, which always brought a sense of relief. "Hey, Inglis," Brice joked over the radio, "your toes cold yet?"

They dropped down through the First Step, moving to a narrow sidehill stretch of track, little more than one boot width across. Medvetz was struggling with his balance, his damaged foot, knee, and back giving him continued trouble. Halfway along the traverse, he yanked on the rope to steady himself and promptly felt slack come into the line; a piton had popped from the rock behind him. Medvetz and Dorje Sonam tumbled backward off the path and began careering down a steep slope of hard snow toward the North Face. They slid only about ten or fifteen feet before the next set of anchors caught, but it was far enough that Medvetz thought, *This is it, this is how it's going to end*. He lay on his side on the slope. He could see Dorje Sonam nearby, upside down on the slope, his safety leash taut on the line. Had the two men not been clipped in, they would have shot over the cliff looming directly below.

"My heart is pounding and I look down at that drop," Medvetz recalled. "Then I looked at Sonam and he kind of flips himself around. And all of a sudden I just started peeing, man, right in my suit."

The fall shook Medvetz deeply. He collected himself and scrambled to the route, each stride now a struggle. He could barely connect ten steps before he had to sit and rest. He couldn't let himself think about what might have happened had he continued to ignore Brice and run out of oxygen. As it was, he was already racing to reach Mushroom Rock, where his second cylinder awaited.

When he finally arrived at the Rock Cave, a little ways beyond Mushroom Rock, Medvetz knew from the recent radio traffic that he would encounter the incapacitated climber lying next to Green Boots. Medvetz had regrouped with Phurba by then, and he stood by as the Sherpa scooted past the others and approached the alcove. Without hesitation, Phurba began trying to pull Sharp from the cave. Another Turkish climber and a Sherpa from his team had also arrived, and they stepped in to help. The three men managed to drag Sharp out from under the rock and into the sun, though he remained contorted, frozen into the position in which he'd been sitting for God only knew how many hours now.

Phurba attempted to straighten Sharp's legs, but they might as well have been cast in bronze. Medvetz watched it all with horror.

Far below at Base Camp, Dick Colthurst, the executive producer from the film project, and a few others were receiving the first images of the gruesome situation, transmitted from Phurba's helmet camera to the wooden shack the crew used as a makeshift studio. Transfixed, they watched with a mix of heartbreak and repulsion as the scene unfolded on the monitor in grim, grainy detail.

Phurba tried to get Sharp to speak, but despite repeated attempts he could glean nothing. Finally, after the Sherpa had fed him oxygen and sat with him for another half an hour, Sharp mumbled a few barely decipherable words: "Asian Trekking" and "Just want to sleep."

Around this point, Dorje, Inglis, and Woody arrived, moving slowly. The ends of Inglis's legs were now blistered and shredded where his prosthetics attached, his stump socks soaked with blood. The pain was excruciating, but Inglis knew he had to keep on toward Camp Four and the safety of lower altitude.

The trio crept past the scene at the Rock Cave. Sharp was on all fours now, facedown, immobile as a figurine, Phurba tending to him. The others could hardly watch; most who came upon the scene just quietly kept moving along. As Chaya had said back at high camp, it was one thing to pass by someone long dead, the corpse welded to the landscape; it was a different experience entirely to pass by a man still dying.

Medvetz remained for a short while as Phurba Tashi replaced Sharp's oxygen mask and then took the man's frozen hand and forced it up so that it cupped the regulator and held the apparatus more or less in place. Sharp's sunglasses had slipped down his frostbitten nose as Phurba worked and the dying man's eyes flicked toward Medvetz. The two climbers looked at each other, a glance that bored all the way down to Medvetz's DNA—not desperate or pleading or frightened but resolved, almost at peace. Here were two men, united in their obsessive enterprise, their trajectories intersecting for just an instant, but an instant that contained some fundamental understanding: the long journey full of failures and setbacks, injuries and disfigurement and pain, propelled by a commitment beyond reason. Here were two men in this inhospitable place, the wind raking across the ridge, the shadows lengthening—one departing his life, the other walking back into it.

"God bless you," Medvetz murmured. "Good-bye."

And then he faced down the mountain and resumed lumbering along the route, toward Brice and Brett Merrell and Mogens Jensen and all the others waiting for him in the world below.

PART TWO

LINCOLN HALL
AND
THOMAS WEBER

Gone was the radiant world of gossamer.
So with all pleasures of life.
All things pass with the east-flowing water.
I leave you and go—when shall I return?

—*Li Po, "His Dream of Skyland"*

CHAPTER 6

HIGH CAMP

David Sharp died sometime during the night of May 15. Phurba Tashi had plied him with oxygen, pulled him into the sun, and tried to get him on his feet, before realizing that the climber could not be revived enough to walk, even with assistance. He and another Sherpa from the Turkish team had placed Sharp back inside the alcove, still visible but at least a few feet removed from the route. Early the next morning climbers on their way up confirmed that they had passed two lifeless bodies in the Rock Cave.

Death from hypoxic hypothermia comes slow. In the beginning, hands and feet begin to tingle and throb, then ache as if squeezed by a slowly closing vise. Speech slurs. Balance slips. As the brain starves and swells, you're gripped by persistent dementia. During the 1933 Fourth British Expedition, Frank Smythe, a writer and photographer, imagined pulsating teapots floating in the air at 28,000 feet. Maurice Wilson, the Brit who had made an ill-fated fatal solo attempt to ascend the Northeast Ridge in 1934, described sensing a benevolent presence with him as he withered on the mountain. In 1996, during the lethal May 10 storm, Sandy Hill Pittman, a New York socialite, thought that she was at a garden tea party listening to Beck Weathers play a flute. In truth, they were both trapped on the South Col, desperately trying to stay alive.

As the deep cold intrudes, nerve endings go numb and the pain recedes as circulation retreats toward the core. Often, ironically, it is around this point where freezing feels like being tossed into a furnace. Victims tear at their clothes, throw away gloves and hats, and frantically unzip their parkas, accelerating the slide. Flesh farthest from the heart—toes, fingers, nose, cheeks—freezes first, death advancing from the perimeter. Skin turns pale with frostnip, white during the full throes of frostbite, red and purple with chilblains and blisters, and ultimately black with gangrene—cellular necrosis, doctors call it, the point at which living tissue is permanently destroyed.

In the final stages, limbs become insensate and immobile, freezing into place as your body shunts blood toward the lungs and heart, trying to preserve the vital organs. Vision blurs and darkens. Involuntary shivering ensues, a last-ditch attempt to generate heat through movement. Your mind swirls deeper into the subconscious, a deep dream state. A few who have returned from the brink of hypothermic oblivion have recounted their last conscious moments as almost pleasurable. "You really do start feeling warmer," Weathers wrote in his memoir *Left for Dead*. "I had a sense of floating. I wondered if someone was dragging me across the ice."

The end arrives a few hours later, quietly, in the dark waters of unconsciousness. Your blood runs chilled; most brain activity has ceased. The heartbeat slows, fluttering erratically, a wounded bird. This action might continue for a while, the vessel destroyed by the encroaching cold while the heart presses courageously on. At last the pump shuts down, and with that the limited circulation ceases. Internally, there is perfect stillness, equilibrium returning between a delicately calibrated but dissonant energy field in the form of a man and the larger energy field around him—the mountain, the air. The only movement now is wind, ice crystals skittering over rock and snow, a jacket flap rustling, a clump of hair, stiff with rime, flicking across the forehead.

Reams of medical literature document cases of those who were believed to be dead, or irretrievably near to it, recovering from a hypothermic coma. Beck Weathers may be the most famous example in mountaineering. No one can quite figure it out, including Weathers himself, a pathologist by training. "The awakening is something I don't understand," he told the London *Observer* in 2000. "And I've looked at it from most spiritual and physical angles."

Humans are particularly temperature-sensitive mammals—not much hair, not much fat. Coordination falters when an individual's core temperature hits 95 degrees. By 86 degrees, you pass out and, now incapable of regulating your own temperature, require external heat to rewarm. By 82 degrees, liver and kidney failure are likely, as is a heart attack. Drop a few more degrees and most hypothermia victims die from cardiac arrest.

But not everyone who freezes dies, as has been the case on numerous occasions. One of the most memorable recoveries on record occurred near Chicago in 1984, when four-year-old Jimmy Tontlewicz chased his runaway sled onto the frozen surface of Lake Michigan, punched through the ice, and sank like a stone to the bottom. He'd been submerged for nearly half an hour by the time paramedics plucked him from the water—ghost white, pupils fixed, no pulse: clinically dead. But little Jimmy Tontlewicz didn't die for good that day, despite the fact that his core temperature had bottomed out at 85 degrees. Within a week, doctors had revived him and started him on his way to a slow but full recovery. In 2001, a toddler from Edmonton, Alberta, wandered into her backyard on a night that reached nearly 20 below. She was found at three A.M., facedown in a snowbank, with no pulse. After several days in intensive care, she was walking and talking.

Freezing quickly and being small help, but they aren't a prerequisite. In 2000, a twenty-nine-year-old Norwegian skier named Anna Bagenholm tumbled down a snowy gully and became trapped in an ice-covered river. She fought her way into an air pocket, where she lasted for forty minutes before falling still. It took rescuers another forty minutes to pull her from the water. Bagenholm's core temperature had plunged to 56.7 Fahrenheit—the lowest ever recorded in a living human being. She spent two months in intensive care, but the only lasting effect was a tingling sensation in her hands.

"In our world, we don't declare somebody dead until they're warm and dead," said Dr. Peter Cox, director of the critical care unit at the Hospital for Sick Children in Toronto.

If freezing to death left so much room for hope that the end was not really the end, why, then, was Everest so rife with tales of climbers stranded high and left to die—many in better shape than David Sharp? Had Beck Weathers not risen miraculously and marionette-like from the snow, stumbling close enough to his camp to be discovered by his teammates, he surely would have joined the list of casualties. Dozens of others weren't nearly as fortunate. Cold and oxygen restriction are twin mallets that deter the kind of heroics most people like to imagine—the fireman carry, the piggyback, the ingenious litter of webbing and rope, soldiers hauling their brothers off a battlefield by their boot heels.

Kiwi camerman Mark Whetu might well have died alongside Mike Rheinberger on the Northeast Ridge in 1994 had it not been for a subtle canard by his teammates. Over the radio, they urged him to descend to the First Step, where he could gather more oxygen and, ostensibly, bring it back up to the disabled climber. But everyone knew he wouldn't. He couldn't; he was lucky to climb *down*.

There were other examples, worse ones in which the best course of action wasn't quite so cut-and-dried. One afternoon in May 1992, an Indian team abandoned one of its climbers near the South Col. The weather was deteriorating and the light fading. The climbers left their companion, whom they would later describe as "beyond help," lying in the snow within a hundred feet of the tents. They departed the col the next morning, heading for a lower camp, believing their teammate deceased and so informing a few other teams. One of those groups was a five-man Dutch expedition preparing for its summit attempt. That morning one of the Dutch team's Sherpas left the tent to relieve himself and returned visibly upset.

"There is a dead man waving," he said.

The Dutch climbers were incredulous, but they peeked outside the door flap. To their horror, they could see a man lying on his side in the snow, one arm raised and gesturing slowly in the air.

"He was only between twenty and thirty meters from their tents," wrote Joe Simpson in his 1997 book *Dark Shadows Falling*. "There were five Dutch climbers and two Sherpas in residence on the col, sufficient to get the man into a tent. Instead there followed a bizarre radio conversation between [team leader] Ronald Naar and the expedition doctor at base camp. Having established that dead men cannot make involuntary movements, Naar asked about the man's physical condition. The experts at base camp advised him that since the man had lain exposed to the fury of the elements for so long, it would be quite impossible to revive him or do anything to save him."

Two of the Dutch climbers and two Sherpas promptly descended, distressed by the dying Indian and wanting no part of any of it. But three of the team remained, planning to depart for the summit that night. They filmed themselves discussing their options and strategy. "They did not go outside again until their attempt on the summit, the next day stepping past the man's body on their way," Simpson wrote. "They were forced to retreat some hundred meters below the South Summit."

May 1998, on the north side: another dire situation.

That season, Sergei and Francys "Frankie" Arsentiev—a Russian climber and his American wife—both reached the summit without oxygen via the Northeast Ridge. Frankie was the second woman ever to accomplish such a feat, but she became ill during the descent and collapsed at around 28,000 feet. Sergei stowed her there as well as he could, clipping her to a fixed line. He then stumbled down to their high camp, where he collected oxygen and eventually proceeded back up the ridge to try to help his incapacitated wife. He was never seen again.

Frankie lived for two more days, itself an incredible feat of endurance and stamina. At least ten climbers passed her as she lay alive but incapacitated among the rocks. If anyone tried to help, the effort went unreported, until two days later, on May 24, when a South African named Cathy O'Dowd investigated what she thought was just another body. When she reached the figure, she bent down and brushed the woman's hair away from her face. Frankie's eyes flashed open and fixed on her would-be rescuer. "Please don't leave me," she wheezed.

Frankie was bent violently at the waist, torso and legs pointing down the slope, the safety leash taut between her harness and the fixed line above. Her face was ashen, wind-burnished, encased in a mask of frostbite. A spent oxygen tank lay nearby. Two of O'Dowd's teammates, Ian Woodall and Jangbu Sherpa, arrived and helped move Frankie so that her back was propped against a rock. The footing was precarious, if not downright dangerous—loose shale covering a steep slope—and the effort left them gasping.

The trio worked on Frankie for nearly an hour. Their oxygen system was incompatible with hers, so they poured fluids into her mouth and yelled at her to do anything she could to help them, to try to stand and walk. But she sat completely limp, murmuring comments that seemed only marginally coherent: "Why are you doing this to me?" and "I'm an American. I'm an American." Three climbers from Uzbekistan passed by on the route above but refused to get involved. "We tried to help yesterday," one said. "We left her with oxygen. She is too far gone to help."

They were in the shadow of the First Step, no sun, the wind howling. Finally, O'Dowd realized the inevitable. "Perched on the steep slope, I could not even stamp my feet for warmth," she wrote in her memoir *Just for the Love of It*. "My fingers were almost totally numb. Orders from my brain to wiggle them met with a lackluster response, a minuscule, slow-motion movement. I had full body shivers and my teeth were chattering behind my oxygen mask."

"What do you want to do?" Woodall finally asked her, though the question was not in reference to Frankie, who had by now fallen unconscious.

"I want to go down," O'Dowd said. "Will you go down with me?"

The climb was over, though O'Dowd would return the next year and make it to the top, Frankie's body still lying where they'd left it. O'Dowd eventually became a minor climbing celebrity. She had weathered the infamous 1996 storm while climbing on the south side, though that climb had cost her a teammate, Bruce Herrod, who died after taking a fall on the Hillary Step. After the 1999 trip, she went on to write her book and work the Everest speakers' circuit. And more often than she would have liked, she found herself fielding hard questions regarding Herrod and Frankie Arsentiev.

"Within a group of climbers who have chosen to tackle a challenge on the level of Everest, no one can be held accountable for the others," O'Dowd wrote.

Each step higher is a personal choice and a personal responsibility. We need to be very clear about that before we venture out. As mountaineering becomes more of a spectator sport, due to websites and satellite telephones, we will increasingly have to answer questions about choices and responsibilities to a curious, largely ill-informed audience.

Whose choice is risk in the end? Is it not that of the person who goes out to do it? We live in a blame society, which demands explanations and accountability, finding scapegoats if necessary. If I walk on the narrow edges of life, I do it because I choose to. If that edge breaks under me, I accept that as a consequence of my choice. I cannot blame others for what happened. Nor do I expect that those who accompany me on that edge, if they do, should carry blame for my decisions. I make a choice and I live or die by it. Death is not the intention, but is accepted as being a possibility, given the risk of the activity. Don't pillory my companions for my choices. I am simply glad they were there to accompany me as far as they could.

It is so difficult to bring a body or an immobilized climber down from above 8,000 meters that it defeats even the most concerted attempts. In the spring of 2004, three Korean climbers perished on the Northeast Ridge. One had gone snow-blind and "stopped going down," while a teammate continued his descent only to collapse several hundred feet below. The third climber, waiting at their high camp, ascended the ridge with hopes of rescuing his companions. By the next day all three were dead.

The following year, a fourteen-person Korean expedition pulled into Base Camp on a specific mission to recover the bodies. They could locate only one of them, thirty-four-year-old Mu-Taek Park, lying on his back along the route at 28,700 feet, still clipped to the fixed lines. It took the team three hours just to chip the body out of the snow and ice. When they tried to move him, they managed to descend only about 500 feet before they gave up and sat down in the snow, drooling into their oxygen masks.

The team leader, Hong-Gil Um, an old friend of Park's, told the others to clear a patch of stones on the ridge so they could make a shallow grave. They dragged Park over and placed him in the clearing. His gloves had disappeared, so Um placed his spare pair on his friend's hands. The climbers covered the body with stones and then conducted a brief ceremony for the dead man while Um sobbed beside him. They returned to ABC by nine o'clock that night.

"I never understood the controversy about David Sharp," said Himex client Mogens Jensen, who had been on Everest during the Koreans' recovery attempt in 2005. "There is no controversy. You want to know what it takes to carry a man off the ridge, all you have to do is look at the Koreans."

On the afternoon of May 15, Russell Brice loaded his backpack and made his way down from his perch on the col. His climbers were safely ensconced at Camp Three or lower now, and he was eager to get back to the sanctuary of ABC. He was always exhausted after summit day, but this year had been particularly trying. Brice had put twenty-seven people on top—one of his best years yet—but not without a price: Mark Inglis, Gerard Bourrat, Bob Killip, and Shaun Hutson all had frostbite, the severity of which was still unknown.

That night, Phurba Tashi and a few of the Sherpas also made it down to ABC. It had been a long day. After his ordeal with David Sharp, Phurba had come to Inglis's aid. The bones had pierced the skin at the ends of the amputee's legs, leaving him almost entirely debilitated. Hutson and some of the others were able to drag-slide him down the snow-covered sections of ridge, but Phurba simply hoisted Inglis onto his back and carried him across the rocky bits. The others could only follow along behind, shaking their heads at the Sherpa's strength.

Phurba and Brice debriefed the next morning. The Sherpa told Big Boss how Sharp's arms and legs had felt like wood, frozen firm, that he had done all he thought he could do. Brice and Phurba hadn't spoken during the rescue attempt, though Brice had been able to see some of what was taking place through his scope. The only person with whom he had discussed Sharp directly that day had been Max Chaya.

Brice could have shrugged off the issue of the dying man easily enough—it certainly wasn't the first such situation, and his responsibilities extended to his own team, not beyond. No one associated the Himex leader with the dead man other than by sheer circumstance, at least not yet. Still . . . he wanted to establish the man's identity before the "fucking Web sites," as he often referred to them, made a mess of things. Brice knew how quickly news traveled now, and how easy it was for hearsay and conjecture to be misconstrued as fact. After breakfast, he and Phurba set out to establish the climber's identity.

Brice had a pretty good idea where to start. He and Phurba walked to the Asian Trekking camp, where they found George Dijmarescu, Dave Watson, and a few others preparing for the hike back down to Base Camp. "Are you missing a climber?" Brice said. Dijmarescu shrugged—how would he know? The independents were not his responsibility. Then he added that, actually, there were three solo climbers from their camp currently unaccounted for, but they could be anywhere on the upper mountain.

Dave Watson, the American who had befriended Sharp earlier in the expedition, chimed in when Phurba began describing the climber's appearance, clothing, and old Berghaus backpack.

"Sounds like David," Watson said.

Watson took Brice and Phurba to Sharp's tent, ducked inside, and found the Brit's passport. Phurba studied the photo.

"Yes, this is man," he said.

"Well, it appears it's your man who's died," Brice told Dijmarescu. He asked him if he was going to get involved and begin the notification process, but Dijmarescu refused.

"He was no help whatsoever," Brice said later. "So I asked for the passport and everything that belonged to the missing man, and then I went to call Asian Trekking."

Office personnel at Asian Trekking confirmed that Sharp had been on their permit, and they provided Brice with contact information for the family, though they offered to make the first call. "I'll do it," Brice told them. He rang the number and John Sharp, David's father, picked up. Brice explained who he was, and then he said he was calling with some very bad news.

Spotty details about a missing climber broke on the Internet as early as May 16. By the next morning, ExplorersWeb had posted Sharp's name, though any other information was slim. Reports of Sharp's death were almost immediately diluted by a succession of other tragedies. A Swedish climber named Thomas Olsson had disappeared on May 16 while trying to ski the Great Couloir, a prominent snow gully on the North Face. Three days later, another north-side climber was reported dead: Vitor Negrete, a thirty-eight-year-old Brazilian attempting to become the first person from his country to summit without oxygen, died in his tent at high camp after growing ill descending the ridge.

Negrete's climb, supported by Asian Trekking and connected with Sharp's, had been fraught with dark omens. A Malaysian climber that he'd befriended in camp had suffered serious frostbite on his summit bid; his friend David Sharp had perished; and, on his own summit attempt, Negrete had arrived at Camp Two to discover that someone had looted his cache of gear and food. The trouble had left him so rattled, he'd almost bailed on the climb altogether.

"All these events have affected me deeply," he reported on Explorers-Web. "I even considered calling the attempt off."

Negrete kept with it, though, departing high camp for the summit at around ten-thirty P.M. on May 17. He had no oxygen and no radio, and the batteries in his satellite phone—his only lifeline—were nearly dead. "I'll be careful," he said in one of his last dispatches. On the way down the ridge the next morning he collapsed between the First and Second Steps. Negrete's Sherpa, Ang Dawa, and the Sherpa's brother, Pechumbi, who had come up from high camp, managed to rouse Negrete and get him down to their tent by one A.M. They gave him fluids and then sandwiched the Brazilian between them for warmth. An hour later Ang Dawa heard Negrete "take three short breaths and then become motionless."

As of May 19, the high-altitude body count was tracking to exceed that of 1996, when twelve people died, Everest's deadliest season. The toll now included the three Sherpas killed in the Khumbu Icefall earlier in the season, Himex's kitchen boy Tuk Bahadur, Sharp, Olsson, and Negrete. News had also emerged that an Indian climber with the Indo-Tibetan Border Police, constable Sri Kishan, had died after allegedly jumping off the Second Step on May 14, and that a French climber named Jacques-Hugues Letrange had collapsed and died on the ridge while descending on May 16. Some who were keeping tabs, like ExWeb and EverestNews, also noted that a Czech climber named Pavel Kalny had perished on the south side after falling from the Lhotse Face, which technically didn't count as an Everest death, since he was on his way up 27,923-foot Lhotse, Everest's next-door neighbor.

The season's rapidly escalating mortality rate alarmed even the thick-skinned Everest veterans, and the busiest summit window—typically the last week of May—had yet to come. Some speculated later that the weather was almost *too* good in 2006, luring the less experienced onto the upper flanks of the mountain and providing few excuses to bail on a summit bid. No one wanted to stay on the mountain any longer than they needed to, bitter and unforgiving place that it is. With the cooperating weather, many climbers focused on getting the job done and getting the hell out of there.

The Himex team was on its way. The climbers had returned to Base Camp by May 19, and Brice organized a celebratory soiree that ran late into the night. After a month above 20,000 feet, Base Camp felt like a beach resort—warm, comfortable, with air so thick and rich it felt as if they had just arrived in Rio. Their mirth would be short-lived. A firestorm of controversy awaited them in Kathmandu.

While the Himex members partied in Base Camp, Alex Abramov's 7 Summits Club climbers moved into position on the upper mountain. Like Brice, Abramov had orgazined his large group of clients into two teams. The A Team, as they'd dubbed themselves, included five Russians, three Brits, two Norwegians, a South African, a Dane, and two Americans—Slate Stern and David Lien. The B Team included the Australian quartet—Lincoln Hall, Michael Dillon, fifteen-year-old Christopher Harris, and his father, Richard—plus Harry Kikstra and his German client Thomas Weber.

Abramov had addressed the first team at ABC a few days earlier, reminding them of the dangers above and providing another overview of the oxygen system. Like most teams on Everest, 7 Summits Club relied on the Russia-based company Poisk to provide its oxygen equipment. Few other systems were available; Poisk had largely cornered the high-altitude mountaineering market. Its products were effective to a degree, but at least one climber interviewed considered them archaic and unreliable. "In the fifties it would have been a great system," said 7 Summits Club climber Kirk Wheatley, who worked as a commercial diver. "But this is 2006. The bottles were heavy and cumbersome, and the regulators were unbalanced and would freeze. In the diving world, you would never be given a regulator like that, and if you were you would send it straight back.

The Poisk masks were large and awkward and, even with working regulators, it was a challenge managing the oxygen flow. The regulators screwed onto the top of the canisters, which were typically carried in a climber's pack, meaning you had to either stop and remove your pack to adjust the flow and check the oxygen level or recruit someone else to do it for you. Variations in barometric pressure brought on by, say, an approaching storm further affected the flow rate. To add to the complications, many commercial clients get limited hands-on time with the gear until a few days before they start their summit push.

"Alex gave quite a lengthy talk about delivery rates, how long a cylinder should last, things like that," Wheatley added. "Afterwards, I think at one point or another at least half the expedition came over to me and said, 'Can you explain this again?'"

On May 18 Abramov sent his first team up the hill. "Weather forecast is quite favorable now," he wrote cheerily on the expedition Web site. "Let's wish good luck them—good luck!"

The B Team—essentially the two microexpeditions under the 7 Summits Club umbrella—was still on its way up to ABC after several days of rest down in Zhangmu, near the Nepal border. All but a couple of the climbers were in good shape, the major exception being Thomas Weber, the German financial adviser, who had struggled to acclimatize since the beginning of the trip. Many on the expedition considered Weber something of an enigma. He seemed intelligent enough—he spoke lucidly about international money markets and U.S. politics—but he could be aloof and even haughty. A few of the Sherpas called him Nasty Thomas. Weber's guide, Harry Kikstra, who arguably knew him best, dismissed it as a typically German disposition, stoked further by Weber's elite education (he told Slate Stern that he held an MBA from Wharton and a PhD from Oxford) and his involvement in high finance.

More curious, perhaps, was Weber's poor physical condition. Anyone could struggle with acclimatization or succumb to the many viruses and bacteria crossing the climbers' paths on the way to Everest. But Weber seemed simply unfit for climbing to 29,000 feet. The bio on the Web site that he and Kikstra had developed, SightOnEverest.com, noted that Weber had already climbed four of the Seven Summits—Aconcagua, Kilimanjaro, Elbrus, and Mount McKinley. Yet he had come to Everest, the most difficult and dangerous of the lot, overweight and undertrained.

Most puzzling of all was Weber's vision impairment. He had told Kikstra that he had had a brain tumor removed several years earlier and that low-pressure environments, such as high altitude, caused his sight to blur. He predicted that he might lose his vision altogether at extreme heights, but he provided few other details—no specific name for his condition, no date of surgery—and few members of the 7 Summits Club team noticed any eyesight problems while he was on the mountain. "I was always a little suspicious of it," said Slate Stern. "It seemed like such an unusual condition. I'd never heard of anything like it before. And his vision seemed to be working fine up until summit day. I never made much of it because he seemed like a credible guy."

Kikstra intended to make his summit push with Weber and two Sherpas around May 25, weather permitting. Their two cameramen, Kevin Augello and Milan Collin, would not go above ABC. The plan itself smacked of profound hubris, if not unconscionable naïveté, considering that Kikstra had been above 8,000 meters exactly once, narrowly escaping with his life. He now intended to take a climber with limited experience who had been struggling at lower altitudes to the Northeast Ridge—and his client could well be blind by the time they got there. When Eric Weihenmayer, a blind schoolteacher from Golden, Colorado, had ascended Everest via the South Col in 2001, he had been climbing sightless for nearly twenty years. On his summit bid, he was surrounded by a ten-man team that communicated via helmet-mounted radios. Kikstra was bringing one Sherpa per man, and a few extra bottles of oxygen, for a client who had never climbed blind, unless you counted the one day in The Hague in February 2006 when Kikstra blindfolded Weber, hitched him to a top rope, and had him scale a fifty-foot ice wall—indoors.

Kikstra was well liked by others on the 7 Summits Club expedition, but several members expressed reservations about climbing with him. "Harry is a really friendly, nice guy," Slate Stern said, "but I would never hire him as a guide or retain him as an expedition organizer. I would want as competent a person as I could find, someone who has proven that they can perform in difficult circumstances. Harry, in my opinion, has not done that."

For others on the trip, in addition to his lack of experience at extreme altitude, Kikstra undermined his credibility at the outset of the trip when he'd struck up a relationship with a female trekker en route to Base Camp, smuggled her through Chinese security (only climbers with permits are allowed beyond the Base Camp checkpoint), and proceeded to host her weeklong visit at the 7 Summits Club camp.

According to Stern, one evening in early May, Weber had himself expressed reservations about Kikstra as a guide. Stern and Weber had been sitting in the 7 Summits Club mess tent in Base Camp, chatting long after their expedition companions had headed off to bed.

"Have you talked to Harry about this?" Stern asked.

"Not yet."

"You need to have a heart-to-heart with him," counseled Stern. "If you don't have a relationship of trust, you shouldn't be climbing with him."

Weber nodded. He would bring this up with his guide as soon as he had a chance.

★　★　★

Kikstra and Weber weren't the only climbers addressing midexpedition issues. The Aussie posse had developed a problem or two of its own.

For the most part the quartet had done remarkably well, but by the time Richard Harris, son Christopher, cameraman Michael Dillon, and high-altitude cameraman and de facto guide Lincoln Hall were reestablished at 21,000 feet on May 18, Richard's nagging cough had blossomed into laryngitis and then bronchitis. It seemed unlikely that he would go much higher.

Christopher and Dillon were both doing fine, though Dillon never intended to climb higher than the North Col. Hall had also acclimatized well, a relief considering he had signed on to the trip so late. He had crashed himself into shape in a mere six weeks, repeatedly hauling a backpack loaded with water jugs up 600 vertical feet of steps chiseled into a cliff behind his house in Wentworth Falls. "I knew my aerobic fitness had just come in the weeks leading into the trip," Hall said later. "Really, the rest is in your mind. How far I got on the mountain depended on how much I was prepared to suffer."

Hall knew the suffering could be severe. He hadn't been on an 8,000-meter peak since 1999, when he'd attempted to climb Makalu and had been forced back by bad weather at around 24,200 feet. Before that, it had been the famous first Aussie Everest expedition in '84. Still, his climbs on myriad lesser peaks, decades of guiding, and countless trips to the Himalayas had to count for something. What he lacked in training miles Hall made up for with a lifetime of knowledge and experience. And herein resided the difference between a marginally prepared climber of Hall's pedigree and the increasing number of amateurs who had little to no concept of what they had gotten themselves into—like Sunday joggers stepping into the elite field of the Boston Marathon.

"Why Everest attracts so many people from the general public is beyond me," said Slate Stern, an ex-marine who'd climbed all over the world. "For athletes, though, Everest is this incredible challenge. Climbing at that altitude is like having the worst case of flu you've ever had and then having to move through a really difficult place. If you can do it with grace, it really says something about your character."

Gracefully or not, the Aussies were going up. On May 21, about the same time the A Team was reaching the summit, Hall and Dillon walked out of ABC with Christopher and Richard Harris, headed for the col. It was a short trip. They hadn't climbed more than a few hundred feet above camp before Christopher, trailing sluggishly behind, sat down on a large rock, complaining that he was having trouble breathing. Richard Harris had pushed farther up the trail, so Hall, sitting behind Christopher, instructed the boy to position himself in a way that would help expand his lungs. Within an hour they had all returned to ABC.

The 7 Summits Club doctor, Andrey Selivanov, told them that Christopher had experienced a sudden blood-pressure crash—alarming, though not uncommon at such altitude. He put the boy on oxygen and sent him to rest in his tent. By dinner Christopher had fully recovered. Hall didn't like the prospect of Christopher continuing on, but Richard Harris was insistent that they try again the next day. The next morning, the foursome lit out for the col, only to turn around a short distance out of camp when Christopher started feeling woozy.

With the Harrises unplugging from the climb, Hall had to make a difficult decision: continue up on his own or descend with them and hang up his Everest dream, at least for this year. Hall feared that Richard Harris might frown on the idea of his continuing up—it was the Harrises' expedition, after all—but Richard told Hall they'd all support his summit bid if that was what he wanted.

When Dillon had e-mailed him about the expedition back in February, Hall had understood that this might be his last chance at the Big E. Back in 1984, he had turned around less than a thousand feet from the summit while two of his teammates had pushed on. Not only were they the first Australians to reach the top of Everest, they did it by an unclimbed route on the North Face—without oxygen. By any yardstick, it was an extraordinary achievement.

But try to tell a climber who's turned around on Everest that his trip was really about the journey, not the destination, and the reply may well be a punch in the mouth. Hall was often introduced as the first Australian to climb Everest, but the next question was almost always "Did you make it?" Answering in the negative had been a tough burden to bear, particularly when mountains had defined you, inspired you, educated you—when you'd spent your life, and often risked it, participating in the complicated and dangerous act of ascending them. It only mattered privately that you'd climbed well, or strong, or smart, or turned around in order to save yourself, or your teammate, or someone else's. Publicly, all that resonated was whether you'd reached the top. No wonder trying to explain why you hadn't made it, or why you felt good about not making it—which you probably didn't, anyway—was a lesson in futility. You hadn't made it, and you hadn't died trying, and that invariably prompted the most deflating response a climber can hear: "Oh."

On the afternoon of May 22 Hall hiked out of ABC, bound for the North Col.

On the upper mountain, the first 7 Summits Club group had remained almost entirely intact; only the American David Lien had bailed at this point. Lien had reached Camp Two, the first stop above the col, at 25,600 feet, but he had been too exhausted to carry on. He had just returned to ABC on May 20 when he had run into Hall in the mess tent. It was one of the only times they'd had a one-on-one conversation, and Lien asked the Aussie if he thought Lien had made the right decision by giving up and coming down.

"Lincoln is very even-keeled, mild-mannered, and intelligent," Lien recalled, "but he wasn't very forthcoming. In retrospect, I think he must have been like, This guy turned around, and I don't want to sit around talking to him because the same thing might happen to me.

"Turning back was brutal," Lien continued. "My strength was draining fast, I could feel it. I tried to rationalize every way I could, but I'm certain I would not have gotten down if I had gone up on the ridge that night. It was one of the hardest decisions I've had to make, but it was the only decision I could make. I couldn't have made the round-trip."

Just after midnight on May 21, 7 Summits Club's A Team had left high camp at 27,200 feet. By ten A.M. sixteen climbers had summited, including Slate Stern and Kirk Wheatley. Among those who had come up short that morning was Igor Plyushkin, a fifty-four-year-old Russian climber from Krasnodaz. Plyushkin was an honorary "snow leopard," a designation bestowed by the Russian Mountaineering Federation on individuals who have climbed all five 7,000-meter peaks located in the former USSR. He had been moving slowly that morning and had turned around at 28,700 feet when he realized he didn't have enough oxygen to make it safely to the top and back. Slate Stern, the quickest among the summit team, had come upon Plyushkin during the descent. The Russian was hunkered down among some rocks, clipped to the fixed line, not far from the Rock Cave.

"*Horosho?*" Stern said. Good?

"*Horosho,*" Plyushkin nodded wearily.

Plyushkin spoke no English, and Stern had picked up only a few words of Russian during the expedition; their conversation had gone about as far as it could go.

Others from the first team were just a short distance behind the

American, including Sergei Kofanov, one of the Russian guides. "I thought, They'll deal with him if he really needs help," Stern recalled. "We weren't far from high camp, so I figured worse comes to worse, he could get there."

By early afternoon, all the members had made it off the ridge, but they were now struggling to pick their way down to the col. Kirk Wheatley, his South African teammate Ronnie Muhl, and a few others were the last to depart high camp that afternoon, and they soon found themselves engulfed in one of the worst squalls of the season. "We made it down to about 7,900 meters, where Russell Brice usually puts his tents, and the wind now must have been approaching seventy miles per hour," Wheatley recalled. "We were literally hanging on to rocks to try to keep from getting blown off. We came across Igor there. The fixed line had snapped, so we had to free-climb down through the rocks until we reached the point where the rope was back intact. We were all sort of frozen there, wondering what to do, wondering if a guide would come, is there anybody around. The Sherpas just wanted to jump into the nearest tents that didn't belong to us. In the end, Ronnie and I carried on down and made it to our tents. Igor was still up on the plateau and we'd been screaming and shouting at him to come down, but he was just like in a trance."

Plyushkin eventually crawled into one of the nearby tents, a couple hundred feet above his own camp, where he rode out the night alone. The next morning, the 7 Summits Club guides circulated through their camp, checking on the team, but it was almost an hour before they realized that Plyushkin had never arrived. By the time they found him up above, Plyushkin was severely dehydrated and had spent the night without oxygen. They roused him enough for Plyushkin to continue the descent, but only fifteen minutes out of camp the Russian crumpled to the ground. Two Sherpas and a Russian guide gave him shots of dexamethasone and put him on oxygen, cranking the flow to four liters per minute. "Struggle for life proceeded for one and a half hour," Abramov reported later. "Unfortunately, Igor's condition was not improved. At 13:45 guides were forced to verify death."

Plyushkin was Everest's tenth fatality that season. Abramov dutifully posted the news on his Web site on May 22, almost immediately after it had transpired. By that evening, ExplorersWeb had picked up the news of Plyushkin's death and posted it on the site, along with a running tally of the season's casualties. ExWeb, meanwhile, was starting to raise hell about the deaths, privately querying outfitters like Russell Brice for more information, and publicly demanding details and accountability. The next day, May 23, an ExWeb editorial read, "For years, ExplorersWeb has been fighting the silence surrounding some deaths in the mountains. Each time, we have been told that the secrecy is only a concern for the victims' families and we have no respect. . . . Time after time, it has turned out that the hush has served much less noble agendas: To cover up foul play in mountains without law."

What foul play they were referring to in this case wasn't exactly clear, but they were lobbing some pointed questions. They harped on the old oxygen bugaboo—faulty equipment (7 Summits Club had swapped out about a third of its regulators during the trip), the unreliability of refilled canisters—but the thrust of the editorials was becoming less about technical issues and more about the ethics behind the action.

Earlier that month, when Himex's second team had returned to ABC, Cowboy, speaking by satellite phone with a New Zealand TV journalist, had commented offhandedly that they had passed a dying man near the summit. The initial comment garnered little response, but by the time the group had returned to Kathmandu, the controversy surrounding the dying climber had ignited.

A few days after his arrival in Nepal, Mark Inglis sat in the lobby of the Hotel Tibet, participating in an exclusive on-camera interview for a New Zealand–based program called *Close Up*. The reporter, John Sellwood, confronted him with the questions people had started asking about the dying man they'd walked past.

Inglis: ". . . It was like, what do we do? You know, we couldn't do anything. He had no oxygen, he had no proper gloves, things like that."

Sellwood: "Someone suggested that maybe you should have stopped the ascent and rescued this man."

Inglis: "Absolutely. Yep. It's a very fair point. Trouble is, at 8,500 meters it's extremely difficult to keep yourself alive, let alone keeping anyone else alive. On that morning over forty people went past this young Briton. I was one of the first, radioed, and Russ said, 'Look mate, you can't do anything. You know, he's been there X number of hours, been there without oxygen, you know, he's effectively dead.' So, we carried on; of those forty people that went past this young Briton, no one helped him except for people from our expedition."

The feeding frenzy had begun. In New Zealand, the media turned to the one authority everyone most loved to hear from during an Everest flap: Edmund Hillary. Sir Ed was hardly sympathetic. He had long ago asserted that the rapid commercialization of Everest was destined for trouble. In the late 1980s, he'd urged officials to consider closing the mountain for five years. In 1993, when he was serving as New Zealand's ambassador to Nepal and India, he proposed drastically curtailing permits—one per route, per season—indefinitely. Neither suggestion had exactly been embraced. By 2006 there were no caps on climbing permits on either side of Everest.

On the *Close Up* program, which aired on May 24 in New Zealand, Hillary voiced the gathering cynicism that had haunted Everest since the 1996 disaster. "I don't think it matters a damn if [the dying climber] was from another party, if he was Swiss or from Timbuktu or whatever,"

Hillary said. "He was a human being and we would regard it as our duty to get him back to safety."

It was a scathing indictment, even if it was based on sensational early reports, and one that few in the climbing community could dismiss, particularly those from New Zealand, where Hillary was revered. Brice was still largely oblivious to the trouble that was brewing; he had remained in Base Camp with the last of his clients. Inglis, however, was catching it full in the face. He had been publicly criticized by his hero, and his impressive achievement had been diminished by those who should have been celebrating it as a mountaineering milestone. Throughout the interview in Kathmandu, Inglis kept holding up his frostbitten hands, his fingertips looking like they'd been dipped in black paint, as if to show the world what he'd been through. Those who were implicating him in David Sharp's death had no idea what it was like up there or how harsh the circumstances. But it would prove nearly impossible to shake the stigma now attached to his climb.

Far above the burgeoning scandal, Lincoln Hall, Harry Kikstra, Thomas Weber, and the others were doing the Everest shuffle up to the North Col. Kikstra, Weber, and their two Sherpas, Pasang and Pemba, had arrived at the col camp on May 21 but had delayed for a day when Igor Plyushkin died. On May 22, Kikstra had radioed down and encouraged Hall to come up and join his group. They could climb to the summit together, a safer and more enjoyable option for everyone. Hall agreed.

Many teams had cleared off the mountain by now, but a final wave of climbers were pushing into position at the high camps, taking aim at a summit bid around May 25 and 26. Those remaining included fourteen climbers from Jamie McGuinness's Project Himalaya expedition (McGuinness himself had summited on May 18 with a tandem group, dubbed the Everest Peace Project), Dan Mazur's five-person SummitClimb team, the 7 Summits Club crew, an Italian duo, an Ecuadorean, and an Austrian.

It defied all expectations that Weber had made it even as high as the North Col. On his way back to ABC, Slate Stern had passed Weber. "There's a ladder just below the North Col, and when I got there Thomas and Harry were coming up," Stern recalled. "When he [Thomas] got to the top of the ladder he looked exhausted. I was exhausted too. We gave each other quick hugs and I said, 'Good luck.' That was the last time I saw him." When Hall arrived at the col the next day, Weber told him that his vision had deteriorated to the point where all he could see was shapes.

Nevertheless, Kikstra and Weber continued up, arriving at Camp Two on May 23. The next morning, not long after they had struck out for high camp, they passed a small sarcophagus built out of loose rocks—Igor Plyushkin's grave. Bits of clothing showed through the slight layer of stones covering the climber. "It made a big impression on me," Kikstra wrote later, "as a strong reminder of the dangers of Everest and high altitude, no matter how good the weather."

The weather, in fact, had become clear and a little warmer, but a steady, vicious wind lashed the North Ridge, which was fully exposed to the persistent westerlies blowing over Everest. Still, Kikstra felt great, and he scrambled ahead of the others, periodically facing back down the route to snap photos of the climbers, the mountain, and the increasingly stunning view.

Kikstra, Weber, and Pemba arrived at high camp on the afternoon of May 24, followed by Pasang, who had been racked with a cough and slipped behind. Kikstra interviewed Weber at his tent—he had brought a small video camera along—and Weber said that he was feeling good and looking forward to the summit push that night. Hall rolled in a short while later. "Welcome to high camp!" Kikstra called. After Hall had himself sorted out, he stopped by Kikstra's tent, where the two sat discussing the day to come, passing a single oxygen mask between them as if it were a hookah.

Hall had considerably more climbing experience than Kikstra, but virtually none using supplemental oxygen. He asked Kikstra to review the equipment with him, just to make sure he had it all down, and then they went over the setup again. Before long Hall returned to his own tent, settling in for the all-too-brief preclimb rest.

High camp is hardly a camp at all—just a small cluster of tents listing pitifully on hastily constructed platforms of broken shale. It's unnervingly high, and many climbers psych themselves out here. Best to try to do something, anything, other than dwell on the hours ahead.

Hall sought temporary solace by phoning home. It was his son Dylan's eighteenth birthday, and while he and Barbara had agreed that he would not call until he was safely down from the summit, this occasion was too important to let pass in silence. He dialed the number on the satellite unit and spoke to his son in Wentworth Falls. What an extraordinary convenience to be able to talk with his family from one of the highest places on earth, as if he were just down at the corner store. Later, when he tried to call Barbara, the answering machine picked up. Hall listened to his wife's greeting, then left his brief message: feeling good, weather's great, much love. Perhaps better that he didn't speak with her directly. Hearing his wife's voice might have been just a bit too much.

The night before, Hall had lain in his sleeping bag, mulling over his reasons for pursuing such a dangerous goal. Having been a writer most of his life, he had long been in the habit of jotting down his thoughts, and he now penned twin columns, his list of pros and cons. He could die—definitely a con—and leave his wife widowed, their boys fatherless. He could wind up maimed or disfigured. He could come up short again. But he had traveled this far now, and if he made it he could close the file for good. Lots of great mountaineers had taken multiple swings at Everest before they stood on the top. Now, lying in his tent, Hall considered his list. In the end, the risk of his own death didn't outweigh the overwhelming motivation for proceeding up—that otherwise he would have to go on living having once again fallen short of the summit.

CHAPTER 7

THE SECOND STEP

Just after midnight on May 25, Harry Kikstra, Thomas Weber, Pasang, and Pemba gathered outside their tents at high camp. The sky was clear and moonless, salted with stars. The valleys below were filled with pools of gray cloud, the surrounding peaks barely distinguishable in the inky night. Something seemed off, but Kikstra couldn't quite figure out what . . . and then it struck him: There wasn't a breath of wind. The night was completely still, a rare experience at such altitude. He had only just taken note of the conditions when Weber and the Sherpas began their slow trudge toward the Exit Cracks and the Northeast Ridge. He set off to join them.

Odd that feeling too good, too soon, and for too long would register as a sign of trouble, but when Kikstra and Weber flashed up to the ridge, Pemba and Pasang humping to keep up, it was their first indication that something was amiss. When Kikstra checked their regulators, he discovered that they had jacked the flow up higher than intended. True, they'd gotten off to a powerful start, but they'd paid for it by blowing through more than half of their first oxygen canister in the initial two hours.

Hall was climbing just a short distance behind, with three Sherpas—Lakcha, Dorje, and Dawa Tenzing. They also gained the ridge in a steady two hours, though without the flow-rate issues experienced by Kikstra and Weber. Hall was moving with such determined focus that, once on the ridge, he strode past the Rock Cave containing David Sharp and Green Boots, oblivious to the bodies.

Throughout the start of the climb, Hall found himself commingled with other climbers, most of them presumably from the large Project Himalaya group. He encountered Kikstra just above the First Step, sitting in the snow, waiting for Weber, who was now straggling behind. The two men sat next to each other, not saying anything, tucked inside the claustrophobic world created by their oxygen masks, goggles, and down suits. Finally Kikstra pulled his mask aside and told Hall he might as well keep going—he was going to be considerably faster than Weber.

The Project Himalaya climbers were led by Scott Woolums, a forty-eight-year-old guide from Hood River, Oregon. Woolums had a brushy mustache, a mellow disposition, and a reputation as one of the sturdiest guides on Everest. This was his fourth trip to the mountain, and his pending third summit, but it was his first trip up the Northeast Ridge. His predominantly American team included Chris Klinke, from Royal Oak, Michigan, a thirty-six-year-old former vice president at American Express who had quit his job in order to climb mountains full-time; Laurie Bagley, an Internet consultant from Mount Shasta, California; Anne Parmenter, a college hockey coach from Bristol, Connecticut; Hans Fredrick Strang, a Swedish industrial worker and photographer; and a Swedish student named Johan Frankelius. Eight Sherpas accompanied them.

Woolums's team was loosely organized into two groups—slow and fast, with the slower climbers pulling out of high camp nearly an hour ahead of the others. But by the time they had reached Mushroom Rock, at 28,200 feet, not far above the top of the Exit Cracks, the groups had merged back together. Woolums urged them to climb as a group until they were past the Second Step; traveling as a pod through the most technical terrain would help keep the team from becoming too spread out along the ridge.

It was, by all measurable criteria, a glorious morning to be climbing Everest. The temperature was still firmly in the negative double digits, but the wind was light or altogether absent. The forecast indicated that conditions were due to deteriorate later that day, but not until the afternoon, by which point the climbers intended to be long gone.

By five A.M. Lincoln Hall and his Sherpas had moved ahead of everyone else on the ridge. Kikstra saw the light from Hall's headlamp dancing on the rock as he ascended the ladder at the top of the Second Step. He and Weber were not far below, confronting the step's lower ledges—the blocky, vertical buttresses where Medvetz and the Himex climbers had bottlenecked behind the Turks a week and a half earlier.

Weber had been making reasonably good progress, but Kikstra knew his client was going to need help through this section. When Weber began flailing at the first ledge, Pemba pushed the German from below, while Kikstra yanked on him from above. In this way, they reached the ladder, but by the time they'd ascended this final pitch, they were all wasted from the effort. By now the ridge was bathed in salmon-colored light, and Kikstra looked up the route where he could see Hall arriving at the Third Step.

Hall and the Sherpas threaded their way through the uppermost step, climbed the snow slope, and at last picked their way past the dihedral, which deposited them on the final, dazzling section of ridge. Lakcha had led most of the route, but now he let the Aussie move ahead so that Hall would be the first of their group to reach the summit. They were all moving strong, and Hall could see the top straight ahead, the last of the technical climbing now behind him. It would still take at least thirty minutes to get there, but at this point it was a mere formality. This was it: the end of "Oh."

A little before six A.M., Laurie Bagley, the first of the Project Himalaya climbers, arrived at the top of the Third Step. Above her, the route continued up a broad white triangle of snow. Not far ahead, she spotted several climbers, one of them on his hands and knees, clawing his way foward: Weber.

"When I saw them, my heart just sank," Bagley recalled. "I thought, Oh my god, we're not going to summit. I had already made a decision that if anyone was dying, I would stop, I would help them, I would do whatever I could. I was not going to cruise by and say, 'Okay, have a nice life, I'm on my way here.'"

When Bagley and her Sherpa, Chhiri, reached the climbers, they asked Kikstra if he needed help, but the guide told them that he had it under control.

"He was honest," Bagley said. "He said, 'Our climber is in trouble, but we don't need anything.' There's nothing you can do for us right now. So we kept going."

Chris Klinke arrived at the top of the Third Step about thirty minutes later. He did not recognize Kikstra and Weber—they didn't appear to be anyone from his team—but he was aware that the trailing climber was in some difficulty. He watched as Weber veered dramatically off the boot track, caught his weight on the fixed rope, then staggered in the other direction, making wobbly progress up the slope—"like a fish on a line," Klinke related later.

When Klinke caught up to the man, he was surprised to see that his goggles were off—an invitation for snow blindness—and that his oxygen mask was pulled down, away from his face. Klinke said he tried to speak to Weber, twice, but the climber didn't acknowledge him. He seemed to be gazing somewhere else, out toward the horizon.

When Klinke reached the second climber, he realized it was Kikstra. They had spoken briefly at high camp the evening before. Klinke told Kikstra that he thought his client high-altitude cerebral edema.

"He's always like that," Kikstra reassured Klinke. "He's okay."

While Klinke stood there speaking with Kikstra, Weber arrived, still not saying a word. Kikstra reached for Weber's jumar and moved the device around an anchor; the client appeared to Klinke to be unable to do much of anything for himself. The situation didn't seem right, but Klinke deferred to Kikstra, who believed Weber's condition was still manageable and was related to his sight problems, and pressed on. He would find out later that his friend Fred Strang had a similar encounter, although Weber responded to Strang, saying that he was having trouble seeing. Strang had echoed Klinke's concern about edema and had told Kikstra that he needed to give his client some dexamethasone and get him down the mountain immediately. Then, like Klinke, he pressed on.

Lincoln Hall topped out a little before seven A.M., the first person to reach the summit that day, though in only a few minutes Sherpas began crowding onto the mountain's modest crest alongside him. Now visible just down the route was Laurie Bagley. The rest of her team was no more than an hour behind.

Hall had arrived comfortably within his turnaround time. He radioed down to Abramov and gave him the good news. The Russian radioed back congratulations, then urged him to get going on the descent. Hall was experienced enough to appreciate that his day was going to get harder before it got easier; he would still be fighting with gravity, just in one direction rather than another. The Australian spent twenty minutes on the summit, and then he did as Abramov had instructed.

Hall shuffled back down the ridge, past other climbers, strangers all, and he simply nodded or waved. The rest of the Project Himalaya team, Laurie Bagley, Chhiri, Scott Woolums, and Anne Parmenter, waited on the summit. By eight A.M. the remaining Project Himalaya climbers had made it, Fred Strang sobbing with joy over the radio to his father down in Base Camp.

Weber, meanwhile, had ground to a halt just at the top of the snow slope. Kikstra asked him what he could see.

"Nothing," Weber replied.

Kikstra worried that Weber was now posing a problem not only for him but for the climbers who would soon be returning from the summit. He and Weber were a mere 300 vertical feet from the top, but even that short distance would likely require another two hours. He told his client they were turning around.

"[His blindness] was not useful, but it was not unexpected," Kikstra reported later. "What was unexpected was that Thomas was also suddenly totally exhausted and unbalanced, when just moments before he was going up the quite steep slopes unassisted and steady. And worse, he did not listen to any directions Pemba and I gave him, even though they were simple, like 'stay on the track, do not move, we will take your carabiner,' etc. I looked at Pemba and decided that under these conditions it would be too dangerous to continue on to the rocky and very airy traverse as well as to the final exposed snow-slope."

Weber stated that he was feeling better and wanted to go higher, but the guide was adamant. He was pulling the plug.

Kikstra set up a short-rope system, with Pemba in back, the guide leading. Pasang, whose cough had continued to beat on him during the climb, trailed behind. They led Weber back down the snow slope and through the Third Step, Kikstra barking directions. It was early in the day, and, despite their snafu with flow rates earlier, they still had ample oxygen. Provided things didn't get worse, Kikstra was confident they could get back to the safety of their camp at 25,600 feet, if not down to the col.

Then things got worse.

By the time they arrived at the Second Step, the German was ambulatory but off balance, and now evidently without vision. Getting back onto the top of the ladder involved what many considered the diciest maneuver on the entire route. Reaching the top rung required inching out onto a snow-covered rock ledge partially blocked by a bulging rock. Climbers are unable to see their feet, and the tattered fixed lines attached to the rock offered little support.

Kikstra had brought a spare length of thin rope, which he now anchored at the top of the step. Then he expertly lowered himself so that he could assist Weber from below using a "fireman's belay"—a technique that would allow him to control the speed of the client's descent simply by tensioning the rope running through the German's rappel device.

While Kikstra worked on his system, Laurie Bagley arrived and sat down on the snow slope near the tricky section above the ladder. She was almost shoulder to shoulder with Weber, although neither of them spoke. She recalled, as others would elsewhere on the route, that Weber's oxygen mask was pulled down away from his face.

"I so regret not saying, 'How ya doing?' " Bagley related later. "But I think we were all so much in that place of survival. I wish I could have extended that little bit of compassion."

Kikstra finished rigging his rope, and he and Pemba lowered their packs to the bottom of the step before turning to Weber. Pemba helped hitch Weber into the line, and they managed to descend the ladder and most of the two rock ledges beneath it. But shortly before the bottom of the step, Weber's foot became tangled in the spaghetti of old ropes draped down the cliff. He began thrashing, trying to free his foot but only making matters worse, until Pemba scrambled down to him, produced a pocketknife, and cut the cords away. After Weber had calmed down, Kikstra called up to Pemba to check the climber's oxygen. Only three bars showed on Weber's gauge—about fifteen minutes' worth of gas.

They had a solid stance again, and Pemba began replacing the climber's bottle with a fresh one. The next thing Kikstra recalled was his client looking at him with a panicked expression.

"I'm dying," Weber said.

And then Weber's eyes closed and the big German fell forward, away from Pemba, and began to slide down the slope toward the abyss.

A few hundred feet above, Lincoln Hall had downclimbed the dihedral to the thin traverse leading over to the top snow slope and was beginning to make his way down that section when he was suddenly overwhelmed by extreme fatigue. Lakcha yelled at him, "Hurry, hurry," but he simply could not. The deleterious effects of altitude had arrived powerfully and without expectation. Whatever clarity he'd held on to above was suddenly gone, all sense of time and place slipping from his grasp.

The Project Himalaya climbers overtook Hall on the way down, but none understood that the Aussie was on the verge of a full-scale meltdown. "He just indicated he was taking a rest," recalled Scott Woolums. "So we continued on." Besides, Hall was being trailed by three Sherpas; even if a problem developed, there appeared to be sufficient help on hand.

Hall snapped in and out of present reality. Time sped up and slowed down. He was there, descending the ridge, and then he was back in Australia, or nowhere at all, slipping through lightless wormholes of lethargy and incoherence. In Hall's book about the climb, *Dead Lucky*, he speculated that the Sherpas must have assisted him down to the bottom of the Third Step—he had no recollection of it himself. All he knew was that the apparent dangers looming below suddenly brought the task at hand back into focus. Hall descended through the rocks, temporarily lucid, the Sherpas driving him on. In the brief mental clearing, he saw Pemba, one of Thomas Weber's Sherpas, approaching along the gentle traverse from the top of the Second Step. It was a mystery why Weber, Kikstra, and Pasang were not with him.

In the brief moment between Thomas Weber's final words and his ensuing collapse, Harry Kikstra thought the German was joking. They had reached the bottom of the Second Step, and while Weber had been moving with some difficulty he was still operating more or less under his own power. The Second Step wasn't just the most significant physical obstacle on the route; it was a psychological threshold as well. Reaching the top of it during the ascent was an inspiring occasion— the last of the real barriers between a climber and the summit. On the descent, reaching the bottom of the step was a point of great relief. It was preposterous to die here. A long day still lay ahead, but the hardest work had been done.

It wasn't until Weber's full body weight bore down on the fixed rope that Kikstra realized this was no joke. His client was in serious jeopardy.

Weber hit the snow-and-ice-covered slope with a thud and began to slide headfirst toward a lip of rock pitched precipitously down the North Face. He was still clipped to the fixed line, but the rope ran horizontally, fastened at the ends to a broad rock face at the bottom of the step, and it sagged significantly under the load. Pemba was holding the line from above to keep Weber from sliding directly over the edge, but he was bearing the brunt of the fallen man's weight and could maintain his grip for only a few minutes before his strength faded and he had to slowly let Weber slip further down the slope. The line came taut at the anchors, Weber suspended at the fulcrum, bent sharply at the waist, head and feet aimed downhill, face burrowed in the snow.

As Kikstra recounted it, he tried to catch Weber as he fell but could not manage to hold him for more than a few seconds. The guide also said that he promptly went to Weber and tried to right him, but the slope was too awkward and dangerous and the German too big to move. He called out to Pemba, but neither he nor Pasang came to help.

"Thomas is dead," Pemba said bluntly.

Kikstra said he scrambled back up to the track and then called Abramov on the radio to inform his expedition leader and seek advice. Abramov was stationed at ABC. Several of the other 7 Summits Club expedition members, including Slate Stern and Richard Harris, were gathered around the radio down at Base Camp, listening to the crisis unfold.

"Make massage of his heart!" Abramov told Kikstra. "Massage his heart. Over."

"He's down the slope," Kikstra said, gasping. "He's facedown in the snow for more than five minutes. There is no color in his face, and he's not breathing. Over."

Abramov: "He's not breathing, but make massage of heart. Over."

Kikstra: "It's impossible! He's hanging down on one small wire. I'm almost falling down myself now!"

Abramov: "Harry, make photos of Thomas for insurance company! Make photo of his face. Make photo with ropes and with summit of Everest, and if you are sure he is dead, go down!"

Kikstra: "I understand, Alex."

Down at Base Camp, Stern turned to the others in the communications tent. "What a fucking tragedy," he said, shaking his head.

Shortly before Weber's collapse, Chris Klinke had descended the ladder and pulled up next to the German, who was paused in the middle of the step, above the lower rock ledges. Klinke was slightly panicked.

He was critically low on oxygen and had already waited for about twenty minutes at the top of the step. His spare bottle awaited him at the bottom of the step, but it was nearly impossible to bypass Weber; the process of getting him through the technical pitch was complicated and congested. Klinke was hoping to make up time by following as closely as he could.

He and Weber were both waiting on a broad ledge in the middle of the step while Kikstra and the Sherpas moved down below to help guide Weber through the last section. Klinke was about ten feet away from the German. "His goggles and face mask were off," Klinke recalled. "We were there for at least twenty minutes. I was like, 'Hey, how ya doin'?' but again he was not responsive to me. How he got down to the bottom, I'm not sure, but it must have basically been a controlled fall."

Klinke waited until it appeared that the climber had cleared off the rock, and then he followed behind. He'd reached a blocky ledge, the last big step before the bottom, when he saw Weber only a few feet below, his foot tangled in the rope. Klinke watched as Pemba hacked away the line and Weber moved down the last bit and took a step away from the buttress.

At this point, Klinke's account of the next twenty minutes diverges from Kikstra's recollection. According to Klinke, Kikstra was not next to Weber but twenty to twenty-five feet away, where the route flattens and traverses along the side of a large rock. Weber was leaning against another rock at the very base of the step, his head crooked into one arm, looking down. Klinke recalls Weber sinking down onto his butt while rotating slightly inward, so that his face wouldn't scrape the rock, and then he began to slide down the slope.

"I know Harry said that Thomas looked at him, but that wasn't what I observed," Klinke recalled.

Pemba was next to Weber and was holding on to the fixed rope running along the traverse, loaded with Weber's body weight. Klinke said he began shouting over to Kikstra, "Do you have injectable dex? Do you have injectable dex?"

Kikstra indicated that he had only oral. Klinke had the injectable variety in his pack, so he scrambled down the last few feet of rock and hurried past Weber and over to Kikstra. By the time he reached the guide, Kikstra was speaking on the radio with Abramov and ignoring the American. "I'm working on the assumption that Harry is the guide, he is supposed to be in charge," Klinke said later, explaining why he didn't go to Weber himself. "I have emergency response training, and that's where I went with chain of command. In my mind, if Thomas had been a solo climber, I would have been the one going down and injecting him. But I knew he had a guide and two Sherpas, so where do I step in? I knew he was in trouble, but I thought the proper course of action was to get the drugs into the hands of someone who could administer them. At this point, I'm screaming up to Scott [Woolums], saying we have a big problem and he needs to get his ass down here," Klinke recalled. "So Scott bypasses everybody, and he downclimbs the step, and then clips into the rope, and it's not until then that Harry starts to go over to Thomas."

A little earlier, when Woolums had arrived at the top of the ladder he'd found most of his climbers queued up and waiting for Weber, Kikstra, and the Sherpas to clear off the technical terrain below. After waiting for fifteen minutes, Woolums stepped past his team to investigate the holdup. He could see that there was some kind of problem below, but his immediate concern was helping his client Laurie Bagley make the first exposed and frightening move required to get down the step.

Woolums got Bagley descending safely, then moved down ahead of her as quickly as he could to check out the situation below. When he reached the bottom of the step, he clipped into the rope leading to

Weber and began the delicate downward scramble over loose rock and snow. "It was extremely dangerous," Woolums recalled. "He was hanging over the edge on a pretty manky piece of fixed line, kind of right in the middle of it. And we're hanging on this line as well. It wasn't that steep where we were, but the whole thing could have just snapped and gone."

After a few minutes, Kikstra arrived. Woolums had managed to lasso Weber's backpack using some spare rope. With great effort, he and Kikstra hoisted the stricken climber into a seated position. Woolums checked Weber over. He couldn't detect a pulse, and the German was no longer breathing. The man appeared dead. Woolums climbed back up to the track and radioed down to Jamie McGuinness at ABC. He had alerted the trip leader earlier that he was going to investigate a problem, and now he gave McGuinness more details and the approximate time of Weber's death.

"I'm not sure where Harry was when I got down," Woolums said later, "but I want to give him the benefit of the doubt. He was pretty shook up. I think he did what he could, under the circumstances. You know, everyone's right at their edge up there.

"What was confusing was that Harry had two other Sherpas right there, and together I think they could have gotten Thomas upright," Woolums continued. "It probably took me twenty minutes to get there from about the middle of the step, and Thomas died during that time. He was still warm when I reached him."

Weber died at approximately ten A.M. In the grim aftermath, there was little for Kikstra to do but document the deceased, as Abramov had instructed. "I have never been more appalled at taking photos than at that moment," Kikstra wrote on his Web site.

"The pictures needed to be taken," Kikstra recalled later. "But I think Alex also realized that I was in shock and that it was important that he give me something to do, something to focus on other than what had just happened."

In the ensuing months, much debate would swirl around what had, in fact, just happened. Though Klinke and others from the Project Himalaya team speculated that Weber had been suffering from edema, Kikstra felt his client had suffered a heart attack or stroke, given his sudden and total collapse. The truth would never be known.

As Kikstra sat by Weber in disbelief, Abramov also informed him about the situation with Lincoln Hall, who was still above, at the Third Step, no longer moving down the route. He told Kikstra that he should send Pemba up to try to help Hall, and then descend with Pasang.

Abramov now had an unmitigated debacle on his hands: One man had just died and a second was stranded even higher on the mountain. He began to tap all the resources he had left to keep the damage from getting any worse. Though almost all of the 7 Summits Club climbers had returned to Base Camp by now, Abramov remained at ABC, where he held a three-way conversation between the Sherpas tending to Hall on the ridge and the climbers huddled around the radio in Base Camp. Abramov had scrambled more Sherpas who had been up on the North Ridge breaking down the camps. They rounded up as much oxygen as they could and began to make their way up the mountain in hopes of intercepting Hall that afternoon.

Hall was not making his rescue easy. As his mind spun away, he became irascible and aggressive, fighting with the Sherpas who were literally trying to pull him along the fixed line.

While Abramov spoke with his sirdar, Mingma, about the pending rescue, Ludmila Korobeshko stood by the radio at ABC. Much of the specific information was being relayed between the Sherpas on the ridge and Mingma, and then Korobeshko would communicate the details to Base Camp. But Harris and the others could also speak directly with those on the ridge.

"Come in, Lincoln," Harris said. "Do you copy?"

Korobeshko: "Richard, it's Luda. Do you know the situation with Lincoln, or should I describe it to you?"

Harris: "Go ahead."

Korobeshko: "So, the situation is that he's maybe kind of a bit crazy, because he is holding to the rope by the jumar, and all three Sherpas are trying to drag him down. But he is very stubborn. He sticks to the rope because he is afraid the rope will end and he will fall down the mountain. Over."

Harris: "Can you get a Sherpa to put a radio to Lincoln's ear so we can talk to him, please."

Korobeshko: "They have enough oxygen; it's just his imagination [that he's running out]."

Harris turned to the others in the tent. "He's going fucking nuts with oxygen, and three Sherpas are trying to get him down the fucking rope. These poor people. He's got plenty of oxygen, he's just lost."

On a snow ledge below the Third Step, Hall had stopped struggling with the Sherpas and had now lain down and fallen unconscious, a development that left Abramov at a troubling crossroads. Hall remained above the perilous Second Step, and his condition appeared to be deteriorating quickly. The four Sherpas could conceivably drag him along more level terrain, but they certainly were not going to be able to wrangle an unconscious climber down the Second Step. Any rescue effort entailed a certain degree of risk, but none so much as the one now confronting the Russian expedition leader, at such great heights, as the morning stretched into afternoon.

Shortly before Hall collapsed, Pemba's arrival just below the Third Step had reinvigorated the rescue efforts. The Sherpa seemed to have a particularly good rapport with Hall. He promptly informed the Aussie of Thomas Weber's death, and Hall burst into tears, throwing his arms around the Sherpa and weeping. It was, perhaps, the last surge of energy his battered body could tolerate. What little conversation he had with those below soon became almost completely incoherent.

The Sherpas managed to revive Hall enough to get him to the top of the Second Step, where they confronted the most formidable and lethal challenge. Through much prodding, he was able to scoot to the top of the ladder and arrange himself on the rappel line. Whatever condition his mind was in, Hall's decades of climbing experience—the deep cerebral programming that was somehow insulated from the deleterious effects of edema—were now dredged to the surface.

Through his fog, he lurched and spun his way down the vertical rock face, Pemba abseiling next to him. At one point, in a brief panic, he kicked out with a boot and sent a crampon spike into Pemba's leg; instantly he recognized what he'd done and stammered apologies under his oxygen mask. Hall later recalled being dimly aware that others had arrived, or were already there—Sherpas perhaps, but in their high-altitude suits it was impossible to know for sure. He heard voices, one of them speaking English, surprisingly—his old climbing friend Peter Adamson, from Australia, with whom Hall had shared many a rope. Adamson encouraged Hall to focus, insisting that everyone there was trying to help him. This was not a game. Hall could hear his friend clearly, but where was he?

There was more tricky climbing below the ladder, but again Hall managed to navigate the rock and suddenly found himself at the bottom of the step. His exhaustion was all-consuming. Hall understood that he needed to try to reach the safety of the camps below the ridge, and that to get there it was essential he keep moving, but the temptation to stop and rest was irresistible. What he could not understand was how each rest was not the momentary break he believed it to be but a full stop during which he would lie down on the trail, prompting the Sherpas to shout at him urgently. It was still a long way, they said, and he must keep moving, no matter what.

It was now mid-afternoon, and the Sherpas were worried that staying with Hall much longer meant that they would be caught on the ridge after dark, in the predicted deteriorating weather. Pemba began to indicate a spot where it would be safe for Hall to spend the night, where the exposure rearing up on both sides of the ridge was slightly less severe. The climber was no longer able to speak, but if he could have, he would have protested adamantly.

Down at ABC, Abramov wrestled with the dilemma. To send more Sherpas to try to reach Hall could cost even more lives, and while it was one thing to lose yet another climber, it was another to send Sherpas to their deaths in the vain attempt to remedy a hopeless situation.

Richard Harris radioed Abramov.

"Alex, you need to give some orders, mate," Harris said. "You're the expedition leader."

"This is very difficult for me," Abramov said. "But Lincoln doesn't move, and the Sherpas may die."

Now Russell Brice, who had not yet departed for Kathmandu, arrived in the 7 Summits Club tent at Base Camp bearing an updated weather report. "At about seven o'clock tonight, your wind speed's going to about double," he announced flatly, adding, "It drops a little bit tomorrow morning. And then it triples."

Abramov: "Mingma say for half an hour, Lincoln's breathing very ill-normal. Maybe only four, five, six times during one minute."

Harris: "We understand, Alex. I think the only thing we can do is get the Sherpas down. Over."

Brice: "It's coming on twenty hours now that he's been up there—"

Harris. "Yeah. Understood."

Up on the ridge, once he was alone, Hall believed he heard a voice informing him that there was a nook among the rocks where three women had made a camp and were waiting for him. But there were no women here, no campsite. In fact, now there was no one, not even the Sherpas. The light was seeping from the sky, the intense azure afternoon softening into layers of pink and purple and gold. Hall lay on his side, facing the horizon, detached from his own circumstances, dimly appreciating the extraordinary view, drifting into the evening's transcendental moment. Above him, along the crest of the ridge, the winds were blowing hard, lifting the familiar flag of snow and ice from the summit. For a short period the mountain burned red under the last rays of the day, then the color bled out and Everest returned to darkness.

Earlier, after Harry Kikstra had sent Pemba up to help Hall, he sat next to Weber simply staring in disbelief. Finally, he gathered himself together enough to take the photos Alex had requested, and then he scrambled back to the track and headed down the ridge.

The descent was a blur. He was alone, for the most part, Pasang having gone on ahead. He came to the Rock Cave, which contained Green Boots and David Sharp. Someone had moved Sharp's backpack to the front, to cover him, but the pack had dislodged and slipped down, exposing the climber's face. It seemed like an eternity now since he had passed this spot on the ascent, the sight of the dead men earlier that morning giving him serious pause. How easily Kikstra could have shared their fate in 2005, when he had so narrowly escaped the clutches of the ridge himself. He thought of his friend Vitor Negrete, the Brazilian who had died only a few days ago. He thought of Marko Lihteneker, a Slovenian from his 2005 expedition, now also dead, sitting bolt upright near the top of the Third Step.

A little farther down the ridge, Kikstra encountered Pasang lying in the snow, flat on his back. His heart jumped.

"Are you okay?"

"Yes," Pasang said. "Just resting."

Kikstra was parched and nearly out of fluids—Weber had consumed most of his supply—and he told the Sherpa that he wanted to just keep moving and get down to high camp, where there was a stove and fuel, which would allow him to melt snow and make a drink. Now he lost vertical quickly, tottering down through the gullies, rocks, and ledges of the Exit Cracks, veering toward camp.

Kikstra had warmed up significantly by the time he arrived at the tents, and he lay with just his head inside the vestibule, the rest of his body against the snow. He was spent beyond words. He had not spoken with anyone from his team besides Pasang since he had left Weber's body hours earlier. Kikstra would state later that his radio had not been working—he could hear incoming calls, the concerned voices of his friends and companions below, but he could not call out.

Kikstra melted water while waiting for Pasang, and soon the two of them were sharing a drink and preparing to move lower. They listened to the radio traffic between the Sherpas, still up on the ridge, Abramov and the others at ABC, and the Aussies down at Base Camp. Eavesdropping on the dialogue was yet one more bizarre experience in a day filled with trouble and tragedy.

It was getting late, and the clouds were coming in again. Kikstra knew he had to get going, so he departed high camp ahead of Pasang, clomping down to the next camp in an hour. He hooked up another half bottle of oxygen, gathered his stash of personal items—some food, an extra jacket—then he moved out again. With luck, he might be able to get all the way down to ABC by nightfall.

Kikstra began to descend the snow ridge toward the col, directly below. It was an easy slope, smooth and snow-covered, with a moderate pitch and a well-defined track. This is the point where many climbers begin to feel truly safe again, nearly home, but Kikstra felt as though he were continuing to move through an enduring nightmare. "It was snowing, but there was no sound," he recalled. "Every rock looked like a hand sticking out of the snow. Every knot in the rope looked like a body. I remember feeling like I was hallucinating. I thought I was going crazy."

When he at last reached the North Col, Andrey Selivanov came out of the mess tent to meet him. He helped Kikstra inside and gave him a hot drink. It would be too dangerous to try to descend any farther this evening, he informed the climber. The snow was posing too much of an avalanche hazard, so the guide would need to spend the night on the col and head to ABC in the morning. The doctor told him that he wanted Kikstra to use oxygen while he slept, and he gave him a cup of tea laced with supplements that would help him sleep.

As Kikstra's blood began to course with the comforts of the sedative, the doctor said that he had also received more bad news: Lincoln Hall was dead.

CHAPTER 8

DARK SUMMIT

Though it was spring in the Himalayas, the austral winter seemed to be arriving early at the Hall household in Wentworth Falls. On May 25, once the cool afternoon had faded into a crisp evening, Barbara Hall built a fire and settled into a chair by the hearth. She had spent the last few hours on the phone, receiving updates on her husband's progress and relaying it to Dylan and Dorje, Lincoln's colleagues, and family friends. She knew he had reached the top—Mike Dillon had informed her from Base Camp—but then Cheryl Harris, Richard's wife, had called to tell her that Lincoln was having trouble getting down off the ridge. When she had last heard from Dillon, just a couple of hours earlier, the report was more promising. He had spoken directly with Lincoln, he told her, and her husband was making progress again, with the help of four Sherpas. Everyone at camp seemed optimistic about the outcome. But was she?

Barbara Hall wasn't a mountaineer, but she understood the dangers involved. When the offer to join the Everest trip had arisen in February, there had been less a debate about whether or not Lincoln should go than an effort to clear the logistical hurdles—time off from work, fitness and training. When he left at the end of March, his parting words had included a heartfelt pledge to Barbara and the boys that he was coming back, no matter what. "Barbara knows I'm a safe person," Hall said later. "I've always been a cautious mountaineer. I turned back on Makalu. I turned back on Everest in '84."

As in most periods of crisis, the waiting was the worst, the mind flipping ahead to a future rife with frightening possibilities. Lincoln and Barbara had first met in an Eastern philosophy seminar that Barbara, a history teacher, was conducting. They shared a deep interest in the East's long tradition of meditative spirituality, and had learned to rely on yogic breathing and relaxed concentration to help them through times of duress.

Barbara moved close to the fire, the warmth enveloping her, facilitating her mental state—*mushin*, martial artists called it, a "mind of no mind," free from anxiety, fear, and ego. Try as she did, though, images of Lincoln continued to force their way in. She and her husband were embracing, surrounded by bright light. It was so real she could feel the broad expanse of his back, his long arms wrapped tight around her, his chin against her head—comforting and terrifying all at once.

The sensation was so powerful that it snapped her out of the moment. She tried an alternative strategy, picking up the book by her chair, the one she had been reading for the last few weeks, Salman Rushdie's *The Ground Beneath Her Feet*. But she could not concentrate on the pages, either, so she submitted to the situation and sat staring into the flames.

A little while later, at nine forty-five that night, the phone rang again, the sound erupting into the silent room.

"Oh, Barbara . . ." Mike Dillon said on the other end of the line, his voice cracking.

* ★ *

Pemba, Lakcha, Dawa Tenzing, and Dorje had returned to high camp late on the night of May 25. At around seven that evening, Abramov had decided to stop the rescue effort and had ordered the Sherpas to leave Hall and descend. They had finally abandoned the climber near Mushroom Rock, at around 28,200 feet. Even as he lay prostrate in the snow, the Sherpas had shouted and shook him. They'd fed him oxygen. They'd pried open his eyelids and poked his eyeballs with their fingers. Hall had not been able to walk or speak for the past two hours. Now he was completely unresponsive, and the Sherpas had left and were descending the rest of the ridge in almost total darkness.

The Sherpas had been above 28,000 feet for more than twenty-two hours. Dawa Tenzing was so exhausted and snow-blind, he had virtually no recollection of how he had made it back to camp. Pemba was in equally bad shape, having been without oxygen since he'd given his own supply to Thomas Weber that morning. At one point, he had considered lying down next to Hall and dying on the ridge with his friend, but thoughts of his family had driven him to leave with the others.

After the Sherpas were back at camp and Hall's fate appeared to be sealed, Mike Dillon had made his call to Barbara. Once they had spoken, Alex Abramov wrote another dispatch for his Web site, posting the unwelcome news that 7 Summits Club had now lost a third climber:

> From 9:30 till 19:20, almost 9 hours, four Sherpas tried to get Lincoln lower. A crest here is very complicated technically and in condition of Lincoln it was possible to lower him for 9 hours 300–400 meters. Sherpas could lower him from the Second step on height of 8700 meters. During descent Lincoln two times talked on a portable radio set to friends. Conversations were addle, there was an obvious loss of orientation in time and space. After 5 P.M. Lincoln has ceased

to reply. Movements have got chaotic character. Sherpas continued attempts to move Lincoln along a crest, but at 19:20 the death was verified. The probable reason: brain cerebral edema, pulmonary edema. Now 21:30, Sherpas have gone down to camp 8300, they are outside of danger though have got awfully tired. Harry Kikstra is in camp on 7000 m on North Col.

The season's death toll now appeared to equal the same troubling number as 1996's, and although official reports and tallies were still coming in, opinions were taking shape, indictments being hurled. ExplorersWeb, which had been closely tracking events, had simply reproduced Abramov's post—what more needed to be said?—but a few hours later the site followed up with a lengthy editorial aimed at all the commercial operators on the mountain. It drew comparisons between the events surrounding Hall and Weber and those involving David Sharp a week and a half earlier.

"Only today, we have seen two more climbers lost on Everest," it read. "Thomas Weber and veteran Lincoln Hall . . . succumbed to altitude above 8000 meters. The difference however to the night David died, was that a detailed, official report was provided within 24 hours of the accidents, and it showed a battle for both climbers to the very end. Everest and Himalaya are tough places and people die there, but this season the biggest debate was not about that. This year, Everest displayed a weakness much more dangerous than death to human kind: Lack of compassion, selfish ambition, and silence."

The news was still sinking in early the next morning as the first wave of 7 Summits Club climbers rambled out of Base Camp in a convoy of jeeps, headed back to Kathmandu. The slow acclimatization process generally requires a four- to five-day trip up to BC, but the journey back—to abundant oxygen and hot showers and hearty meals—is concluded as quickly as possible, typically in two days. Climbers are delayed by immigration in Zhangmu, the wild border town, its steep narrow streets lined with squalid hotels, massage parlors, and cellar bars with red neon signs flickering above their grimy stairwells. They are a captive clientele, a few more than ready to indulge in the services offered. They wake the next day to wicked hangovers, then file through immigration, walk across the Friendship Bridge, and at last board a bus headed for Kathmandu.

Only a few teams remained on the mountain at this point, chief among them the SummitClimb expedition, led by American Dan Mazur. His climbers included Jangbu Sherpa; twenty-five-year-old Myles Osborne; Andrew Brash, thirty-seven, a teacher from Calgary; and Phil Crampton, thirty-five, a Brit who tended bar in New York City. The group had been up to high camp once already, a few days earlier, on May 18, but the winds had come up and Mazur had suggested that they descend and wait for the next weather window rather than sit in camp burning up all their oxygen. They'd recovered at ABC and had now returned, rested, healthy, primed for their shot.

Since teams typically operated on different radio channels, the SummitClimb members were oblivious to the events involving Weber and Hall earlier in the day. Mazur and his team were planning to depart for the summit at eleven o'clock that night, but by the time they were melting water and hydrating for the climb ahead their prospects began to look dim. The snow had started again, and with it came more wind. No one really thought they were going to make it any higher. Then, around nine P.M., the squall cleared out and the weather stabilized. Mazur looked outside, at a clear sky now filled with stars. Maybe they were going to get their chance after all.

When Mazur and his clients pushed out of camp that night, conditions were about as good as Everest allowed. The temperature was bracing—somewhere around 20 below—but the wind was light, the route covered with a few inches of loose snow. They were alone on the route, heading up toward the Exit Cracks. The team climbed together, oxygen cranked, warming up. Mazur had a good feeling about the day; he was already looking forward to expedition success.

In the blackness above, Lincoln Hall began to dream.

"A man appeared from the direction of the Second Step, a Westerner with a beard wearing mountaineering gear," Hall recounted in *Dead Lucky*. "I knew that I was the only Westerner alive this close to the summit of Everest, but . . . I did not think this was strange. He stopped and looked at me but did not speak at all."

Hall sensed that the man wanted something, and he led the other climber along a trail contouring a low wall built from meticulously stacked stones, as if bordering a country estate. Soon, the stone wall merged into the side of a house and Hall entered the building where an interior doorway led to another room, inside of which burned a large fire surrounded by people who were talking and laughing. Hall worried about losing the bearded man, so he went back outside to where the mysterious climber still stood, still silent. Together they walked back up to the spot where Hall had been sitting earlier, and the Aussie watched the stranger dissolve into the darkness.

Hall continued to drift through his edema-induced reverie, each dream waking into the next. Now he was gazing out across the shallow valleys of Australia's Snowy Mountains, where he had learned to ski and climb as a boy. There seemed to be others nearby again—Hall could see figures moving among the rocks—but he could not hear anything, and he could make out only a few familiar faces. There was his dear friend and teammate Mike Dillon, with whom he had first come to Everest twenty-two years earlier. What a comfort to have his mate so close by; they had shared so many trips and tents and close calls, surely they would come through this, too. And there was Hall's sister, Julia, a lawyer. She knew how to handle serious situations. He had always admired her diligent organization, her ability to manage a demanding career while raising three kids with unwavering grace. But Hall could not reach them, nor they him.

For brief periods, he would snap back toward some degree of lucidity. The peaks of the Snowies suddenly morphed into high Himalayan spires, Everest's 8,000-meter neighbors rising above a blanket of clouds. There were no houses or people around him any longer, just a barren ridge, falling away for thousands of feet on either side, horrifically exposed. The awareness filled Hall with dread. With the vision came a gathering but palpable recognition that he was in grave danger, alone, high on Everest, in the middle of the night. He was profoundly tired, as if his limbs had been draped with sandbags, but he knew that going to sleep now meant going to sleep for good. He tried to focus on the simplest tasks: staying awake, staying warm. Hall pulled his knees toward him and hunched forward to channel more heat toward his core. And then—

He was sitting on a mat made of grass inside a crude wooden hut in Nepal's lush lowlands. The structure had only one wall, rough-hewn planks nailed up behind him, but Hall was relieved to discover that he had found at least minimal shelter. In the distance, he could see tiny diodes of light—villages, no doubt, or individual farms. Either way, if he could make his way down to them he was likely to find someone who could help. He spoke passable Nepali, and he resolved to set out for the nearest homestead at dawn.

When Hall woke next, he realized with a sudden and terrifying impact that the lights were not houses in the valley below but stars shimmering above him. He was still tethered to the real world, and he came flying back into it as if on the end of a bungee cord. He had nothing with him now besides his clothes, a balaclava, his goose-down suit. Believing him dead, the Sherpas had taken most of his belongings with them in order to pass them back to his loved ones: his pack and extra mittens, his headlamp, ax, and oxygen. The cold was ferocious, unrelenting. Hall could not feel his toes or fingers beyond the first knuckle. He removed a glove and looked at the strange appendages protruding from his hand, attempting to move them with pitiful results.

Hall grew acutely aware that he wasn't simply stuck in deadly circumstances but was nearly dead himself. This was it, the situation he had dodged so many times before, the mountaineer's endgame. So few survived an ordeal like this that had Hall been even slightly more lucid, had he understood what it would take to endure until dawn, he might have succumbed to the sheer historical odds stacked against him, taking the path of least resistance, nodding off into eternity. His friends below had already resigned themselves to this outcome, but Hall was not yet willing to concede. If nothing else, he remained well enough to tap the vast reservoirs of experience he'd acquired during countless climbing trips, the limbic memory burned into his brain. How many times had he bivouacked on a mountainside during his years on high peaks? Enough, at least, to understand that surviving the night was going to require immense effort and concentration. In the past, under less severe circumstances, he would sing to himself, anything to focus his mind. But Hall's voice was trashed, a locust in his throat, so he began to rock back and forth, then to rotate slightly, forcing more blood through his veins, generating one more precious degree of warmth.

Whatever tricks Hall's personal history had taught him, it may have been something else entirely that kept him alive through those critical hours. Buddhism teaches the principle of nonattachment, the idea that we are born into a world of desire and that desire is the root of all suffering. But here, alone on the ridge, it was the strength of Hall's attachment to the world below that sustained his fight. For at its center was an element so profoundly important to him, so necessary in this life or any other, that it transcended everything else, including his own death. It was not an abstract notion, like faith or hope or even God. It was specific and absolute. He could point to it, name it: Barbara. Dylan. Dorje.

Around four that morning, Dan Mazur and the other Summit-Climb members reached the First Step. They were climbing strong; only Phil Crampton lagged behind. Crampton had already been up to the Second Step once that season, on May 18, when he had aborted his climb to help a teammate who had developed cerebral edema. The ordeal had left Crampton with frostnip on his right hand, but he had recovered enough to return with Mazur and the others. A second attempt, however, was proving to be too much. He told the others he was turning around.

As Crampton headed back down on his own, Mazur, Osborne, Brash, and Jangbu pressed upward. They were moving slowly but steadily, notching their way along the ridge as the horizon split open with the first striations of daylight. The quartet crept past Mushroom Rock, moving along a stretch of low-angled track toward the Second Step, straight ahead. What a moment—approaching the towering buttress, the crux of the climb, the dawn light beginning to illuminate the ridge in all its awesome detail. Then another sight caught the climbers' attention.

"Sitting to our left, about two feet from a 10,000-foot drop, was a man," Myles Osborne later wrote. "Not dead, not sleeping, but sitting cross legged, in the process of changing his shirt. He had his down suit unzipped to the waist, his arms out of the sleeves, was wearing no hat, no gloves, no sunglasses, had no oxygen mask, regulator, ice axe, oxygen, no sleeping bag, no mattress, no food nor water bottle. 'I imagine you're surprised to see me here,' he said. Now, this was a moment of total disbelief to us all."

The man told them his name—Lincoln Hall, from Australia—but

when they approached him, despite his apparent coherence, they realized that he had not arrived there that morning but had been on the ridge overnight, and was now in serious condition. How long he had been without his hat and gloves, his suit open, they could only guess, but he was shivering violently and waving his hands in the air, his fingers ghastly white, rigid with frostbite.

Osborne and Brash were crestfallen. There was no question about the course of action—the man needed help, and they were resolved to provide it—but they wouldn't be going to the top of Everest today. Worse, perhaps, was the prospect that Hall could keel over at any moment, and they'd have to stand by and watch him die.

The four of them scrambled up to the climber and set him up with one of their spare masks and oxygen. They replaced his hat and gloves, which he kept inexplicably removing. It seemed no small miracle that he had lasted the night perched on this cornice without simply rolling over the edge and plummeting down Everest's Kangshung Face.

Mazur radioed down to ABC, where he was eventually able to raise Abramov. The Russian was incredulous. This man couldn't possibly be Lincoln Hall; when the Sherpas had left, Hall had been unconscious, as good as dead.

"They were like, 'You mean he's alive?'" Mazur said later. "It took us half an hour, forty-five minutes to convince them. We're telling them, 'Yeah, he's *alive,* he's moving around, he's talking. We've got him on oxygen. He's looking better all the time and we need to get him out of here. C'mon, let's get this thing going.'"

By the time Mazur spoke with Abramov, Phil Crampton had returned to high camp. Mazur had briefed him by radio on the situation with Hall, and Crampton combed the tents to see who else might be around to help. Pemba and the other 7 Summits Club Sherpas had not descended yet, but they were still wrecked from the effort the day before.

They couldn't be of much assistance themselves, but they were willing to accept Crampton's argument that Hall was still alive, and they helped persuade Abramov to send up more men and oxygen.

Within the hour Abramov had dispatched eight more Sherpas to try to bring Hall down. Jamie McGuinness and Russell Brice also pitched in, offering manpower and oxygen, coordinating a ground rescue on a scale never before seen on the north side. With the season all but over for the commercial outfitters, the clients home or on their way home, they could throw their remaining resources at the Hall rescue without risking their own customers. It had been a grim year, with all its fatalities, but perhaps now there was a chance to snatch one back.

On the ridge, the climbers tried to stabilize Hall while they waited for assistance to arrive from below. They gave him warm Gatorade and Snickers bars, which he thrust in his pocket; his appetite was meager at best. Two Italian climbers approached, the first on oxygen, the second without. Mazur said later that he had solicited their help but they had replied, "No speak English," and kept walking. Later, the Italians released a statement, translated from Italian, attempting to clarify their point of view. "As I passed them, they made way and I noticed nothing out of the ordinary," wrote Marco Astori, the climber who had been using oxygen. "A climber (who we only later discovered was Lincoln) was sitting and looking in his jumpsuit for something and talking with the others. I was asked no questions and no request for help."

Although Hall was sitting up and responsive, he remained only marginally coherent. "Do you know how you got here?" Mazur asked him at one point. "No, do *you* know how I got here?" Hall said.

Throughout the morning, the Aussie communicated through the haze of edema. He was on the ridge, then on a boat, swaying with the waves. Now he was standing on the wing of a plane, about to step off. He made a move toward the cornice. "You need to stay put," Mazur told him, placing a hand on Hall's shoulder.

The climbers led Hall away from the cornice and hitched him to the fixed line, understanding the entire time that his fate was still undetermined. They could try to prevent him from leaping off the mountain, but he could easily suffer cardiac arrest or a stroke or simply slide into a hypothermic coma at any moment. They were afraid to move him very far; it would be too dangerous. And so they sat with him for nearly four hours, casting disappointed gazes toward the summit while the perfect day came up, the sun warming the ridge. Meanwhile, from below, a small platoon of Sherpas worked its way toward them.

In Wentworth Falls, Barbara Hall was hunkered down in her home, surrounded by close friends who had shown up with soups, casseroles, cakes, and flowers, the outpouring of condolence and concern exceeding her expectations. The circle of well-wishers continued to expand through the day; calls flooded in, e-mails filled up her in-box. Barbara was grateful, but it was all she could do to remain gracious and welcoming.

In her bereavement, she was several layers removed from the outer world, where by now the media interest in Hall's apparent survival was approaching a rolling boil. Several of Barbara's friends, including Simon Balderstone, the chairman of the Australian Himalayan Foundation, had received the news but were attempting to shield her from it, given the dubious sourcing and unconfirmed details. To learn that her husband was dead, then miraculously alive, then dead again would be too much for Barbara, even given her tough emotional constitution. And besides, her friends who had caught the latest news about Lincoln knew the mountaineering world well enough to understand that even if he was alive, even if they were attempting to get him down from the ridge, it was impossible to know what kind of condition he was in, or whether he would survive the descent.

Around four P.M. at the Hall home, Dorje called out from his room for his mother to come take a look at something. His voice was animated, excited, and Barbara's pulse rose immediately. On her way to the room, Lincoln's sister, Julia, caught Barbara and told her what she was about to learn from her son.

That afternoon, a friend of Jamie McGuinness's, who also ran Everest expeditions, posted a Web report stating that Hall had been found alive and that a rescue was under way. The dispatch was quickly picked up by ExplorersWeb, which relayed the post in its entirety— including the erroneous information that Dan Mazur had left Hall and continued on to the summit. That morning, ExWeb received so many hits that their server crashed.

Dorje had been tipped to the news by a friend with whom he'd been chatting online. He immediately pulled up the *Sydney Morning Herald* Web site, where, sure enough, the home page blared: "Lincoln Hall Found Alive." When she saw the headline, Barbara's heart leapt, though outwardly she stayed cool. She remarked on what a nice picture of Lincoln they had posted. And then she told her son not to get his hopes up just yet; they couldn't be certain. Barbara was telling herself the same thing.

Around 9:15 A.M., the first two Sherpas arrived at Mushroom Rock to help bring Hall back down the ridge. The Aussie was sitting up and sucking oxygen, his head clearing more by the hour. It struck him that the Sherpas were mildly perturbed. They spoke rapidly with Jangbu. Hall believed that they were on their way to the summit but had been redirected to deal with the ailing climber.

Osborne and Brash had already left and headed down, brimming with disappointment. They had been feeling good and had contemplated going for the top regardless of the long delay, but it seemed a fool's errand. To head up now would put them on top much too late in the day, when the winds were likely to come up again and they could get caught in darkness on the descent. Had they not been interrupted by Hall, they certainly would have made it that morning; now they had no choice but to descend. By the time the Sherpas were able to get Hall on his feet, Mazur and Jangbu had started to make their way down to the camps below.

The two Sherpas had brought Hall's rucksack back up, and with it more oxygen. Hall still had to traverse nearly half of the ridge, much of it a fragile path of rock and ice tracking precipitously along the top of the North Face. Provided he made it that far, he then had to descend the North Ridge nearly a vertical mile before he reached the sanctuary of the North Col and the attention of 7 Summits Club doctor Andrey Selivanov. He was dangerously off balance, and he could not move more than a few steps along the track before he needed to stop and rest. The day already seemed too short.

Hall did not know these Sherpas. One appeared young, the other a bit older. The younger of the two moved in front of him, while the other trailed closely behind. They made their way from Mushroom Rock across the first section of ridge to the First Step, the next technical obstacle, a horizon line at their feet, the rock face dropping straight away. The younger Sherpa clipped into the rappel line and dropped over the lip. Hall was next, but as soon as he peered over the drop he knew he was going to have to muster all his remaining resources to reach the bottom safely. His hands were a mess, his fingers frozen solid at the tips, with no feeling and no mobility. He also knew just how fragile the tissue was by this point. There might still be a chance to save his fingers, but only if he kept them carefully protected. Any impact or abrasion now would destroy the flesh for good.

Before he could psych himself out, Hall arranged himself on the rope and dropped over the lip, only to arrest his descent when he saw the exposure, and the other Sherpa, directly below. Hall was worried that he had set up his braking device wrong—for speed rather than control. In his poor condition, he would slide down the line too fast and risk tearing his hands apart or, worse, plummet to the bottom and batter himself against the rocks. Dangling on the rope, which was now bearing nearly his full weight, he began to try to switch modes, an interruption the Sherpas could not understand. "Go down! Go down!" they yelled at him, but he could not communicate the dilemma and they became incensed. Hall tried to grab hold of another rope next to him, to unweight the line from which he was hanging, but the older Sherpa above snatched the rope first and sliced it away with a knife, grinning maniacally down at Hall.

During their stalemate, Roby Piantoni, the Italian who was climbing without oxygen, appeared at the step. He was wasted from his oxygenless ascent, and when he saw that Hall and the Sherpas were clearly making little progress, he pushed past them, lowering himself by hand on the old ropes and then stumbling off down the route below them. At last Hall managed to persuade the Sherpas to let him lower himself down the rock ahead of them, and, after a nearly thirty-minute effort, he reached the bottom with his hands in good order.

Hall proceeded along a gently sloping section of the route, though the footing was awkward and, in his bulky suit and crampons, he had a hard time walking without stumbling. Every step exhausted him, and he leaned on his ax as if it were a cane. Each time he stopped to rest, the Sherpas harassed him. The younger one in front was particularly agitated, while the older one mostly kept quiet. After he'd covered only a short distance with numerous rests, the young Sherpa grabbed Hall's ax. "You go fast," he insisted. "No stop."

The Aussie tried to do as he was told, but the fatigue was profound. Hall pressed his mask tight to his face so that he would benefit from as much oxygen as possible. He tried to focus on the path at his feet, but several times he tripped and fell to the ground. After one such fall, he was particularly slow to rise. "You go, or I hit you," the young Sherpa growled at him, brandishing Hall's ax.

Even in his hypoxic condition, Hall could not believe the threats coming from these men. When the Sherpa appeared to back off, he got up and staggered along the path, but the pace they forced upon him was too much. He stumbled and fell again and again, which raised their ire further. The effort required to regain his feet each time only made the situation worse. He begged the Sherpas to let him move more slowly, which would prevent him from falling over so often, but they forced him to keep walking, more like captors than saviors.

Again Hall stumbled and fell to the snow, and again the Sherpa wielding Hall's ax threatened to use it against him. He lay on the ground and saw the tool being raised above him, but this time it was not an idle threat. The Sherpa swung the ax down into the back of the climber's ribs, then cocked it above his head for the next blow. Hall had been too exhausted to protect himself, but now he screamed and thrust one arm up, intercepting the ax as it came down. He succeeded in deflecting a strike that would have landed squarely on his head, then rolled out of the way.

What insanity was this? Later, Hall would wonder if the outrageous incident had only been a part of his high-altitude dream world, but his painful bruises convinced him that he hadn't invented the encounter. "It was for real. No doubt about that," Hall said later. "It could be that Alex told them to do whatever it takes to get [me] down alive and they went overboard with it. Particularly since Alex's English is just adequate. Even if it was that, they went way beyond that line. I was certain I was going to die and it didn't seem fair. I should have just died up higher with a little bit of dignity."

Clearly, the Sherpas were not thrilled about escorting the Westerner down from the ridge, putting their own lives at risk in the process. Perhaps they considered the threats and violence to be the only sure means of prodding him onward under such serious circumstances—a kind of extremely tough love. Or perhaps they could not fully appreciate the severity of their actions. Or perhaps they were simply bad men. Sherpas have a well-earned reputation for routine heroics, but that does not preclude a handful of unsavory characters from mingling among them. Everest certainly sees its share of burglaries and petty crime, and anecdotes occasionally surface of Sherpas abandoning their clients or refusing to help them.

Hall and his escorts continued down the ridge, still moving fast. If the altercation had been intended to jump-start the Aussie again, it had worked. His heart raced, the adrenaline surging. These men could be just as willing to kill him as rescue him, and he knew now that he had to be careful. Presently, the other Italian climber, Marco Astori, came past on his descent, offering them what little oxygen he had left, but the Sherpas declined. They had enough, they said. Hall considered stopping Astori and telling him what had just happened, but he feared that the Italian was in too much of a hurry and would not want to get involved. And he was even more afraid of angering the Sherpas again. In his condition, this high up, he was simply too vulnerable.

At last Hall reached a spot along the traverse where he could see others gathered a few hundred feet below, where the route doglegged off the Northeast Ridge and angled down through the Exit Cracks toward the North Ridge. He rounded some rocks and spotted a lone climber approaching along the fixed lines: Lakcha. The Sherpa had been one of his stalwart companions the day before, struggling to save him. He must have regained enough strength to make the trip back up from high camp. Hall couldn't have been happier to see him. He trusted Lakcha implicitly, and he was so eager to greet him that he tripped and fell again, landing downslope of the track. The two Sherpas glowered, but he just lay there waiting for his friend.

"Why you so slow?" Lakcha said when he arrived, his tone serious, as if the last twelve hours hadn't even happened. "You climb fast on way up, but too slow coming down."

Hall was so relieved and energized, now that he had been delivered from his persecutors, that he got to his feet, snatched his ice ax from the young Sherpa, and took off down the route. Somehow, he managed a kind of half trot, as much as such a thing is possible at 8,000 meters, across the remaining flat track leading to the group of Sherpas milling around just below. They appeared quite happy to see Hall, though not nearly as happy as the Aussie was to see them. He was safe, for the time being, but now he sat wheezing at the top of the rappel lines, so spent from his effort that he could not move another step.

Mike Dillon, the Harrises, Slate Stern, Kirk Wheatley, and a few other 7 Summits Club members had rolled out of Base Camp by eight that morning, none of them suspecting that Hall would soon be found alive on the ridge. It was a long, dusty drive from the Rongbuk down to Zhangmu, the Tibetan Plateau rolling by outside the car windows, Richard Harris pledging to return and build a memorial to Hall on the Mound.

Beyond their insular convoy, however, the news about Hall whipped around the globe at digital speed. Because the Chinese were obsessed with technology, cell-phone service was available through many areas of Tibet. Not long after the 7 Summits Club group arrived in Zhangmu, Kirk Wheatley received a text message from his wife, back in England. He and the others had just eaten dinner at one of the local restaurants that catered to Western tourists, decorated with mountaineering posters tacked up on wood paneling. "We were sitting in a bar, sort of drunk," Wheatley recalled, "and we were like, 'Oh my God—Lincoln's alive.'"

They couldn't do much besides try to glean more information and confirm details. Mike Dillon began talking about arranging a helicopter evacuation once they got back to Kathmandu. The Harrises called ABC and confirmed that Lincoln had made it off the ridge but was still above the col. It was too soon to ascertain the full extent of his condition, but they knew it was serious. They tried to keep their hopefulness in check. The sudden demise of Igor Plyushkin a few days earlier had left everyone wary of premature assumptions.

At around eight P.M. on May 26, Hall and his fresh entourage of Sherpas stumbled into Camp One, on the North Col. He had navigated the snow ridge above the camp under his own power, and while he was a mess—he'd barely eaten for three days and continued to suffer hallucinations—he was now at least in a place where he could stay the night. Andrey Selivanov, who had been waiting for him, led Hall to the makeshift infirmary he had set up in the mess tent and began Hall's next big challenge: a long and painful recovery.

Abramov was ecstatic. "Yes! Lincoln Hall has passed without assistance the whole snow slope, from 7500 m!" he wrote on the 7 Summits Club site. He went on:

> In camp on the Saddle doctor Andrey Selivanov met him and led to a dining tent, which is now as a field hospital. As he said, the first problems of Lincoln is an acute psychosis, a disorientation in space, also he shows resistance accompanying and now to the doctor. First of all it will be necessary to calm him. The reason—an acute edema of a brain and hypoxia. The doctor have examined his hands— frostbitten 2–3 degrees. Legs to the moment of communication were not examined yet. On a question on prospects Andrey has told: 'We shall overcome!'. Now Lincoln is in heat, in spacious tent with electric illumination, 10 person are engaged in his service. Descent is planned for tomorrow's morning, when there will be a sun and will become warmer. Under last message, for today, Lincoln Hall has fallen asleep in warm tent in camp on North Col. Necessary and possible (in this place) medical aid was rendered to him.

On May 27, Hall picked his way carefully back down to ABC, flanked by Andrey Selivanov and Mingma. His mental clarity was retuning, and he prattled on to Mingma in Nepali as they negotiated the fixed ropes anchored to the icy slope below the col. In camp, Selivanov set him up in the medical tent for another day and night of critical care, jabbing his frozen digits with vasodilators, feeding him measured amounts of warm, sweet liquids, even though Hall could have consumed a river.

One of those in camp was the Briton Kevin Augello, who had been helping film the documentary about Thomas Weber. Augello and Hall had become casual friends during the expedition, and now the filmmaker was charged with the long-overdue but highly anticipated task of calling Barbara Hall in Wentworth Falls. He introduced himself awkwardly, then passed the phone to Hall, who croaked into the receiver. Hall's voice had been reduced to such a hoarse whisper that at first Barbara was not convinced she was speaking to her husband. But soon she came around, Hall sobbing on his end of the line. He told her he was okay, though some of his fingers might be coming off from frostbite. It didn't matter, she sobbed back. She would love him regardless.

Three days later Barbara boarded a plane for Kathmandu to help bring her husband home.

On the afternoon of June 3, a Saturday, Alex Abramov hosted a party to celebrate Hall's survival and honor the fifteen Sherpas who had been involved in the rescue. The soiree was held on the roof of the Radisson Hotel, near Kathmandu's Thamel District, just across the street from the Hotel Tibet. The worst was behind them now. Hall had recently arrived from Everest, his hands wrapped in twin mittens of bright white gauze, and he joined the Sherpas at the table; it would be their first real chance to share their account with him.

Hall had not yet told Abramov about his assault by the Sherpas.

He had tried briefly back at ABC, but they had been interrupted, and now hardly seemed like the time. The Sherpas who Hall believed had beaten him were there, but during a slightly confused period of questions and answers, emceed by Mingma, the Sherpas claimed it had been Hall swinging the ax at *them*. When Hall showed them his bruises, they only became more perplexed. Abramov simply shrugged. Hall had survived a great ordeal and this made him quite a man, he indicated. The bruises would fade soon enough. The damage to his fingers and toes would not.

Earlier that day, Abramov had also said farewell to Russell Brice, who had arrived back in Nepal by May 30, unprepared for the press corps that had now descended on the Everest teams. Most had been waiting for Hall's return, but a handful chased after Brice as well, given all the speculation associated with David Sharp's death.

Ordinarily, Brice enjoyed the layover in Kathmandu; he kept an apartment in the city and still had many friends there. But now he simply wanted to get away, to leave the mess of 2006 behind and move on. Everest was getting almost as much attention as it had ten years before, only this time Brice was caught in the spotlight. Somehow, he had emerged as the villain in all of this, and he needed to think about how to handle it. He dodged reporters but intended to provide a statement to the media. He had already begun to contemplate the memo as he walked across the tarmac at the Kathmandu airport, toward his plane and the start of his long trip back to France.

Only one important task remained for Brice. He had agreed to speak with John and Linda Sharp, who were meeting him at the Hilton at Heathrow Airport. They had asked only that Brice return a few of their son's belongings: David's passport and his Bible. If Brice could make use of the other equipment, then that was for the best.

Brice sat with the Sharps for four hours, drinking coffee, explaining what had happened. He tried to lay out the facts as he understood them. Yes, David had been alive when his climbers had passed him and, yes, he had been able to speak, just a few words. Brice explained how dangerous it is for everyone at that altitude, how risky a rescue would have been. He told them how Phurba had tried to give David oxygen and get him to his feet but simply could not, even though Phurba was one of the strongest climbers on Everest. He told them not to believe everything they read and urged them to bear in mind how the media could spin the truth, or misunderstand the truth, in their eagerness to get the story out.

Brice told the Sharps that he had brought the video footage with him. The filmmakers who had been following his expedition had wanted them to have the tape and were not intending to use any of it in their documentary series.

The Sharps wanted to know only so much. They were grateful for Brice's explanation, but they told him that they held no one accountable and simply wanted to get on with their grieving and with their lives. They told Brice a little about their son: his lifelong love of adventure, how he had discovered climbing in school, how it had been his third trip to Everest—like George Mallory. They thanked him for taking care of the death certificate that had to be filed with the Chinese. And they said they were glad that he had not put others in danger on the mountain.

"They just wished everyone would stop talking about it," Brice said later. "They were in huge distress about the whole situation. But they deserved to hear the truth. And I did that willingly, making a twelve-hour flight, because it's very useful for the parents to know that at least someone was caring."

When it came time for Brice to leave, there was still one more matter to discuss. If the Sharps were willing, Brice could move the body off the ridge, interring it on the mountain, as he had done for so many others. If nothing else, it might provide the Sharps a little more peace of mind to know that their son was no longer visible on the ridge. If they liked, they could even come with his expedition to Base Camp next spring, where it was tradition to erect a memorial to fallen climbers. But these details could all be worked out later.

Despite the public setting in the busy hotel, theirs was a private and largely anonymous affair. How many other stories floated amid the cacophony of voices—strangers striking up conversation, colleagues talking shop, parents tending to their kids. It didn't matter. It was time for Brice to go, and he said his good-byes and at last was off on the last leg of his long journey—back to his home in Argentière, back to Caroline, back to his paperwork and accounting, back to the crush of reporters who would hound him for weeks by phone and e-mail, demanding details, exegesis, accountability.

How could they even begin to understand what he had done and what he had tried to do, not just for David Sharp and his family but for so many who came to his mountain?

By the next day Brice was back at his desk, composing his statement for the reporters, for all those now looking to him for answers, doing his best to summarize the facts, even while he knew that trying to clarify it all was nearly futile. The complete account would require a lifetime to convey—no matter how much he was willing to say, no matter how careful his explanation.

EPILOGUE

Just days after the deadly season ended, on June 9, Russell Brice released his statement to the press. Entitled "Reflections on Everest 2006," it began with a note about the rope-fixing job, for which Brice had accepted sole responsibility, per his agreement with the CTMA. The project had taken forty days, he wrote, and required "30 cylinders of oxygen, many yaks and associated support logistics," all of which cost him a total of $32,160. He acknowledged those who had contributed $100 per climber and tallied the amount he was still out of pocket: $17,360.

Brice then rattled off a list of additional support he'd provided for others during the season, most of it gratis: the climbing equipment for the Ecuadoreans after their camp was robbed; the oxygen for the Turks on May 15; the critical care given to the Indian climber on the North Col; the emergency care for one of Dan Mazur's Sherpas who had fallen and lacerated his head; the artificial legs he, Inglis, and

Cowboy had given to Tilly, the Tibetan amputee. He noted that he had been involved in at least fifteen "major" rescues on Everest, and finally he concluded with his most revealing point yet: that he had not been aware of David Sharp until his team was coming down off the ridge.

"If I had known there was a problem on the way up I am sure the structure of the day would have been very different, and most certainly I would have investigated the chance of a rescue," Brice wrote. "At that stage we would have had fresh Sherpas, guides, and members, and ample oxygen as opposed to exhausted people and very little oxygen when we were returning. It was still early in the season, and so if we had carried out a rescue we could have all returned for another summit attempt later in the season with remaining oxygen, food and resources."

When I first read Brice's statement, I had the same reaction as a few others who had been captivated by the recent events on the mountain: Big Boss doth protest too much. "Reflections on Everest 2006" ran upwards of twelve pages, much of it freewheeling through the long list of services, resources, and equipment Brice had provided to other teams and climbers, generously and free of charge. It seemed all that required clarifying on the record was that Brice had not known about Sharp until around 9:30 A.M. on May 15, too late to initiate a rescue.

Almost immediately suspicion began to swirl around Brice's press release. Some people suggested that Brice could simply be lying about when he first learned about Sharp, despite the fact that he'd offered up his own logbook detailing the communications he'd had with his team during those two days. Critics pointed to Mark Inglis's recollection of a radio conversation that morning, when he said his group had been advised to continue their climb after encountering the stricken Brit. It also seemed hard to believe that lead guide Mark

Woodward and the others from Himex's second team would have in-
teracted with a dying man on the ridge and not made mention of it to
Brice. *Oh, right—that.* Deeper conspiracy theories focused on the fact
that Brice supplied his guides and lead Sherpas with backup satellite
phones in case of radio failure—or, at times, to communicate sensitive information they didn't want overheard on the airwaves. Most
conspicuous, perhaps, was the sheer statistical improbability that, after some forty climbers had walked by Sharp early that morning during the ascent, word had not traveled down the mountain until nearly
eight hours later.

All of which, of course, presupposed that a rescue was even feasible, a topic that spurred another rondelet of speculation and analysis.
"Could David Sharp have been saved? Definitely," exclaimed the lead
story on ExplorersWeb on June 14, citing José Ramón Morandeira,
a specialist in high-altitude medicine and head of research at University Hospital in Zaragoza, Spain. "David would have had many possibilities of being saved if someone had cared for him on the spot, and
then helped him down," Morandeira said. "I've seen people in the
mountains in a much worse state—and they made it." That the Rock
Cave containing Sharp was located "only" about 500 vertical feet above
high camp became another point of contention, although it was rarely
noted what was *between* those two points: specifically, the Exit Cracks,
some of the steepest and most technical terrain on the route. Nor did
many people acknowledge that, even had it been possible to get Sharp to
the tents at 27,500 feet, it would hardly have ensured his survival. Above
it all hovered one of the most vexing questions—not about what could
have been done but, as the reporter John Sellwood had put it to Inglis,
what should have been done.

*"Some suggested that maybe you should have stopped the ascent and res-
cued this man."*

"Yep. It's a very fair point."

Though the accusations were disturbing, the implications were darker yet. Commercial outfitters and their Everest clients had already been stigmatized in the wake of the 1996 disaster, but the circumstances surrounding the David Sharp incident seemed, on the surface, far less forgivable. There had been no deadly storm; the climbers had come upon Sharp early in the day, when they were arguably at their strongest and had the most resources and manpower at their disposal; and, most damning, they were still on their way up. What's more, one of Everest's most established operators had been calling the shots—someone who already had a reputation for proprietary behavior and caginess with the media.

But what tended to prompt the most intense discussion, beyond the course of action, beyond even the lurid spectacle of men and women suffering slow deaths at high altitude, was the suggestion that the modern circus on Everest had exposed something essential about who we are as human beings—an insight that reverberated among climbers and nonclimbers alike. More specifically, the cavalcade of deaths during 2006 raised the highly uncomfortable possibility that, in fact, we are *not* all in this together—that we are simply the latest edition of a complex species tenuously drawn together into social systems that mask our genetic predilection toward selfishness and competition. The argument, followed to its logical conclusion, had less and less to do with climbing mountains and more to do with the foundations of human sociology, and it challenged some of our most cherished assumptions about the roots of compassion and altruism.

Because Everest was such a grand stage, one on which players performed so close to the limits of self-preservation, it had the unique ability to magnify—or perhaps *isolate* is the better word—basic drives and behavior. Those who took the stage were no longer professional adventurers and elite alpinists but, rather, an increasingly broad core sample of the world's middle class. Whether these individuals sought the summit of Everest for private reasons mattered about as little as if they publicly trumpeted every step. In both situations, all that really counted was the achievement—in the first case because of its cathartic potency; in the latter because of its undiminished power to impress. What did that imply when it came to the welfare of others?

In March 2007 I traveled to Brice's home in Argentière, France, a quaint mountain hamlet a couple of miles upvalley from Chamonix. Brice put me up in his sister-in-law's vacation condo; he and Caroline lived across town, in a modest but tasteful rent-controlled two-bedroom apartment. I spent a week visiting with them and others, including Brice's old friend Harry Taylor, several members of the documentary film crew (who were in town to prep for Discovery Channel's follow-up show on Himex), and Brice's staff at Chamonix Experience, a.k.a. Chamex, the guiding business that he ran in tandem with Himalayan Experience. Chamex occupied a one-room office behind a ski shop on Argentière's main drag, where Brice also operated a small coffee bar. During the days I was there, we sipped endless cups of espresso while talking about Everest, skiers clomping by on the sidewalk outside.

"Two years ago, there were a lot of climbers at Base Camp, maybe two hundred people," Brice told me. "We had a big party in camp and I invited everyone to come—the Indians, the Bulgarians, et cetera. The only stipulation I said is that you've got to bring a national dish. So we started the party at three in the afternoon, and it went through to midnight and everyone came and had a great time and this is all hunkydory, eh. And then when the wind came and the ropes weren't going up the mountain, all these same people who were in my camp having a great time, drinking my beer, were going, 'You haven't fixed the ropes. You are a horrible man.' So what's that about? It's really disappointing. You make an effort to be friendly and people just shit on you. And you go, Why be friendly?"

The more I heard—not just from Brice but from many of those I spoke with—the more it seemed to me that Brice's largesse emanated from some central part of his character, an expression of his personal achievement, perhaps, but also just the way he socialized. I knew he was putting his best foot forward, since I had a tape recorder running most of the time. But I think he would have acted the same regardless. He seemed to draw a great deal of satisfaction from ensuring that those around him had a good time.

His generosity was, however, coupled with high expectations. He judged swiftly, and his assessment of his critics and the conduct of others on Everest could be harsh.

"We do this year in and year out," Brice said. "People have gone missing and they go to my Sherpas, 'Can you go around and check all the top tents?' And you check the tents, and here's these guys lying there. We give them oxygen. We give them drinks. That's all they need. They're just too tired. We get them back to life and we say, 'Get down the hill.' We've been doing this for a long time, and we've never said anything about it on our Web site. And these people, they don't come and say thank you and put it on their Web site—'Thanks to Russ's Sherpas we're alive.' So where did this cult of laying blame on someone come from? What happened there?

"These Web sites that report this stuff, I don't believe them and I don't trust them," he continued. "This Thomas and Tina [from ExplorersWeb], I have nothing to do with them and I want nothing to do with them. I think they are horrible, nasty people with weird ideas. When you read what they write about oxygen, they have no idea what they are talking about. And no one ever says, 'Hey, mister, stop—you are wrong.'"

We had relocated to an apartment above the Chamex office, where the film crew was staying. They had been out training all day, and Brice and I were going on our third or fourth hour of conversation.

"We've always been slow putting information on our Web site about what is happening on the mountain," Brice said. "It's like the

David Sharp thing. Everyone's talking about, well, when did you hear about David Sharp? I didn't know the name of that man until the next day, after I found his passport, after we found a picture and had a description and so on. It was me that went around and did the detective work. Well, how come I struck jackpot the first camp I went to? Here's a camp that's in such a shambles, I guarantee it's from them. Boof, straight there. How many times have I gone around saying, 'Who's missing a man? Whose bloody glove is this?' So why am I being criticized? I'm the only person who took any notice."

A little more than a month later, I went to Everest with Himex. I paid Brice $8,000 to join his North Col trip, which was folded into the larger climbing expedition. I fantasized about trying to go to the top, but I lacked the experience—and the $40K—it required. Several people from the previous year's trip had returned to try again, including Tim Medvetz and Mogens Jensen. Guides Bill Crouse and Mark Woodward were also back, as were several of the film crew from the Discovery Channel project.

I joined the expedition in progress at the beginning of May, traveling out from Lhasa with a friendly young Brit named Nick Bonner, the engineer behind the Sherpas' helmet-cam kits. When we arrived at the upper Rongbuk, the Himex Base Camp was even more luxe than the year before. Brice had purchased a large hexagonal group shelter from a Swiss company called Whitepod. It was twenty-five feet across, and Brice had furnished it with a bar, Tibetan rugs, lounge chairs, and a flat-panel TV hooked up to a DVD player and a surround-sound speaker system. It had been dubbed the Tiger Dome.

The other camps were scattered around the gravel flats, as usual. A large contingent of Chinese had come that season to try to make a test run with the Olympic torch, which they hoped to carry up to the summit in 2008 as part of the opening ceremonies for the Beijing Games. Another group of Chinese had set up a large relay tower in Base Camp, and a Brit on the Himex team intended to make the first cell-phone call from the top. ("Can you hear me *now?*") Directly behind Himex's spread was a much smaller camp composed of one grimy pitched-roof tent and two small dome tents. The pitched-roof tent listed and sagged and looked as though it would blow away in the slightest wind. Someone told me it was George Dijmarescu's camp, but I never saw him.

Much discussion still revolved around the events of 2006. John, Linda, and Paul Sharp had accompanied the Himex team to Base Camp at the beginning of the 2007 season, but they dodged the debates about the year before. They simply sought closure, and perhaps a glimpse of the thing that had so obsessed their son. Brice had built a new cairn on the Mound, and the Sharps held a small private ceremony, placing a rectangular plaque on the rocks.

David Sharp 1972–2006
"Sleep serene amid the snows untrod"

It was just the three of them on the Mound that day, huddled together under Tibet's turquoise skies, the wind sweeping down from Everest's North Face, which rose in front of them like an enormous headstone. They left Base Camp shortly thereafter, heading back on the Friendship Highway to Kathmandu, and then home to England.

By the end of my trip, after dozens of interviews, I came to side with the opinion succinctly voiced by Mogens Jensen: The more I learned about the particulars surrounding Sharp's death, the less controversial it seemed to be. Sharp had known the risks the ridge presented, yet he had chosen to climb without support and with minimal oxygen. He hadn't even carried a radio. If he had wanted to court the dangers of Everest, he had done so with determined forethought.

Of the handful of people who acknowledged having seen the

dying climber during their ascent, all the descriptions indicated that he was in a hypothermic coma, fully catatonic. If anyone—Woody and the Himex climbers, the Turkish team—had been inclined to initiate a rescue, it would have required upending their entire expedition, derailing months of planning and costing thousands of dollars. It would have placed clients at risk and required a dangerous operation in the middle of the night where the apparent odds of success seemed slim at best. Fifty years of Everest history warned against a rescue attempt as well. No nonambulatory climber has ever been brought down from above 8,000 meters.

"It's played on my mind many times," Mark Woodward told me at Base Camp. "Could I have done more? Should I have done more? Even somebody said to me one day, if it was somebody you knew, would you have done more? And that's quite an interesting question. But David was completely unresponsive and he appeared more dead than alive, so there just wasn't much we could do.

"Every time I've been on Everest, I've seen something quite horrible," Woody continued. "The first year, as I came down the Second Step, there was this Bulgarian woman and she wanted me to check that her oxygen was done up properly and everything. And this woman, she just biffed her empty cylinder down the North Face. I checked her oxygen and screwed it all up for her and said, 'Yeah, that's all fine,' looked at the gauge—she had about an hour's worth—and I said, 'You can't go up.' I explicitly shook this woman, because she just didn't seem to be responding. I said, 'Don't go up, you don't have enough oxygen.' Blondie carried on up, and I never saw her again."

I often wondered whether David Sharp would have made as many headlines had Lincoln Hall not pulled off his astonishing return from the dead. Hall's story prompted the largest news cycle Everest had experienced in ten years, and it illuminated the other problems on the mountain, confusing much of the public in the process. The predominant notion seemed to be that if Hall had been rescued, surely more could have been done for Sharp, who was lower on the ridge and who, at the time he was first seen that morning, had been incapacitated for less time than Hall.

But several important differences distinguished the two situations. While exact readings are nearly impossible to confirm, the night Hall spent on the ridge was some 15 to 20 degrees warmer than the night Sharp was out. Not a great difference perhaps, considering both nights were intensely cold, but possibly just enough to account for the severity of Sharp's frostbite. Sharp had also been ascending lethally late in the day. If he had in fact summited, it would not have been until late afternoon or early evening, meaning he would have been ascending for approximately fifteen hours, nearly twice as long as it took Hall to reach the top. The physical toll that would exact cannot be overstated.

In May 2007, Phurba Tashi and other Sherpas fixing the route moved Sharp's body from the Rock Cave, interring it on the mountain, and retrieved his old Berghaus backpack in the process. Inside, they discovered dexamethasone, extra gloves, and a bivy blanket. Sharp had obviously been prepared to overnight on the ridge, but when he'd climbed inside the alcove next to Green Boots, he hadn't had the presence of mind to deploy the precious few items that might have saved his life.

In Lincoln Hall's case, the bulk of the news reports revolved around what had been done to help him, as if he were another hapless client hauled down on the shoulders of Sherpas. Very little was said about what Hall had done to save himself. When I spoke to him in the fall of 2007, the Aussie was mildly uncomfortable that so much ado had been made about his rescuers. Dan Mazur, who had appeared with Hall on NBC's *Dateline* in June 2006, seized the chance to turn the rescue into a PR windfall: "There was never a point where I wondered whether or not to help Lincoln," he told interviewer Matt Lauer. "I wasn't raised like that."

Hall didn't want to be misunderstood—he was enormously grateful to those who'd helped him; without a doubt, had Mazur and the others from the SummitClimb team not stopped on the ridge, and had Abramov not dispatched Sherpas to bring up more oxygen, Hall would still be on the mountain. But he had done much to help himself, too. Despite the fact that he had been blitzed by cerebral edema near the summit, with help from the Sherpas he had somehow made his way down to Mushroom Rock, on the lower part of the ridge. After he'd been abandoned, he'd been able to hang on to whatever small embers of rational thought remained, enough, at least, to keep up the fight. During his brief windows of consciousness he'd focused on his ingrained practice of yogic breathing. More important, throughout the course of the expedition Hall had been particularly mindful of nutrition, eating well at camp and supplementing his diet with various vitamins and herbs, including one called cordyceps, long used in Chinese medicine to help improve strength, endurance, and vitality. Finally, he'd trained his mind on his family, the thing holding him most firmly on this side of oblivion. It's hard to believe that any one of these factors made the difference between life and death for Lincoln Hall, but it's hard not to think that the combination of them may have helped sustain him just long enough to survive.

"I've thought about this a lot," Hall said. "There are eleven other people dead up there, and four of them from pretty much what I almost died from. I think those little bits of vital fuel keep those neurons firing and hormonal and endocrine processes going. . . . You are putting your body in the most extreme set of circumstances that you can imagine, and at those heights, your body's starting to self-destruct. You don't even have to do anything; it's doing it automatically. You just have to get out of there before it destructs to the point of no return."

What remained most troubling to me about the events of 2006 was not the men who had made the most news but the one person who had made the least: Thomas Weber. The German's death had emerged as the most enigmatic of any of those on the Northeast Ridge that year. On June 29, Chris Klinke, the climber from Project Himalaya who had witnessed Weber's collapse and the effort—or, in his opinion, inadequate effort—to save him, filed his recollection of those events to ExplorersWeb, concluding, "It had been approximately 20 minutes from the time that Thomas had first started to collapse to the time that [Kikstra] actually went to his client and only after an experienced guide with another company had started to make a rescue effort. At no point did Harry give Thomas dex, nor did he make any effort to save Thomas's life from my vantage point on the scene."

As I probed further, the Weber case only became more bizarre. At one point, I received an e-mail from Volker Heggert, a German who identified himself as the husband of Weber's former girlfriend and said that he was trying to find out more information about what had happened on Everest. His primary motivation was that his in-laws had spent years embroiled in a lawsuit with Weber, who had allegedly lured the family into an investment scheme that had gone belly-up. Heggert cited a list of grievances against Weber, including a supposed history of fraudulent business practices. He even went so far as to speculate about whether Weber might have faked his own death on Everest in order to dodge a mountain of debt he had accrued in Germany. Heggert also suggested that Weber's claims of prior mountaineering experience were specious, suggesting that Weber had never put on a climbing harness before 1999.

Naturally, I was dumbfounded by all this, but also suspicious. It sounded like an inflated case of sour grapes. Several people had witnessed Weber's death, and climbers in 2007 had confirmed that a body remained where Weber had collapsed, so the most fantastic allegations appeared groundless. But other questions weren't as easily resolved. Weber had told several members of the 7 Summits Club expedition that he held an MBA from Wharton, but when I called the business school, officials there had never heard of him. He had also told Harry Kikstra that he had climbed Mount McKinley, but when I called the Talkeetna Ranger Station, which maintains a comprehensive database of all climbing permits issued for McKinley since the early 1980s, rangers were unable to produce a record for anyone named Thomas Weber.

Kikstra said he had been unaware of Weber's past, troubled or not. To some extent he had also shrugged off the more immediate concerns that had come up during the expedition, like Weber's fitness and health. Ultimately, Kikstra may have been guilty of little more than poor judgment; however, the accusations coming from Klinke, combined with editorials from ExWeb, pretty much derailed his guiding business. "I have grounds to sue them, if I was that type," Kikstra told me when we talked in September 2007. "They damaged my business and my reputation. Last year, I had no clients on Everest."

If nothing else, the raft of fatalities in 2006 intensified discussions among the operators and the CTMA about what should be done both to prevent deaths in the future and to better cope with emergencies when they crop up. In August 2006, Brice, Abramov, and Asian Trekking's Ang Tshering Sherpa met with Chinese officials to discuss regulations and rescue programs. Though nothing had been established by the following year when I visited the mountain, proposals ranged from the practical to the dreamily high-tech. The most feasible measure would involve requiring mountaineers to have climbed at least one 8,000-meter peak before they could receive an Everest permit. Also practical, if far more costly, was the idea of establishing a rescue team of Sherpas that would rotate every few days on the upper mountain; climbers would pay around $500 into a general rescue fund to offset the costs.

Also in fall of 2006, Mark Inglis had teamed up with Peter Hillary, Sir Ed's son, to launch the Everest Rescue Trust, an independent nonprofit organization dedicated to "saving and changing lives on the highest mountains." Though it was intended to operate exclusively in Nepal, it may not stop there. The project revolves around an unmanned, full-size, remote-controlled helicopter called the Alpine Wasp that can operate at altitudes up to 30,000 feet and will theoretically be able to pluck two disabled climbers at once from the highest peaks and ridges in the world. The Everest Rescue Trust claims that the Alpine Wasp will be ready for deployment by 2008.

At the end of May 2007, while I was still on Everest and just before everyone left Base Camp for Kathmandu, Brice hosted one of his epic soirees. There was much to celebrate. Tim Medvetz had made it to the summit, as had Mogens Jensen and nearly two dozen other clients, Sherpas, and guides on a climb that had taken place pretty much without a hitch. "Some of our team were on the summit without gloves for more than an hour!!! Unbelievable!" declared a report from the Himex Web site.

Brice had stocked the Tiger Dome with extra cases of beer and bottles of whiskey and champagne. We ate dinner and then all piled into the big tent. The film crew hosted a skit they called "The Brice Is Right," one of them pulling off an uncanny impersonation of Big Boss. Next came a rowdy hour of playing limbo under a trekking pole. We threw back countless shots of Famous Grouse. The women on the trip had done themselves up for the party, scrubbed and radiant, dressed in tight pants and shimmery tops. Apparently, after two months, they'd had enough of shapeless goose-down parkas, their hair wadded up under a ski cap. The ratio of males to females was something like fifteen to one; the women never lacked for a dance partner.

At one point in the evening Brice approached me as I stood on the sidelines. "I have no idea what you're going to write," he said. It seemed like a statement and a question at the same time. I told him I just wanted to try to tell the story of the 2006 season.

"Well, I hope you can capture this," he said, indicating the scene in front of us, the shindig in full tilt. The music thumped; Sherpas danced with the women; climbers from various expeditions clustered around the dome, talking and laughing. The plastic windows of the Tiger Dome had fogged up. In a couple of weeks, the spot where we stood would be a barren sweep of gravel.

"This is what I love," he said. "Look at all these people here together. The Sherpas, the climbers, the people from other expeditions. I throw the best parties on Everest."

We stood watching the scene for a minute or two, then he changed topics.

"You think anyone else would have done what I did for David Sharp? Do you think anyone else would have moved his body? Would anyone else have contacted his family, or brought them here? Would anybody else light a candle in his memory at the monastery, or have built the cairn, or made the plaque?

"I live around death all the time," he went on. "Do you know how many bodies I've moved on the mountain? A lot! And you know what? My auntie died today. And you know what her last words were? 'Come down safe.' So now all of my family is dead, and I have to deal with that, and meantime keep all this running. . . . So why am I the bad guy?"

"Because you're the big guy," I said. I didn't know what else to tell him.

"Fuckin' A, right," Brice said. "No one else can do what I do here. They just copy me."

Late that night, as the party wound down, the hangers-on reclined around the edge of the Tiger Dome. Brice had gone off to bed, as had most everyone else. Maybe a dozen people remained. Of slight concern was a thin, bearded climber from another expedition whom no one seemed to know. He appeared barely conscious after the long night of partying, and we just assumed he would sleep it off in the relative sanctuary of the dome. But at some point he stumbled out of the tent, presumably headed for his own camp. Concern mounted among those of us still there. It was cold enough outside to be dangerous.

"We're going to find him dead in the stream tomorrow," said Monica Piris, the expedition doctor, as we stood around wondering what to do.

After a brief discussion, Monica, Woody, a Himex guide named Dean Staples, and I formed a small search party, fanning out into the night and combing the ground with our headlamps. It was two A.M., and near zero. If the guy had passed out somewhere, Monica was right—he wasn't going to last very long.

After about forty-five minutes we regrouped. Several square miles of open ground engulfed us, and we didn't even know where his camp was located. He could be anywhere. We pushed on a little farther until my headlamp faded, making any continued effort completely useless. We turned back to the Himex camp, now a ways behind us. On the return trip, trying to cross a stream of glacial runoff, I punched through the ice and dunked my foot. I felt the water pour in over the top of my boot, soaking my sock, the cold immediate and bracing.

With my headlamp shot, I tried to stick close to Monica as I sloshed back toward the tents. Stars dappled the sky, bright as klieg lights. I could see Everest out in front of us—the snow and ice marbling the North Face glowing softly, the rest of the peak a black monstrosity rising up in the dark night. A few teams were still up there, and I knew that at that moment climbers were working their way up toward the Northeast Ridge, beginning their summit push. A few days earlier, I had stood at the North Col, gazing up at the ridge, wondering if I could make it to the top. Ever since I had seen Everest for the first time a couple of years earlier, my unwavering opinion had been: No way, no way, no way. But as I stood on the col, the summit so close it seemed as though I could reach out and touch it, suddenly, surprisingly, a different thought materialized: *Hell, yes, I can.* It must have been the hypoxia talking. Now, crunching across the gravel in the middle of the night, lightless, tired, my wet foot quickly going numb, all I wanted to do was get back to camp, don dry socks, and crawl into my sleeping bag. Looking up at the ridge only made me shudder.

We walked past the Mound, its constellation of cairns softly illuminated by the starlight. Despite having spent the last year talking with those who'd climbed or tried to climb Everest, I had to admit I felt no closer to understanding why people were so willing to risk their lives to do it. I still clung to the romantic notion that summiting Everest possessed some genuine transformational power, but I had seen none of this among the climbers on my expedition, just a kind of deep, weathered fatigue. If there was any consensus among those who'd succeeded, it was their yearning to return to their families, to sleep in a soft bed and soak in a warm bath. And maybe that was it, after all: to reach that point so close to our own extinction that it made every mundane detail of our lives numinous again.

The next morning, as the Sherpas broke down camp and the climbers started packing, Monica canvassed the other expeditions to see if she could find out about the climber who'd gone missing from the party. It didn't take long. He had turned up in his own tent, hungover, mildly perturbed, eager to go home.

AUTHOR'S NOTE

It's impossible to write about Mount Everest without grappling to some degree with the Rashomon effect—that is, the subjectivity of perception, particularly when it involves individuals who have spent so much time at extreme altitude. On the Northeast Ridge in particular, where atmospheric oxygen is 70 percent less than at sea level (and off-set only slightly by supplemental oxygen), many basic human functions, including memory, can be significantly impaired. Now add to the hypoxia the complications of exhaustion, anxiety, violent winds, and dangerous cold and it becomes clear that nearly everyone who reaches such elevations is operating at barely functional levels.

I am not trying to suggest that all information coming from the mountain is open to debate, or that recollections are always inaccurate. Rather, I want to underscore that the differing accounts that inevitably emerge from Everest may not reflect—as has sometimes been alleged—hidden agendas, cover-ups, or mistruths so much as they illustrate the aftereffects of such a brutal environment—a mind fog that can last for months.

In reporting this book, I tried to speak with as many people as possible who either were eyewitnesses on the mountain or could provide firsthand accounts from a particular vantage point. Where stories about the same incident conflicted, I did my best to corroborate information and establish the most likely sequence of events. In the few cases where video and/or audio recordings were available, I relied on those to reconstruct action, dialogue, and scene. Lastly, several published accounts, most specifically Lincoln Hall's *Dead Lucky*, were available to me while working on this book and helped verify details that only one or two individuals could have known.

My intent in telling this story was not to try to render any final judgment about the events of 2006. In fact, if anything, I set out to try to illustrate, explain, and clarify a series of incidents about which so much judgment had already been issued. On the other hand, the purpose of this book is also not to make excuses for those who may arguably have been in a position to do more to help. The tragic fact remains that eleven people died climbing Everest in the spring of 2006, and several of these deaths, in my opinion, at least in the luxury of hindsight, may have been prevented.

Ultimately, no greater responsibility exists than that which falls on each individual climber—whether he or she is an expedition leader, guide, Sherpa, or paying client. Too much has been written, said, filmed, and photographed for anyone going to Mount Everest not to be fully aware of the risks of climbing to 29,035 feet. Only a fool would put complete faith in someone else to guarantee their safety, or bail them out of trouble if a problem arises, though certainly the mountain continues to attract its share of fools.

Everest is an extraordinarily dangerous place, one where the growing crowds and proliferating number of commercial operators may lend it an illusion of being safer and more carefully controlled than it actually is. Climbers need to conduct their own due diligence when joining an expedition to ensure that they are supported by capable operators, just as commercial operators and guides need to do all they can to ensure that the clients they bring up the mountain are adequately prepared. The same holds true for independent mountaineers and private teams. I believe that much has been improved on Everest since 1996, but the calamitous 2006 season is evidence that more remains to be done.

On one level, I applaud those who moralize and muckrake about Everest; it draws more attention to that small corner of the world and makes it more difficult for those traveling there to act recklessly or inappropriately. Unfortunately, the righteous are not always right, and I fear too much of the world has acquired a warped perception of the business taking place on Everest. Many of those who work there are admirable individuals who should be commended for the standards they endorse, and I hope that mountaineering in general will continue to benefit from their involvement. Climbing Everest is an extraordinary achievement that can enrich and empower the lives of those who do it, and inspire many others who don't. It's my hope that those who lost their lives in 2006 will not become simply another batch of grim statistics, but that a better understanding of how and why they died will help ameliorate the problems that continue to plague the roof of the world, even if the inherent risks of climbing Everest can never be entirely eliminated.

SOURCE NOTES

Composing this book was an expedition in its own right, one that relied on numerous individuals and resources. Inevitably, and for the sake of consistency and continuity, I came to rely heavily on a few key sources. Geographic names were reconciled using *Merriam-Webster's Geographical Dictionary*. For the final ruling on mountain elevations, I turned to *Webster's Geographical*, *Encyclopaedia Britannica*, and the U.S. Board on Geographic Names. Certainly the most significant resource of all from a statistical point of view was the Himalayan Data Base, launched in 1993 but started many years earlier by expat American Elizabeth Hawley. HDB is the most historically comprehensive compilation of Himalayan expedition information available anywhere, and all those who take an interest in Himalayan climbing owe Ms. Hawley a great debt.

While some sections of this book were based on historical accounts of Everest climbs, high-altitude physiology, and the early exploration of the Himalayas, most of it was drawn from the personal testimony of climbers who were on the mountain in 2006—whether in the form of individual dispatches posted on the Web and aired on television programs, interviews I conducted with them personally, interviews others conducted and made available to me, or a combination of all three. Lastly, my own trip to Everest's North Col in 2007 provided me with invaluable firsthand knowledge of the climbing route, the pace of life at the various mountain camps, and the extraordinary landscape in which the story is set.

Prologue

Although much was written about the events that transpired on the Southeast Ridge during Everest's fateful 1996 spring season, very little was reported from the north side that year. The best account—in fact, almost the only account—was Matt Dickinson's *The Other Side of Everest*, which provided important details surrounding Mohinder Singh's Indian expedition. Singh also wrote an account of the climb, *Everest: The First Ascent from North (Col)*, an insightful, if propaganda-laden version published in Delhi by Indian Publishers Distributors. Like many people, I was introduced to the larger themes that emerged from 1996—Everest's burgeoning popularity among amateur climbers, the roll of the commercial operators, human behavior in extreme environments—through Jon Krakauer's *Into Thin Air*, which influenced public opinion about Everest to a considerable degree. But other accounts are critical to obtaining a more comprehensive and balanced picture of that year, most significantly *The Climb*, by Anatoli Boukreev and G. Weston DeWalt. After both books—which took dramatically different views of the events on the mountain—had been published, the Web site Salon.com followed up by publishing a lively exchange of letters between Krakauer and DeWalt. These letters are required reading for anyone interested in what happened on Everest in 1996, a seminal year without which the events of 2006 would never have captured the public interest as forcefully as they did.

Chapter 1

You can't talk about Everest without invoking, at some point, those who ushered high-altitude mountaineering into the contemporary age. For the broadest perspective about the world's highest peak, I turned to Walt Unsworth's *Everest: The Mountaineering History*—the undisputed heavyweight champ for Everest's early history. Only one caveat: It trails off in 1989, about the time commercially guided climbing on the mountain began. For deeper reading into a few of the watershed climbs by some of the modern practitioners of the sport, I turned to Reinhold Messner's *The Crystal Horizon*, a strange, fascinating recollection of the first successful climb of Everest without supplemental oxygen; *The West Ridge*, by Thomas Hornbein, a gripping firsthand account of one of Everest's most audacious ascents; and *The Boardman Tasker Omnibus*, by Peter Boardman and Joe Tasker, which reveals much about the ethos of alpine climbing as it evolved through the seventies.

Chapter 2

Dozens of books inform my abridged history of Everest, specifically its north side, but a handful were essential to the narrative. John Keay's *The Great Arc* is the strongest work I found about the astonishingly complex Trigonometrical Survey of India. Peter Hopkirk's *The Great Game* is a must-read for anyone interested in geographical struggle among Russia, China, and the Raj during the eighteenth and nineteenth centuries. John B. West's *High Life: A History of High-Altitude Physiology and Medicine* is arguably the best and most readable history of high-altitude physiology. I also turned to *Going Higher: Oxygen, Man, and Mountains*, by Charles Houston, and a more academic text, *High Altitude Medicine and Physiology*, by John B. West, Robert

SOURCE NOTES

B. Schoene, and James S. Milledge, for expanded technical explanations of the science.

Patrick French's classic biography, *Younghusband*, is a provocative portrait of one of Britain's most compelling figures. James Hilton's *Lost Horizon* helped popularize notions of Himalayas and Tibetan Buddhism in the West. An excellent discussion about the evolution of the perception of Tibet in Western culture can be found in the translated edition of *Dreamworld Tibet: Western Illusions*, by Martin Brauen, a professor of Asian studies at the University of Zurich, Switzerland.

A small library of books recounts the story of George Mallory. Among the best are Peter and Leni Gillman's biography, *The Wildest Dream*, the definitive source of information about Mallory's life and climbs. *Because It's There*, by Dudley Green, is another well-researched book focused specifically on Mallory. David Breashears and Audrey Salkeld's *Last Climb* is a fine overview of the three initial British expeditions. Julie Summers's *Fearless on Everest* tells the compelling tale of Mallory's final climbing companion, Andrew Irvine. Excellent first-person accounts of the discovery of Mallory's body in 1999 include *The Lost Explorer*, by Conrad Anker and David Roberts, and *Ghosts of Everest*, by Jochem Hemmleb, Larry A. Johnson, and Eric R. Simonson. Several rare volumes chronicle the early solo attempts on Everest, including *I'll Climb Mount Everest Alone: The Story of Maurice Wilson*, by Dennis Roberts, and Earl Denman's *Alone to Everest*. The story of Woodrow Wilson Sayer's 1962 climb is told in his book *Four Against Everest*.

Chapters 3–5

For the most part, narrative details of the 2006 season were derived from interviews with climbers, but I also relied on a number of Web postings and reports, predominantly from ExplorersWeb (www.mounteverest.net) and EverestNews (www.everestnews.com). Also vital to the reconstruction of events during that spring was the docu mentary series *Everest: Beyond the Limit*, produced by the Discovery Channel (www.discovery.com). I gleaned additional information about acclimatization and high-altitude physiology from basecampmd .com and Luanne Freer, who has been providing free, independent medical support at Everest's south-side Base Camp since 2003. Details about Henry Todd can be found in the book *Operation Julie*, by Dick Lee and Colin Pratt, and in the 1978 BBC television documentary *Operation Julie*.

Chapters 6–8

A handful of published accounts describe various situations where climbers have been abandoned on Mount Everest. I drew primarily from Boukreev and DeWalt's *The Climb*, Beck Weathers's *Left for Dead*, Joe Simpson's *Dark Shadows Falling*, and Cathy O'Dowd's memoir *Just for the Love of It*. For Lincoln Hall's story, I leaned heavily on Hall's *Dead Lucky*, though the details were further expanded, embellished, and rounded out by the recollections of others who were either directly or indirectly involved in his rescue. Additional details regarding the death of Thomas Weber can be found on sightoneverest.com and 7summits.com.

Epilogue

My own thinking about the motivations driving human behavior, at any altitude, was profoundly impacted by Robert Wright's *The Moral Animal*. Other writers, thinkers, and journalists whose big ideas will be detected here include Joseph Campbell, Bill Moyers, and Abraham Maslow. For a deeper clarification of the way organized agencies involved in mountaineering view the role of ethics in climbing, I turned to the 2002 Tyrol Declaration, as adopted by the American Alpine Club in 2002, and intended to provide a manifesto for behavior and decision making among those involved in the sport (http://www .americanalpineclub.org/pdfs/aaj/AAJ_2003_Tyrol_Decalaration.pdf).

I would be remiss not to mention Maria Coffey's *Where the Mountain Casts Its Shadow*, an eloquent and deeply thoughtful look at the way climbers' deaths impact those who are left behind. On that note, though the family of David Sharp declined several inquiries for an interview, I did have a brief correspondence with David's brother Paul during the summer of 2006. "In life David was a private individual who avoided publicity and being the centre of attention," Paul wrote me. "He would be dismayed at the attention surrounding his death. Neither I nor my parents wish to add to this. . . . I hope you will understand."

ACKNOWLEDGMENTS

M any people helped make this book possible. Of all the climbers who gave of their time, none was more generous than Russell Brice, who sat for hours of interviews and allowed me to join his 2007 Everest expedition, despite being understandably leery of journalists. I am indebted to others who shared their recollections and insights, including Lincoln Hall, Harry Kikstra, Mark Woodward, Bill Crouse, Brett Merrell, Tim Medvetz, Mogens Jensen, Mark Inglis, Ken Sauls, Terry O'Connor, Max Chaya, Slate Stern, Kirk Wheatley, Alex Abramov, Jamie McGuinness, Chris Klinke, Scott Woolums, Laurie Bagely, David Lien, Eric Simonson, Dave Hahn, Nick Bonner, Tom and Tina Sjogren, Kevin Augello, Volker Heggert, Caroline Brice, Grania Willis, Dean Staples, Monica Piris, Harry Taylor, Geoff Tabin, Pete Athans, Michael Brown, Dave D'Angelo, Elizabeth Hawley, Eric Simonson, Chris Warner, Luanne Freer, Phurba Tashi Sherpa, Dawa Sherpa, Ang Tshering Sherpa, Lobsang Temba Sherpa.

ACKNOWLEDGMENTS

My agent, Sloan Harris, pushed this project out of the gates and delivered it to the hands of a very capable publisher. My editor at Henry Holt and Co., John Sterling, helped steer and shape the story with uncommon intelligence and good humor. Another talented editor, Jennifer Barth, contributed valuable suggestions to the early stages of this book as well. Kevin Fedarko provided astute and thorough feedback when it was most needed. Bonnie Thompson and Will Palmer brought their eagle-eyed copyediting skills to the project. Henry R. Kaufman provided expert legal input. Miriam Beyer, Kristyn Keene, Dana Welch, Christina Erb, and Alicia Carr provided vital clerical and logistical support. None of these pages would have been completed if not for indefatigable research and fact-checking from Katie Cantrell.

I am indebted to Tom Foster and Brad Wieners for making the initial story possible in the August 2006 issue of *Men's Journal*. On that seedling assignment, I benefited greatly from the stalwart assistance of Catharine Livingston, Abe Streep, and Andrew Olesnycky. Their hard work resonates through this version as well.

Others who contributed either directly or indirectly to my introduction to, and appreciation of, Himalayan climbing include Conrad Anker, Jordan Campbell, Kristoffer Erikson, John Griber, Ace Kvale, Dr. Sanduk Ruit and all those affiliated with the Himalayan Cataract Project, Dawa Sherpa, Ang Temba Sherpa, Kevin Thaw, and Abby Watkins. Finally, a sincere shout-out to those who, at one time or another, offered doses of support, inspiration, encouragement, and enthusiasm, especially Bay Anapol, Claire Antoszewski, Dave Cox, Hal Espen, Alex Heard, Elizabeth Hightower, Chris Keyes, Dennis Lewon, Hannah McCaughey, Penn Newhard, Ali Noland, Caroline Palmer, Stephanie Pearson, Bob Shacochis, Hampton Sides, Janine Sieja, and Mary Turner.

INDEX

Entries in *italics* refer to maps.

ABOUT THE AUTHOR

Nick Heil first wrote about the 2006 climbing season for *Men's Journal*. Now a freelance journalist based in Santa Fe, New Mexico, he was a senior editor at *Outside* from 1999 to 2006. He has also worked as a climbing and skiing instructor and has traveled extensively in Europe, Asia, and North America.